AF820118

DRUGS & SOCIETY

ANDREW D. HATHAWAY

OXFORD
UNIVERSITY PRESS

OXFORD
UNIVERSITY PRESS

Oxford University Press is a department of the University of Oxford.
It furthers the University's objective of excellence in research, scholarship,
and education by publishing worldwide. Oxford is a registered trade mark of
Oxford University Press in the UK and in certain other countries.

Published in Canada by
Oxford University Press
8 Sampson Mews, Suite 204,
Don Mills, Ontario M3C 0H5 Canada
www.oupcanada.com

Copyright © Oxford University Press Canada 2015

The moral rights of the author have been asserted

Database right Oxford University Press (maker)

All rights reserved. No part of this publication may be reproduced, stored in a retrieval system, or transmitted, in any form or by any means, without the prior permission in writing of Oxford University Press, or as expressly permitted by law, by licence, or under terms agreed with the appropriate reprographics rights organization. Enquiries concerning reproduction outside the scope of the above should be sent to the Permissions Department at the address above or through the following url: www.oupcanada.com/permission/permission_request.php

Every effort has been made to determine and contact copyright holders. In the case of any omissions, the publisher will be pleased to make suitable acknowledgement in future editions.

Library and Archives Canada Cataloguing in Publication
Hathaway, Andrew D. (Andrew David), 1969-, author
Drugs and society / Andrew D. Hathaway.
(Themes in Canadian sociology)
Includes bibliographical references and index.
ISBN 978-0-19-900788-2 (pbk.)
1. Drugs--Social aspects. 2. Drug abuse--Social aspects.
3. Drug control. I. Title. II. Series: Themes in Canadian sociology

HV5801.H37 2015 362.29 C2015-900377-6

Cover image: © iStock/francisblack

Oxford University Press is committed to our environment.
This book is printed on Forest Stewardship Council® certified paper and comes from responsible sources.

MIX
Paper from responsible sources
FSC® C103567

Printed and bound in Canada

1 2 3 4 — 18 17 16 15

Contents

Preface

Drugs and Society is intended for undergraduate students in sociology and other social science programs taking upper level courses in areas relating to drugs. Many textbooks have been written with similar titles and a standard format: to offer a comprehensive explanation of psychological and physical effects of a variety of drugs. This one departs from the typical approach. Biomedical, psychological, and sociological perspectives ordinarily inform the nature and extent of "the drug problem." The resulting "bio/psycho/social" view involves combining explanations from a wide array of disciplines and theories to define the problem and provide solutions.

Many textbooks in this area include alternative perspectives that are critical of policies outlawing certain drugs. Most provide historical analyses that help shed light on the origins of discriminatory antidrug laws. Many also offer insights into the cultural and moral relativity of attitudes, experiences, and societal reactions to a wide variety of drugs. These same textbooks, however, also tend to reinforce specific, predominant assumptions about the nature of substance use. Ordinarily this means respecting and conforming to biomedical and legal definitions of drug problems, with the emphasis on treatment, prevention, and control.

The present book, by contrast, is guided by the premise that the meaning of all substance use is socially constructed. The claim that drug use is a problem in society, from this standpoint, is a collective definition that must be problematized in turn. A contextual constructionist perspective is adopted, which situates the meaning and experience of drug use within its historical, political, and sociocultural contexts. This approach diverges from other sources by adopting a cohesive sociological framework. Informed by classic and more recent contributions to the literature, the focus is on making constructionism more accessible as a means for examining drug issues in society.

Preparation for this project was facilitated greatly by the efforts of two students, Bethany Cudmore and Trevor Morrison, who overviewed existing sources and their overlapping themes. The insights gained from these impressions—the point of view of students with no extensive background in this area of research—were invaluable in shaping the analysis that follows. Their contributions to the project are most gratefully acknowledged.

The literature consulted in preparation of this book brought to light a number of related themes that are especially compelling for young people. This includes the observation that the war on drugs has not been an effective use of policy or police resources. I have found that students are particularly open to discussing strategies such as harm reduction and decriminalization of certain drugs such as marijuana, for example, which a large proportion of students use.

There is considerable agreement on the need for education *about* rather than *against* drugs. More accurate, unbiased information about drug use is necessary in order to address the misconceptions reinforced by well-meaning parents, teachers, doctors, and others in positions of authority. Providing better education about drugs must go beyond dispelling myths and scare tactics.

It is equally important for young people to receive unbiased, nonjudgmental information about alcohol and other drugs to guide their choices. Increasing use of stimulants, prescription medications, and binge drinking in student populations (and beyond) points to the need for harm reduction education, which prioritizes mitigating risk rather than drug status or criminal consequences.

The book is divided into eight chapters, which are thematically connected but can also stand alone. Chapter 1 presents an inventory of the content found in leading textbooks on drugs and society. It overviews the themes and theoretical perspectives provided in these sources. The emphasis is on explaining drug-related problems from a bio/psycho/social point of view.

Chapter 2 introduces constructionist perspectives, theoretical assumptions, and continuing debates. This framework for researching social problems is primarily concerned with understanding "claims-making" about drug use that define it as a problem. A contextual constructionist position is developed, emphasizing the historical, political, and cultural influences.

Chapter 3 presents a social history of drug use and drug control in Canada. The influence of racial and class conflicts are examined. The constructionist perspective is augmented by the introduction of a critical historical perspective on drug problems. The discussion is informed by recent Canadian contributions to the research literature on moral regulation.

Chapter 4 examines philosophical foundations and political realities shaping drug policy debates. In addition to the recent history of drug law developments in Canada, the challenges and prospects of the harm-reduction movement are examined in this chapter. The current controversy over supervised injection is a prominent example of value conflicts at the centre of Canadian drug policy debates.

Chapter 5 examines the sociocultural environment and social meaning of drug use, from the perspectives of both users and non-users of a variety of drugs. Sociocultural constructions of drugs, such as descriptions of "hard," "soft," "good," and "bad" substances, are shaped by legal, medical, and popular distinctions that are hard to reconcile with scientific facts—or with the actual experiences of many substance users. The remaining chapters of this textbook thereby seek to offer a more in-depth investigation of the social meaning of psychoactive drug use.

Chapter 6 investigates the cultural construction of drug use as a symbol of conspicuous consumption. Psychoactive substances are valuable commodities conveying certain meanings about identity and status. Drug use has been variously constructed as a symbol of conformity, rebellion, and expression of presence or lack of self-control.

Chapter 7 examines the construction of drug problems from a biomedical perspective on addiction. Viewing drugs as symptoms of disorder or disease is a longstanding Western cultural tradition. Throughout the modern era, the drug problem has been characterized as being of a type that warrants punishment or treatment. From a sociological perspective, however, neither standpoint conveys a very convincing understanding of the problem. An alternative to medical (and moral–legal) understandings is to view addiction as a symptom of exploitation and social dislocation in a globalizing world.

Chapter 8 investigates the use of drugs as tools. The explanations given in this chapter significantly differ from conventional assumptions about drugs. Psychoactive drugs are used as instruments or tools for coping, recreation, and transcendence. The arguments presented challenge observed tendencies to oversimplify distinctions between legal and illegal, medical and recreational forms of substance use.

The book concludes with a discussion on better appreciation of the cultural assumptions and reactions influencing substance use behaviour. A more balanced understanding of drug problems will require a better understanding of the benefits of drug use, and of the biases and interests determining the predominant assumptions that pose obstacles to policy reform.

Acknowledgements

In addition to the team at Oxford University Press, I would like to thank my friends and family for their unwavering support. I am grateful to the mentors, colleagues, peers, and many students who encouraged me to write this textbook. In particular, Bob Stebbins, Billy Shaffir, Dorothy Pawluch, Patricia Erickson, Mike Atkinson, and Amir Mostaghim provided inspiration of the kind I dearly needed to take on a project of this magnitude and scope.

This book is dedicated to my children.

1 Studying Drugs and Society

Learning Objectives

- To understand drug use in society from biological, psychological, and sociological perspectives.
- To distinguish between types of drugs in terms of their chemical and behavioural effects.
- To understand how expectations and experiences of drug use are influenced by social learning and environment.

Introduction: What Are Drugs?

It has long been recognized that understanding drug use and drug-related problems requires an understanding of the drugs themselves and the social and cultural context of the people who take them. The topic of drugs and society has inspired an extensive range of academic literature. This chapter provides an overview of the predominant ideas and perspectives in the field. Different disciplines contribute very different points of view. It is important to consider these perspectives before moving toward developing a better understanding of sociological–constructionist perspectives on drug issues.

Like most textbooks on drugs and society, this chapter will examine the topic from a multidisciplinary **bio/psycho/social standpoint**, focusing on contributions from biology (or biomedicine), psychology, and the social sciences. Most of the leading textbooks in this area of study downplay sociological perspectives on drug problems. Emphasizing biological or psychological components of the literature gives more evaluative weight to pathological perspectives that define the nature of the "problem" from the start. However, this book will also emphasize the social processes that determine how we understand drugs. This chapter lays the groundwork for more critical discussion, recognizing the importance of context in how drug problems are constructed and how we look at drugs. The predominant perspective, as we shall see, is strongly influenced by biomedical and legal definitions and distinctions that determine the acceptance or rejection of drug use and users. Understanding what is meant by substance *use* versus *misuse* requires an understanding of how different drugs are classified by medical professionals in terms of chemical effects, which in turn characterizes “types” of use and users. The resulting characterizations influence how one is treated—i.e., as a criminal, an addict, or merely a consumer—depending on the way use of the drug in question is socially defined. On assessment of the facts, it is apparent that existing legal definitions are not based on evidence of harm.

Instead, we must look back in history to understand the early origins of substance use, related attitudes, and efforts to control drugs that shape how we perceive them. In this process, it is vital to attend to the cultural, and subcultural, dimensions that determine the meaning of drug use. Definitions vary between cultures and across different social subgroups within the same culture. Before investigating social scientific theories, this book will first examine biomedical explanations of different drugs and drug effects.

Types of Drugs

Examining connections among drugs, drug effects, and corresponding drug-related problems orients our focus toward scientific evidence. Scientific knowledge about drugs is well-developed, and a great deal of literature is devoted to these facts. From an objective standpoint, it is critical to know the different types of drugs and drug effects, and how we use drugs, as a prelude to examining the harms of drug misuse.

Understanding use trends and user types for a wide variety of drugs is important. We should be familiar with the standard definitions of problem drug use, as determined by clinicians who diagnose and treat substance use disorders. This approach facilitates discussion of appropriate forms of treatment and prevention of drug problems by adopting a medically informed public health perspective, which views drug addiction as a disorder or disease. The focus of this section is, accordingly, on reviewing how scientific knowledge about drugs and drug effects informs the way we look at and understand drug use.

Recognizing drugs as triggers that influence behaviour, or how people think and feel, is a useful starting point to identifying different types of drugs and possible effects. Most “drugs of abuse” (Table 1.1), for example, can be divided into one of five general categories—stimulants (e.g., cocaine, amphetamines); depressants (e.g., barbiturates, alcohol); opioids (e.g., opium, codeine); hallucinogens (e.g., lysergic acid diethylamide [LSD], ecstasy [MDMA]); and cannabis (e.g., marijuana, hashish).

Based on these descriptions, we gather that some drugs get you up, some get you down, and some take you sideways (or affect you other ways that alter your perspective). There are advantages to starting by reducing the matter in this way, emphasizing only the essential characteristics of different types of drugs and drug effects. Things get complicated, however, when the focus of analysis shifts to other characteristics of the substances examined.

Coca leaf and crack cocaine versus alcohol and heroin. Caffeine and nicotine versus LSD and cannabis. Phencyclidine (PCP) and salvia versus steroids. Prescription pharmaceuticals versus over-the-counter drugs. An initial look at how drugs are classified shows that there is no straightforward or discernible relationship between a drug's effects and its legal status. There are far too many differences, and too few similarities, to meaningfully distinguish essential properties of legal and illegal drugs, and approved and frowned-upon use, in terms of chemical effects.

Likewise, whereas some drugs have accepted medical uses, others of the same class are rejected despite corresponding characteristics and effects. To illustrate, alcohol and barbituates are depressants with similar characteristics and physiological effects. One is a widely used relaxant and a mainstay of social interaction, yet has no accepted medical uses. The other is accepted when prescribed by a physician, but is not considered safe for recreation. Classifications sometimes vary depending on the country and whether the user or patient is an animal or human (cf. Hanson et al., 2011; Hart et al., 2011). There are no medical uses for analgesics such as heroin in the US, for example, or for hallucinogens like LSD or mescaline; the same is true of tranquilizers such as PCP and ketamine, unless you are a licensed veterinarian.

Of further interest, cannabis is generally considered to be relatively safe in terms of its toxicity and the potential for its users to develop **dependence** or **abuse**. It has a long history of use for medical symptoms and it is prevalent among a substantial segment of the general population, particularly as a social lubricant. The social status of this substance is remarkably conflicted, and we gain nothing in the way of understanding its effects by referencing medical or legal definitions.

Form (i.e., liquid, vapour, pill) and method of consumption (i.e., sniffed, injected, smoked, ingested) are other characteristics that may influence societal perceptions and acceptance of a drug's use. These considerations may or may not correspond with evidence of harm, physical effects, or other characteristics, such as the risk of overdose or potential for developing drug dependence.

Medical and legal definitions are inseparable from various historical and cultural influences that shape the social status of the substance and its users. Looking at reported trends, use prevalence, and problems with the types of drugs commonly used, it is increasingly observed that the harms of "legal" drugs overshadow those of the drugs most often feared. This is an important observation that facilitates critical reflection and discussion by Canadians about existing policies for regulating drugs.

Rather than allowing legal standards to determine our approach to analyzing types of drugs and drug effects, the strategy adopted here is concerned with developing the broader theoretical orientation that determines how drug issues are ordinarily discussed. It will soon be evident that it is

Table 1.1 Drugs of Abuse: Uses and Effects

	Drugs	Trade/Street Names	Medical Uses	Physical Dependence	Psychological Dependence	Tolerance	Usual Methods of Administration	Possible Effects	Effects of Overdose	Withdrawal Syndrome
Stimulants	Cocaine	Coke, crack, snow	Local anesthetic	Possible	Moderate (oral); very high (IV injected or smoked)	Possible	Sniffed, smoked, injected	Increased alertness, excitation, euphoria, increased pulse rate and blood pressure, insomnia, loss of appetite	Agitation, increased body temperature, hallucinations, convulsions, possible death	Severely depressed mood, prolonged sleep, apathy, irritability, disorientation
	Amphetamines	Biphetamine, Desoxyn, Dexedrine, meth, ice	Weight control, hyperactivity, narcolepsy			Yes	Oral, injected			
	Methylphenidate	Ritalin								
	Phenmetrazine	Preludin								
	Other stimulants	Adipex, Bacarate, Cylert, Didrex, Sanorex, Tenuate, Tepanil								
Depressants	Chloral hydrate	Noctec	Hypnotic	Moderate	Moderate	Possible	Oral	Slurred speech, disorientation, staggering, drunken behaviour	Shallow respiration, cold and clammy skin, weak and rapid pulse, coma, possible death	Anxiety, insomnia, tremors, delirium, convulsions, possible death
	Barbiturates	Amytal, Alurate, Butisol, Mebaral, Nembutol, Seconal	Anesthetic, anticonvulsant, sedative, hypnotic	Moderate to High	Moderate to High	Yes	Oral, injected			
	Methaqualone	Quaalude	None	High	High		Oral			
	Benzodiazepines	Ativan, Dalmane, Halcion, Librium, Valium, Xanax	Anesthetic, anticonvulsant, sedative, hypnotic	Low to moderate	Moderate to high					
	Alcohol	Many types	None	Moderate	Moderate					

Opioids	Opium	Pantofen, Paregoric, Parepectolin	Analgesic, antidiarrheal	High	Moderate (oral), high (smoked)	Yes	Oral, smoked	Euphoria, drowsiness, slowed respiration, nausea	Slow and shallow breathing, clammy skin, constricted pupils, coma, possible death	Watery eyes, runny nose, yawning, loss of appetite, tremors, panic, chills and sweating, cramps, nausea
	Morphine	Morphine	Analgesic	High	Moderate		Oral, injected			
	Codeine	Many brands	Analgesic, antitussive	Moderate	Moderate		Oral			
	Heroin	Many street names	None in the United States	High	Very high (IV)		Injected, smoked			
	Methadone	Dolophine	Analgesic, addict maintenance	High	Moderate		Oral, injected			
	Other opioids	Demerol, Dilaudid, Fentanyl, Percodan, Talwin	Analgesic	Varies	Varies					
Hallucinogens	LSD	Acid, many others	None	None	Low	Yes	Oral	Visual illusions, hallucinations, altered perception of one's own body, increased emotionality	More prolonged episodes that may resemble psychotic states	Not reported
	Psilocybin	Mushrooms, 'shrooms								
	Mescaline, peyote	Mesc, cactus, others								
	Amphetamine variants	DOM (STP), MDA, MDMA, Ecstasy, MMDA, TMA		Unknown	Unknown					
	Phencyclidine	PCP, angel dust	Veterinary anesthetic	Very low	High		Oral, smoked			
Cannabis	Marijuana	Pot, grass, weed, many others	Under investigation	Very low	Moderate	Yes	Smoked	Euphoria, relaxed inhibitions, increased appetite, impaired memory and attention	Fatigue, paranoia, at very high doses a hallucinogen-like psychotic state	Insomnia, hyperactivity (syndrome is rare)
	Tetrahydrocannabinol	THC, Marinol	Nausea				Oral			
	Hashish	Hash	None				Smoked			

DOM (STP)—2,5-Dimethoxy-4-methylamphetamine (STP—Serenity, Tranquility, and Peace), IV—intravenous, MDA—3,4-Methylenedioxyamphetamine, MDMA—3,4-Methylenedioxy-methamphetamine, MMDA—3-methoxy-4,5-methylenedioxyamphetamine, TMA—Trimethoxyamphetamine.
Source: Ksir et al. (2008).

not a simple task to differentiate bio/psycho/social factors for the purposes of better understanding each. Drug properties and drug effects are difficult to separate from psychosocial factors, unless the actual experience of users is neglected.

The effects of stimulants reported in Table 1.1 are increased alertness, agitation, and excitability as well as physiological responses, such as elevated pulse rate and blood pressure, insomnia, and loss of appetite. Users take stimulants to feel more "up." It is not difficult to understand the reasons why users may want to feel more vigorous, or more productive (although motivation is not our main concern at present).

By contrast, alcohol and other known depressants cause slurred speech, disorientation, staggering, and drunken behaviour. Quite apart from the objection that "drunken behaviour" is a circular description of alcohol's effects, many readers may discern other limitations of descriptions of this nature. Interestingly, euphoria is not a noted effect, although it figures prominently in the experiences of drinkers. Lowered inhibitions and relaxation are other effects of alcohol that are probably familiar, but not among those listed in Table 1.1. Drinkers commonly find these effects pleasurable and often stimulating—effects clearly sought by those who imbibe in the most widely used "depressant."

Drug Effects

We cannot depend entirely on drugs' chemical characteristics to describe their actual effects. For example, the most widely used stimulant is coffee, which does not appear in the drugs-of-abuse list (Table 1.1). It is considered safe, of course, if used in moderation and even in large doses (as many late-night workers and students, among other regular users, would probably agree). It is consumed most often in the morning, and, much like tea and other caffeinated drinks, enjoyed continually throughout the day by many people.

When taken as a stimulant it brings about alertness, fights fatigue, and reinvigorates reliably, but these effects can be followed by "crash," or loss of energy, which inevitably leads to having more in order to stay awake. The ceremonial attributes and prominence of tea time, coffee breaks, and other societal arrangements that support its use, even during work hours, is a testament to the cultural pervasiveness of stimulants consumed in this popular manner. It also serves to demonstrate how different expectations can be associated with different types of drugs.

Taking afternoon tea is a calming or relaxing pastime experienced by consumers, even though caffeine is technically a stimulant. A not entirely unrelated matter is the use of stimulants like Ritalin as a medication for children with attention deficit hyperactivity disorder (ADHD) (Hanson et al., 2011).

Because stimulants excite the nervous system, on the surface it makes no sense to give them to a hyperactive child. Children with ADHD, however, react by calming down in response to the internal stimulation caused by the drug. This physiological and behavioural balancing act seems contradictory, and the effect varies when taken by adults and non-ADHD diagnosed children.

These examples illustrate how drug effects are often contingent on individual and situational factors. When most people think of opioids they think of medications. The effects of prescription painkillers are not easily reconciled with those of street drugs such as heroin. Heroin is typically considered the kind of drug experience sought by only the most destitute, alternative, or marginalized members of society—yet it is also an opioid analgesic. Using drugs to numb pain, both physical and mental, is not limited, however, to the lowest social strata.

The effects of hallucinogens are also known to differ depending on the social circumstances of the user (cf. Levinthal, 2014; Lyman, 2011). As experienced by shamans or plant teachers in the Amazon—or by students in their dorm rooms, in the woods, or at a concert—there are clearly limitations to relying on general descriptions of drug effects, in this case visual illusions, altered perceptions, emotionality. These are helpful starting points, but inadequately characterize the full range of effects of drugs in this class.

The effects of cannabis are similarly variable, depending on the circumstances and experience of users. Furthermore, how substances are experienced in laboratory conditions often differ markedly from how they are experienced by users in real-world situations. Taking cocaine, for example, has been shown to improve reaction-time performance in a driving simulator. The use of cannabis under lab conditions appears to have the opposite effect (McDonald et al., 2008). These effects, however, have not been demonstrated under actual driving conditions, for either drug, respectively. Drivers under the influence of cannabis appear to perform better behind the wheel than those under the influence of cocaine. The effects of substance use depend on a variety of motivations, expectations, and characteristics of the user, and his or her social situation.

With the possible exception of euphoria (stimulants, opioids, cannabis), relaxed inhibitions (cannabis and alcohol), and excitability or alertness (cocaine), few descriptions of the potential effects of most drugs would be considered desirable. Rather, the negative effects are most often emphasized, with a focus on descriptions of abuse. The effects of overdose, tolerance, withdrawal, and the potential for developing dependence, where applicable, are described in Table 1.1.

Consistent with maintaining a biomedical perspective on different types of drugs and drug effects, the standard method of examining drug problems is to elaborate on biological determinants and official definitions. This approach consists of distinguishing between dependence and abuse, and includes clinical criteria for differentiating physiological from psychological dependence (Hart et al., 2011).

Box 1.1 presents established clinical criteria for psychiatric diagnosis of substance-use disorders. It is generally acknowledged by clinicians that dependence and abuse are complicated diagnoses. Behaviour varies widely and, consequently, so does the application of these standard definitions. For example, because dependence may occur with or without symptoms of physiological dependence, it appears that tolerance and withdrawal are less essential to the diagnosis than psychological dependence. These concerns or complications do not necessarily conflict with biomedical perspectives on addiction—also known as the **disease model**.

Biomedical interpretations of addiction, which understand drug problems as symptoms of a disease, are unquestionably becoming the

Box 1.1

DSM-IV-TR Criteria

A maladaptive pattern of substance use, leading to clinically significant impairment or distress, as manifested by three (or more) of the following occurring at any time in the same 12-month period.

1. Tolerance, as defined by either of the following:
   a. A need for markedly increased amounts of the substance to achieve intoxication or desired effect
   b. Markedly diminished effect with continued use of the same amount of the substance
2. Withdrawal, as manifested by either of the following:
   a. The characteristic withdrawal syndrome for the substance (refer to criteria for withdrawal from specific substances)
   b. The same (or a closely related) substance is taken to relieve or avoid withdrawal symptoms
3. The substance is often taken in larger amounts or over a longer period than was intended
4. There is a persistent desire or unsuccessful efforts to cut down or control substance use
5. A great deal of time is spent trying to obtain the substance (e.g., visiting multiple doctors or driving long distances), use the substance (e.g., chain smoking), or recover from its effects
6. Important social, occupational, or recreational activities are given up or reduced because of substance use

7. The substance use is continued despite knowledge of having a persistent or recurrent physical or psychological problem that is likely to have been caused or exacerbated by the substance

Diagnostic Criteria for Substance Abuse

A. A maladaptive pattern of substance use leading to clinically significant impairment or distress, as manifested by one (or more) of the following occurring within a 12-month period:

   1. Recurrent substance use resulting in a failure to fulfill major role obligations at work, school, or home (e.g., repeated absences or poor work performance related to substance use; substance-related absences, suspensions, or expulsions from school; neglect of children or household)
   2. Recurrent substance use in situations in which it is physically hazardous (e.g., driving an automobile or operating a machine when impaired by substance use)
   3. Recurrent substance-related legal problems (e.g., arrests for substance-related disorderly conduct)
   4. Continued substance use despite having persistent or recurrent social or interpersonal problems caused or exacerbated by the effects of the substance (e.g., arguments with spouse about consequences of intoxication, physical fights)

B. Symptoms have never met the criteria for substance dependence for this class of substance.

Source: American Psychiatric Association (2000).

predominant perspective. The disease model has developed over the last century, since the first scientific studies began to question the traditional assumption that addiction was a character flaw or moral failing of the addict. As we shall later see, in Chapter 7 in particular, there are benefits and downsides to adopting the disease model in addiction. The individual addict is absolved of blame, supporting investment in less punitive solutions to drug problems. Granting greater scope for biomedical solutions, however, individualizes drug-related problems in a way that minimizes social explanations.

Current understanding of drug issues owes as much to the increasing jurisdiction of the medical profession as it does to pre-existing moral standards that continue to support the criminalization of certain types of drugs. From a critical perspective, the disease model is perhaps better understood as an analogy, considering that addiction shares few characteristics of diseases (as they are more commonly defined and understood). Because addiction lacks the kinds of symptoms found in traditional medical diseases, diagnosing a drug problem offers little indication of how to treat the underlying cause.

Relying on behavioural symptoms makes it difficult to meaningfully distinguish addiction to drugs from addiction to certain behaviours (such as overeating, gambling, and even sex), which are increasingly depicted and treated in the same way. Treating these phenomena in the same way similarly expands the role of medicine in seeking out solutions, while minimizing social explanations for behaviour. Most experts in the field uncritically adhere to the disease model of addiction, despite its limitations. This approach in no way contradicts the theoretical assumptions of a bio/psycho/social standpoint on drug problems.

To support this argument, the following explanation is provided by a highly authoritative source—the National Institute of Drug Abuse (NIDA) in the US. Addiction is defined as a chronic, often relapsing brain disease that leads to changes in the structure and function of the brain; it causes compulsive drug seeking and use despite harmful consequences to the addicted individual and to those around her. Because of these changes, it is challenging to stop abusing drugs. Fortunately for addicts, there are treatments that can help them.

In addition to prevention—or the message that addiction can be best prevented if one never uses drugs—addiction-treatment medications, combined with behavioural therapy, are considered the best way to ensure sustained recovery. The National Institute of Drug Abuse calls for treatment approaches that are tailored to the individual patient's drug abuse patterns and any co-occurring medical, psychiatric, and social problems. The biomedical model is accordingly extended to include environmental and developmental factors (Wilson, 2012). These, in addition to biological factors, are recognized as having an important influence on developing an addiction.

First and foremost, it is noted that genetics, in combination with environmental influences, account for about half of one's vulnerability to addiction. This has been acknowledged by experts and leaves a great deal open for discussion on the relative proportion of genetic versus environmental factors. Other factors such as sex, ethnicity, and the presence of other mental disorders also play a role. Furthermore, genetic and environmental factors interact with critical developmental stages, which means that youth have higher addiction vulnerability. Environmental factors include the influence of friends and family members, socioeconomic status, and general quality of life.

Peer pressure, stress, parental involvement, and traumas such as physical and sexual abuse are all known factors influencing the course of drug addiction. Accordingly, the recommended emphasis on treatment and prevention is supported by a view of drug addiction as a disease shaped by social and developmental factors.

The psychosocial factors that influence drug use behaviour are examined more closely in the remainder of this chapter. Attention to these aspects of the framework does not necessitate a substantial deviation from the perspective of addiction as a disease or pathological condition—this overall perspective on drug problems is sustained due to considerable agreement across academic disciplines on the value of supporting the disease model of addiction.

Psychological Perspectives

The role of psychological dependence in addiction is widely recognized as being more important than biological dependence—at least according to most standard diagnostic tools. Therefore, it follows that psychology should have much to offer for better understanding of drug behaviour. The focus of the first part of this section is devoted to reviewing psychological perspectives (see Table 1.2). Psychological explanations put more emphasis on factors that describe how drug effects and problems are determined by user characteristics apart from their genetics and physiology or the properties of the drug per se.

Psychological approaches to drug behaviour in the literature emphasize the role of personality, costs and benefits, and other expectations about drug use held by users. In order to maintain authoritative definitions, as understood by experts and practised by clinicians, it is important to define the terms with some precision. The term *addiction* is too vague for present purposes; as a word that is used commonly and often rather casually in public conversation, it is ascribed with too many different social meanings. The term *dependence* is considered more precise; *drug dependence* is defined as frequent use, with clear signs of physiological withdrawal when the user stops taking the drug.

Table 1.2 Psychological Perspectives on Drug Problems

Theory	Description
Addictive personality	Assumes that problem drug use is the result of certain deficits (such as low self-esteem and reality avoidance) in the personality of individual users
Expectation effects	Emphasizes individual drug use expectations and motivations in determining experiences of use
Obsessive compulsive disorder	Assumes addiction is a form of mental illness manifested in the repetition of problematic drug behaviour
Reinforcement theory	Assumes that drug behaviour is determined by people's tendency to maximize rewards (or positive reinforcement) while minimizing costs (or negative reinforcement)
Self-medication hypothesis	Assumes the use of drugs is motivated by the need to cope with anxiety, depression, or other painful mental states

Dependence can take other forms. One indication is devoting a considerable amount of time and effort to getting and using the drug. According to the *Diagnostic and Statistical Manual of Mental Disorders (DSM),* other symptoms of dependence include taking more of the substance than originally intended and failed attempts to cut down or control the substance use (Box 1.1). By contrast, the term *abuse* refers to using drugs in ways that cause physical or psychological problems, difficulty meeting obligations at home or work, and legal problems. To receive a diagnosis of a substance abuse disorder, according to ***DSM* criteria**, use must be recurrent and the problems must lead to significant impairment or distress.

The recurring and compulsive nature of dependence, and its causal role in many symptoms of abuse, recommends the value of explaining drug behaviour with reference to reinforcement theories. Like economic models of behaviour, **reinforcement theory** in psychology (Bozarth, 1986) begins with the assumption that behaviour is determined by a natural tendency to seek to maximize rewards while minimizing costs. **Positive reinforcement** is the term used to explain how the pleasurable experience of drug use leads users to want to repeat the behaviour.

Negative reinforcement refers to the connection between avoiding withdrawal symptoms and continuing drug use. Alcohol and opiates are among the drugs most commonly associated with symptoms of withdrawal. It is often difficult to meaningfully distinguish the effects of physical and psychological withdrawal in these and in other drugs, including cocaine, cannabis, nicotine, and caffeine, which also have well-recognized symptoms of withdrawal.

A general description of the role of reinforcement is that while drug use may continue to be pleasurable, as tolerance develops a larger dose is needed to maintain the feeling sought by users (see Goode, 2011). The associated pattern of compulsive and increasing substance use results in the behaviours many experts and others recognize as symptoms of dependence or abuse. The presence or absence of pleasure in drug use is another source of controversy and discussion in research and theory on this area of study.

The compulsive nature of addiction lends itself to the recent tendency to view it alongside behaviours more traditionally aligned with mental illness. Among other implications, this suggests it might be readily diagnosed and treated much like obsessive-compulsive disorder (OCD) (see Berrios, 1985). An alternative to this view draws on evidence that addicts are usually anxious, depressed, or otherwise disturbed. Using drugs might thereby serve a self-medicating function to cope with or alleviate painful emotional states.

The similarity between OCD and drug dependence is challenged by the common observation that while addicts ordinarily describe the drug experience as pleasurable, OCD sufferers describe their behaviours as more distressing. The self-medication hypothesis (Khantzian, 1985), by contrast, corresponds with everyday drug use, which is often motivated by a need to cope. One need not necessarily use illicit substances to understand the function of "nonmedical" consumption of drugs as a way to feel better.

General use of the term **self-medicate** suggests a widespread recognition that medical needs are not always met by drugs that are prescribed and regulated by physicians and dispensed by pharmacies. The self-medication model is especially convincing when the addict's drug of choice correlates with a specific symptom, such as the use of stimulants by people with depression or of depressants in someone with anxiety. It is less persuasive in the case of polydrug use or in instances of switching from one substance to another by someone who is suffering from multiple addictions.

Because many addicts do just that, the lack of specificity lends support to other psychological explanations. One such explanation that is commonly referred to is found in the connection between problematic drug use and what is widely known as the **addictive personality**. Although there does not appear to be a set of unique attributes that correspond with this particular condition, a wide variety of correlates of addiction are identified. These range from antisocial behaviour to rebellion to sensation-seeking and risk-taking behaviours.

Other individual personality characteristics include reality avoidance, low self-esteem, self-derogation, and rejection as predictors of addictive drug behaviour (Lang, 1985). Many drug abstainers also demonstrate these characteristics, however, and it is difficult to prove that the addictive personality is the cause and not the consequence of excessive drug use. Accordingly, the theory of addictive personality is less influential among experts than its use in daily conversation might otherwise suggest.

Despite the popularity of explanations based on psychological characteristics of the individual user, situational and social influences are more important than the personality of people who use drugs. Understanding substance use and misuse requires attention to the social context in which the drug is used.

The Role of Expectations and Environment

It is commonly agreed that the effects of drugs on users must be understood as a three-way interaction between the drug, the individual, and the environment. At high doses, chemical effects and physiological reactions are more influential than psychosocial factors. At lower doses, characteristics of the individual user and the social context have a larger role to play (Hart et al., 2011).

The user's expectations about drug use are an important individual-level factor influencing drug behaviour. **Expectation effects** refer to how preconceived beliefs of the drug's effects influence the user's experience. Positive and negative (or neutral) expectations are predictive of quite different substance-use effects. The role of expectations or beliefs is demonstrated in medical studies with control groups using chemically inert drugs—i.e., taking a **placebo**—to assess the efficacy of another drug.

Just as a trusted, enthusiastic doctor can encourage changes in a patient that are not explained by the curative potential of a particular medication, so can users' expectations influence a drug's effects. If you think that smoking a joint will get you high, the chances are increased that it will do so. If you believe the drug will not affect you, the chances are increased that it will not. If you are highly anxious or anticipate unpleasant drug effects, such outcomes are more likely to occur.

If you believe that you are drinking the finest beer or wine or liquor, as opposed to cheaper brands of alcohol (or "swill"), there is a stronger tendency to rate it as superior even if it isn't. The kinds of expectations that we have about a drug's effects shape our understanding of the experience. Expectation effects help explain why drinking alcohol can be a different experience at a funeral, for example, than drinking at a graduation party, or at other times when we are sad or happy. Drug effects vary according to time, place, and situation.

The influence of drug use expectations is inseparable from the context or environment in which substance use occurs (Levinthal, 2014). Different social meanings attached to different drugs also shape perceptions and experiences of use. Some sociologists have argued that motivations for drug use develop after the behaviour rather than before (see Hathaway et al., 2013). Motivation originates not from within, but from the situation in which users find themselves.

Motivations are descriptions by users to specify preconceived expectations of, effects of certain drugs, thereby giving meaning to use by employing a range of explanations that are culturally appropriate. They describe the consequences of particular actions and the designated nature of the act. These associations are inseparable from social meaning and reaction to drug use. Whether motivation follows or precedes the drug behaviour, understanding social norms and attitudes is central to better understanding the experiences of use.

Rather than fixed elements, users' expectations and motives are, for sociologists, social phenomena that need to be explained. Along with rules and norms of action for various situations, users learn appropriate descriptions of use motives. As socially accepted justifications for behaviour, motives establish the conditions for certain lines of conduct. These interpretations must be situated socially (and historically and culturally).

Although the terminology used to describe motivations are based on cultural representations or general orientations for interpreting reality, different social groups have different vocabularies reflecting different circumstances and situational experiences. From a sociological perspective, better understanding of expectations that determine which motivations for drug use are considered culturally appropriate is a priority.

The role of the environment in determining drug behaviour has been documented by a number of researchers. One important study showed that heroin-addicted American war veterans stopped using heroin completely upon their return from Vietnam, despite its availability (see Robins, 1993). Challenging the popular notion of the "drug slave," this research shows exposure to heavily addictive drugs does not necessarily predict continuing addiction.

Other observations further challenge mechanistic perspectives of addiction, namely that drug use escalates and inevitably results in steadily deteriorating health and certain death (see Peele, 1985). There are many examples of long-term addicts who live long, productive, and otherwise "normal" lives. And there are examples of cancer patients (and wounded soldiers) whose dependence on strong opiates ceased immediately after recovery.

The role of environment is also demonstrated in studies that give animals (most often rats or monkeys) access to powerful narcotics in a laboratory setting. In these studies, morphine or cocaine is self-administered, sometimes to the point of death—with no regard for food, sex, health, or personal hygiene—in conditions experienced as unnatural or stressful. In more natural environments that offer opportunities for social interaction and other pleasurable distractions, the animals disregard the addictive drug.

Recognition of the role of environmental factors does not necessarily result in more attention to sociological perspectives on substance-use behaviour. Rather, the tendency is to limit descriptions of pathological behaviour as the product of deviant social learning or the absence of control. Classic sociological perspectives on drug problems (cf. Goode, 2011; Lyman, 2011) tend to be derived from theories of crime and deviance. Drug addiction is accordingly understood to be a problem with societal dimensions, causes, correlates, and corresponding solutions (Table 1.3).

Questioning the basis of existing definitions as they are conventionally described and understood is not a theoretical priority consistent with establishing a bio/psycho/social point of view. Sociological perspectives that encourage criticism of legal definitions and assumptions about deviance are

Table 1.3 Classic Sociological Perspectives on Drug Problems

Theory	Description
Differential association	Assumes that drug behaviour is the result of social learning and interaction between participants in a deviant subculture
Social bonds	Assumes that problem drug use is the outcome of inadequate development of bonds and controls in early childhood
Social disorganization	Assumes drug problems stem from the breakdown of traditional sources of control based on ethnic ties, religion, and other norms eroded in disorganized communities
Strain	Assumes drug problems are the outcome of frustration that results from social inequality and lack of opportunities

certainly less prominent than those that correspond with a conventional point of view pathologizing drug use.

Classic Sociological Perspectives on Drug Problems

Illicit substance use is often depicted in sociology as a problem caused by breakdown of control. In addition to the failure of the family or community to maintain said control, drug use becomes a product of a socialization process in which deviant values, beliefs, and motives are passed on to other individuals within the social group. Failed socialization to conventional norms is the main cause of crime and deviance in **social control theory**.

Examining community environments with high rates of substance use has often supported the conclusion that drug problems are a product of **social disorganization** (Shaw and McKay 1942). In other words, higher rates of crime, such as illicit drug use, are commonly observed in communities characterized by the breakdown or absence of controls. Traditional controls based on ethnicity, religion, and other norms or values that exist within communities are assumed to be diminished in inner-city neighbourhoods marked by cultural differences, poverty, and a transient population (Jacob, 2006).

Interventions targeting environmental factors at the community level, or else social disorganization, include developing connections in areas that strengthen the traditional controls, ties, and bonds that provide residents with a greater sense of neighbourhood safety and belonging. Investment in schools and after-school programs, recreational facilities, and community associations are among the recommended measures for addressing criminality and drug problems in the inner city.

Classic sociological perspectives and solutions contribute to a better understanding of the social conditions that facilitate drug problems in society. Higher rates of drug abuse and crime in some communities are better understood in terms of social disadvantages rather than individual pathology or biological determinants.

The role of economic disadvantage in particular is targeted in **strain theory**, which posits that disrupted norms and values are caused by a lack of legitimate opportunities for success (Merton, 1938). North American society has long encouraged citizens to strive for meritorious advancement and prestige. The harsh reality is that few actually succeed. Unequal access to accepted means to meet these goals (for example, opportunities for decent education and occupational success) results in failure to achieve them, and they are ultimately pursued through different or unconventional means.

Innovative means of gaining wealth, prestige, or status may include involvement in drug dealing. This type of criminal behaviour is frequently attractive to those whose other options are limited to taking a minimum-wage job in the service industry, with little hope of future advancement or security. Drug addiction is another adaptation to the strain produced by trying and failing to attain legitimate goals.

Rejection of conventional means and goals by addicts is described as a **retreatist adaptation**. Lack of necessary means to succeed in mainstream lifestyles and without the skills and know-how to engage in criminal activity, such as dealing drugs, retreatists seek escape by dropping out entirely. Addressing the conditions that incur such emotional strain through social programs that provide job training and educational opportunities is a common policy suggestion for communities plagued by high rates of crime and drug abuse.

A corresponding weakness of strain (and social disorganization) theory is the problem of uncritically assuming that drug use is more prevalent in particular communities. Information about crime rates tells us more about policing and reporting practices than substance use per se (see Blackwell and Erickson, 1988; Kitsuse and Cicourel, 1963). Drug use is more likely to be labelled as a crime in communities under steady police surveillance. Drug law–enforcement officers target middle- and upper-class neighbourhoods less frequently.

At the same time, open drug use may not attract the same level of attention in a lower-class community, where the police and public are more likely to encounter evidence of street-level use. Formal and informal societal reactions vary significantly depending on the social environment in which substance use occurs. Substance users have a wide range of social characteristics. Social disorganization and strain theories are, accordingly, at a disadvantage when explaining drug use as a kind of social pathological condition similar to other types of crime.

Another sociological perspective often cited emphasizes social controls within the family, as opposed to the community or economic strain. Here the focus shifts to early childhood socialization, and failure to develop social bonds (Hirschi, 1969). Drug use and other delinquent behaviour in youth are explained by failed socialization. Developing attachments to our mothers, fathers, siblings, and other family members facilitates development of ties to the community, and society more broadly, which knit individuals into the social fabric.

The socialized development of bonds to society, which theoretically protect us from using outlawed drugs, is augmented by commitment, involvement, and belief in the value and rewards of conventional behaviour. Primary socialization is the developmental process whereby children are rewarded for coming to the realization that conformity is highly valued and that there is more to be gained than lost by following the rules. Children initially obey to avoid the threat of punishment. Through processes of positive and negative reinforcement, a sense of guilt concerning consequences of wrongdoing extends to include feelings about disappointing loved ones.

Over time, social conscience is internalized, resulting in a motivation for conformity founded on the moral satisfaction of doing the right thing. This sense of satisfaction (and belonging) is arrived at independently of punishment or discipline by parents, teachers, and other respected authorities. Adolescents with a strong attachment to their parents, and commitment to conventional beliefs, can be reasonably expected to have lower rates of drug use and other delinquent behaviour.

Empirical support for this connection (cf. Butters, 2002; Hyshka, 2013) justifies investing in initiatives that target at-risk youth, with the goal of increasing their stake in conformity. Involvement in conventional activities that serve to limit time available for deviant behaviour and reinforce the value of conformity may include school and community-based programs, clubs and sports, Big Brothers Big Sisters, and other recreational pursuits. Developing social programs aimed at strengthening bonds in the family, the community, and the society at large is supported by the primary-socialization model.

As innately social creatures, we seek approval, recognition, and belonging or connection to our social group. As a society, it is increasingly recognized that many social problems like addiction are related to the sense of disconnectedness or alienation experienced by people in a globalizing world (see Alexander, 2000). People's ties to the community and family bonds are weakened, despite the advent of Facebook and other social media aimed at connecting individuals, in a society where transient relationships seem normal.

Children commonly grow up in single-parent families, and are often far removed from the countries and communities where their mothers, fathers, and grandparents were raised. Emphasizing problems due to social marginalization or disrupted social norms within the family and community has considerable appeal from an environmental standpoint. This explanation, however, does not give much insight into the socialization process for substance-use behaviour.

Failed socialization only partially explains drug use and misuse as they are conventionally defined and understood. The family and community, from this standpoint, are assumed to represent traditional standards of morality. These controls deter criminality and drug use, unless they fail to function in a manner that enables normal moral standards to prevail. But what about the influence of social groups that model criminality or deviant behaviour largely rejected by the standards of conventional society? Social bonds promoting drug behaviour are easily formed with deviant others among the family, peer group, or community.

Social Learning and Subcultures

Viewing substance use as an unconventional behaviour overlooks the fact that it often indicates a commitment to extreme conventionality, which does not equate to explanations derived from observations of "peer pressure" to be deviant. Drug use is often motivated by the pursuit of productivity, rather than rebellion. The use of powerful stimulants by students or night-shift workers, or steroids by athletes, is an innovative (albeit deviant) way of meeting the highly valued goals and expectations of North American society.

As noted previously, however, the strain interpretation does not shed much light upon the nature of the process by which substance use behaviour is learned. According to the theory of **differential association** (Sutherland, 1939), illicit drug behaviour, like other criminal traditions, is passed along from one generation to another within the immediate family and peer group. Definitions favourable to substance use are thereby learned through interaction within intimate social groups.

Through participation with more experienced users, novice users learn techniques and moral justifications that facilitate progression from initial experimentation to occasional and regular consumption of the drug. The transition into substance use appears to be augmented when conventional social bonds are weak (Kirst et al., 2009). Deviant social learning is therefore reinforced as the perceived rewards of nonconformity increase.

The frequency, intensity, and duration of interaction with deviant role models further influence the theorized process of transition into deviant behaviour. Age of first exposure to nonconformity also influences differential association. This factor corresponds with the familiar observation that young people are impressionable and hence particularly vulnerable to learning bad behaviour from deviant role models. The more intimate, frequent, and long term the exposure, the larger the potential for social learning.

In addition to the role of reinforcement in creating the optimal conditions for such learning to occur, revisions to the theory of differential association include the role of media and other influences that may be external to the family and peer group. Our relative proximity to criminal traditions may be less important than identifying with them and with the nonconforming definitions they uphold (Glaser 1956). One need not live in the same house, community, or city to be influenced by forces that are favourable to drug use.

Movies, television, music, and the Internet are all potential conduits for learning definitions that enable deviant role models to exist beyond these boundaries. Outside influences need not even be real people. The advent of the Internet has meant that drug subcultures have become increasingly diffuse throughout society and less associated with a particular social group.

The potential for like-minded people to connect through virtual communities, and the growth of social media, has made the role of media increasingly complex. Drug use by popular characters in movies, television, and in music has long been criticized by parents, politicians, and police.

However, there have also been opposing influences—condemning any form of drug use by young people, in particular—that have been transmitted through mainstream media resources.

Since the early days of ***Reefer Madness*** to today's antidrug campaigns that target youth, there has been considerable attention to the influence of media on substance use behaviour (cf. Schlosser, 2004; Starks, 1982). The influence of media advertising is demonstrated in the cultural acceptance of pharmaceutical solutions to all kinds of behavioural problems. We are bombarded daily with ads promoting pharmaceuticals as a fix-all remedy for everything that ails us. Therefore, theoretical discussions on the influence of media and other social learning require further contemplation of the broader cultural context in which substance use occurs. Classic sociological perspectives have contributed a better understanding of the features of the social environment and processes that explain criminality.

Yet these theories shed no light on how our social understanding of drug use as pathological or criminal came to be. To foreshadow the more critical perspective taken here, certain types of drugs and drug-use behaviours are prohibited in order to serve a particular political purpose and to target particular groups. Drug laws serve the interests of the powerful, reinforcing existing institutional arrangements. Drugs have come to represent certain ways of thinking and their users' status in the social world. It will also be observed that drug-related problems are as much a product of the criminalization of drugs as of the use of substances.

Implications for Drug Policy

Official definitions that determine what is "legal" and socially acceptable often contradict the facts. The toll of legal drug use on society, for example—due to the use of alcohol, tobacco, and pharmaceuticals (cf. Haydon et al., 2005; Rehm et al., 2006)—suggests there is a problem with assuming that our drug laws target forms of substance use that cause the greatest harm. Lessons learned from prohibition of alcohol in the United States, and the continuation of the war on drugs today, include rising prison rates, corruption, and increasing violence connected to the policing of the "black market" (Hathaway and Tousaw, 2008).

Accordingly, drug policy observers have increasingly argued for a shift toward prevention, education, treatment, and **harm reduction**, versus criminalizing users, to deal more humanely and effectively with drugs (Box 1.2).

The Four Pillars drug strategy is generally consistent with approaching drug use and drug-related problems from a bio/psycho/social point of view. This multiperspective view suggests a three-way model informed by biomedical and social science disciplines. An emerging public health perspective on drug problems similarly looks beyond biological determinants

Box 1.2

The Four Pillars Drug Strategy

Canada's National Anti-Drug Strategy is committed to maintaining a strong law enforcement framework that focuses primarily on reducing the supply, demand, and crime associated with illicit substance use. Drug policy at every level of society—global, national, and local—is recognized as having a profound effect on the health of individuals and communities.

At the local level, the Four Pillars Drug Strategy was adopted by the City of Vancouver in 2001 to address its open drug scene in the Downtown Eastside, and to reduce drug-related harm. The Four Pillars identified in the City's strategy are prevention, treatment, harm reduction, and enforcement. The most controversial of the pillars—harm reduction—has been explicitly rejected by the new national drug strategy.

The inclusion of the harm reduction pillar in Vancouver recognizes that strict abstinence is not a realistic option for every person addicted to drugs. Harm reduction's primary objective in the context of illicit drug use is to eliminate or minimize the risks of drug use to users and the public. Needle exchanges and supervised injecting facilities are two examples based on harm reduction that have been shown to improve safety and meet public health objectives by reducing harms of injection substance use.

Source: Urban Health Research Initiative (2014).

to consider the role of the *host* and *environment* as well as the *agent* or cause of disease.

Drug-taking behaviour is increasingly interpreted from a multi-lensed perspective that accounts for substance users' genetic susceptibility, vulnerability, and resilience, and their individual motivation to use drugs. The role of social context, or the environment, is another element increasingly recognized as being part of the equation.

The resulting three-way model corresponds with Norman Zinberg's (1984) account of drug experience—in terms of drug, set, and setting—which also takes a bio/psycho/social point of view. It is important to examine each drug's chemical composition and its documented physiological effects. We must account for **set factors**, including users' motives and their expectations of the drug experience. And we need to understand the **setting** or environment in which the use of substances takes place.

As a multidisciplinary framework for examining drug issues, a bio/psycho/social standpoint has considerable advantages. It spans a wide variety of academic areas and it is consistent with the training of many certified professionals—from physicians to psychiatrists to social workers and beyond.

Although still controversial, calls for law reform that challenge punishing drug users based on evidence-based practice are increasingly familiar and accessible to students. They also resonate with other members of the public who may find themselves questioning, or in conflict with, the law.

Despite its evident advantages, this model nonetheless presents an overly simplistic understanding of the social, which tends to reinforce the pathological perspective on drug use I have criticized above. The focus of this text is on better understanding substance-use behaviour with particular attention to the **definition of the situation**, or societal construction of the meaning of these acts.

Chapter Summary

This chapter lays the groundwork for developing a more critical perspective on drug problems in society. The approach adopted here departs from other textbooks by examining the social quite apart from its treatment from a bio/psycho/social point of view. The sociological perspective developed in this book suggests that sociology has much more to offer than simply describing features of the setting or environment that determine substance use behaviour.

The bio/psycho/social theories outlined in this chapter are better suited to describing pathological conditions than to challenging assumptions about drugs. Not only is there room for a more critical perspective, there is also a need for more explicit recognition of the value of refusing to accept—or take for granted—any knowledge that reinforces status-quo assumptions about drugs. This includes uncritically adopting a perspective comprising biomedical and psychosocial theories that often seem to contradict one another.

The aim of this book is to show the ways in which current understanding of drug use and drug problems are problematic. How we understand drugs is the focus of analysis, rather than a sidebar or point of passing interest. We are primarily concerned with the construction of drug problems as a product of collective social definition.

Chapter 2 develops a constructionist perspective on drugs and society that differs from most textbooks by taking a distinctly sociological approach. It begins by asking the fundamental question: how do we know what we know?

Questions for Critical Thought

1. How would someone trained in biology or medicine explain the influence of drugs on human behaviour?
2. How do psychological perspectives on drug use differ from the classic sociological approaches?

3. How would you explain the roles of set and setting factors to someone who has never been introduced to these ideas? Can you give some examples from your own experiences?

Suggested Readings

The five suggested readings are all leading textbooks for students taking courses on drugs and society. Each provides a comprehensive and accessible introduction to biological components of drug use and addiction, as well as psychological and classic sociological perspectives.

Hanson, G.R., P.J, Venturelli, and A.E. Fleckenstein. 2011. *Drugs and Society,* 11th edn. Burlington, MA: Jones and Bartlett Learning.

Hart, C.L., C. Ksir, and O. Ray, 2011. *Drugs, Society, and Human Behavior,* 14th edn. New York: McGraw-Hill.

Levinthal, C.F. 2014. *Drugs, Behaviour and Modern Society,* 8th edn. Upper Saddle River, NJ: Pearson.

Lyman, M.D. 2011. *Drugs in Society: Causes, Concepts and Control,* 6th edn. Burlington, MA: Anderson Publishing.

Wilson, H.T. 2012. *Annual Editions: Drugs, Society, and Behaviour 11/12,* 26th edn. New York: McGraw-Hill.

Suggested Websites

The Canadian Centre on Substance Abuse

www.ccsa.ca

The Canadian Centre on Substance Abuse (CCSA) website provides information and resources with the aim of connecting people with knowledge to reduce the harm of alcohol and other drugs.

The Centre for Addiction and Mental Health

www.camh.ca

The Centre for Addiction and Mental Health (CAMH) website provides information about services for people with addiction and mental health disorders.

Drugs & the Body: How Drugs Work

www.doitnow.org/pdfs/223.pdf

This publication from the Do It Now Foundation offers basic information about how drugs affect the body.

National Institute on Drug Abuse

www.drugabuse.gov

The US National Institute on Drug Abuse (NIDA) website is an authoritative resource with the goal of helping researchers find better ways to prevent and diagnose addiction.

Streetdrugs

www.streetdrugs.org

This website provides comprehensive information on a wide variety of commonly abused drugs.

2 Theoretical Perspectives on Drugs: How Do We Know What We Know?

Learning Objectives

- To understand how sociological perspectives on drug problems have developed over recent decades.
- To understand the contribution of constructionist perspectives to discussions about drug use as a social problem.
- To distinguish between contextual and strict constructionist approaches to examining social problems, and their implications in examining drug issues.

Introduction

There is a scene in *The Matrix* in which the protagonist "awakens" in a fluid-filled pod, with tubes entering his body, facing a most disturbing redefinition of reality. In *The Truman Show,* the hero comes to the shocking realization that his life is actually a reality TV show, and those around him are paid actors. In *The Sixth Sense*, the main character must ultimately face the stunning truth that he is actually dead. These fictional examples illustrate the point that things are not always as they seem.

This may be so, one might object, but real life is quite different. Short of being brainwashed or converted to a cult (and other things at home in the movies), there are few examples in the real world where (sane and lucid) perceptions of reality are so significantly altered. Our knowledge of the world is largely shaped by our experiences, which in turn are shaped by social learning.

What we know about drugs, therefore, depends on who we are, where we come from, the people with whom we surround ourselves, and our individual experiences. Some attitudes about drugs are established early on. By the time children reach school age, drugs are generally seen as "bad." Medicines bought in pharmacies, however, are "good," and are not considered drugs in the colloquial sense of the word. Bad drugs are used by bad people—or criminals. Good drugs are used by people who are sick and who therefore require expert medical treatment.

When we are children, learning to distinguish between good drugs and bad drugs is the same as learning right from wrong. Over time we learn that there are other "in between" substances that can be used when we are older and reach the legal age. Some, like cigarettes, are actively discouraged. Others, such as alcohol, are more socially acceptable but come with warnings to use in moderation to avoid health problems.

Standard definitions of good versus bad drugs are more likely to be challenged as children enter adolescence. It is often understood, at least informally, that some experimentation or experience with drug use is a normal part of growing up. For many youth, standard definitions about drugs and drug use are unlikely to be seriously questioned until they take a post-secondary course in university or college that encourages them to question what they know. Critically examining the social world in which we live is a crucial function of the social sciences. An important role of social scientists is, arguably, to challenge and undermine assumptions about so-called universal truths.

People's understanding of the world is partly altered by exposure to alternative perspectives and new knowledge, which is the aim of sociologists and social scientists. Accordingly, this chapter is devoted to developing the critical perspective adopted in this book. Its focus on the "definition of the situation," or the social context in which substance use occurs, requires an understanding of the nature of the process by which we learn the difference between right and wrong. This includes exploring how our world view is determined by a variety of cultural and social influences that shape attitudes about drugs as a social problem.

Theoretical Developments

Labelling Theory

The sociology of crime and deviance has undergone considerable development throughout the last half-century (see Hathaway and Erickson, 2003). Since the 1950s, sociologists have been increasingly concerned with challenging what they believe to be a naive adherence to an overly simplistic way of looking at the world. Although it had been previously observed in the United States that drug laws unfairly target and affect the disadvantaged, it was not until the 1950s that this view began to flourish. Drug use was defined as a crime first and foremost, on the assumption of a shared or common value system.

Notwithstanding classic contributions to the development of sociological perspectives on criminal behaviour, an entirely different theoretical orientation was required to shift the focus to the process of defining deviance. Previously, sociology was primarily concerned with the study of rule-breaking behaviour (Lemert, 1951). This point of view assumes consensus over the legitimacy of rules that have been broken and seeks to explain the social causes of rule breaking. Because everybody breaks rules from time to time, but does not necessarily get caught or punished, the focus ought to shift to societal reaction and the subsequent influence this has on the rule-breaker.

Howard Becker's (1953, 1955) research on marijuana use provided a detailed explanation of substance use behaviour within a general framework of normal learning processes that depend on interaction within intimate personal groups. Based on interviews with jazz musicians, he shed light on how marijuana users learn to interpret drug effects, define its use as pleasurable, and justify its use despite mainstream social disapproval.

To progress to regular use of marijuana, one must learn how to secure a reliable supply, and how to keep one's use a secret from disapproving others. In the 1960s, Becker's book *Outsiders* (1963) inspired a growing interest in the role of law enforcement and social-control agencies in the process of exclusion from conventional attachments, which facilitates increasing commitment to criminality. A more critical perspective, focused on the labelling process, encouraged sympathetic portrayals of drug users and other social deviants as more "sinned against than sinning."

The labelling perspective emphasizes the emergence of a sense of self that favours criminality through a process of internalizing exclusionary labels. Occasional marijuana use in adolescence, for example, is not unusual. Some experimentation with illicit drug use is considered normal. But what if the occasional pot smoker gets caught using by a parent, teacher, or law enforcement officer who is required to recognize and punish the behaviour?

Whether the punishment is formal or informal, through official labelling and subsequent rejection, the resulting stigma theoretically does not necessarily deter future marijuana use. The experience of social disapproval and exclusion might, on the contrary, result in more commitment to the habit and increased association with marijuana-using friends. Over time, the "pothead" label may even start to stick, as our hypothetical wayward adolescent comes to identify increasingly with marijuana users and less and less with her non-using peers.

Taken to its logical extreme, the labelling process eventually results in more commitment to the label or deviant identity so that it becomes one's **master status** (Becker, 1963). Being labelled as a pothead (or a hooker, or a junkie, or any colloquial term for an undesirable behaviour), therefore, becomes the central attribute determining one's outlook and how one is viewed by the outside world (see Box 2.1). This may explain why tough-on-crime approaches do not work. The implication is that less control, not more, or harsher punishment is needed to avoid assigning formal labels that lead to amplification of deviant behaviour.

The criminalization of illicit-substance users, and others engaging in victimless crimes, spurred a growth of studies on the negative effects of formal (and informal) stigma. This shift in focus from the previous emphasis on causes of criminal behaviour to the process of defining deviance represented a significant challenge to the legitimacy of law and related moral norms. If labels served to amplify commitment to the behaviour that is

Box 2.1

The Stigma of Addiction

> I am not what I think I am. And I am not what you think I am. I am what I think that you think I am.
>
> —Charles H. Cooley

Stigma is a form of *bias* or *prejudice* against others. Like *discrimination,* these terms typically refer to negative assumptions that are made about members of a group who subscribe to a set of characteristic values and behaviours that are perceived to be different from those of the cultural norm. Most people are treated as individuals, with distinct qualities and faults. When stigma intervenes, however, individuals are no longer seen as multifaceted, but rather as a stereotype. Perceived as being "not like us," these individuals are dehumanized. This reaction creates problems not only for those stigmatized but also for their families and their communities. Stigma is destructive because it forces people to live on the margins of society.

The term stigma is particularly relevant to addiction and how people with drug problems are viewed. Society's condemnation of illicit drug use is not simply about punishment, for it may help prevent or change harmful substance use behaviour. Stigma, though, can easily create a greater obstacle to change. The assumption "once a junkie, always a junkie" puts a burden on those in recovery as they wrestle with their addiction. Treating addicts as outsiders further marginalizes people whose substance use is often symptomatic of the very psychosocial problems caused by being cast aside.

Source: Seymour (2012).

defined as criminal or deviant, the solution was to stem the emphasis on punitive societal reaction to the act and the actor.

Excessive monitoring and punishment that is disproportionate to the societal harms caused by the action is not only ineffective, but also counter-productive. From this perspective, crimes without victims, including drug use, ought to be decriminalized to avoid the formal labelling and process of exclusion leading to the formation of a criminal identity.

In the 50 years since publication of *Outsiders*, the liberal agenda of the labelling tradition has been roundly criticized by mainstream criminologists, who object to what they believe to be a distraction from the primary objective of explaining causes of criminality. From this standpoint, labelling theorists, whose agenda seems to be winning sympathy and tolerance for criminal behaviour, are no more than apologists for crime.

Although less sharply critical, most liberal sociologists were more focused on environments and conditions that encourage criminality than on critiquing criminal justice institutions. By the end of the 1960s, however, liberal sociology—**labelling theory** in particular—was being reproached for its complicity with the state in failing to challenge social inequality in American society. The labelling perspective was disparaged for promoting a man-on-his-back attitude that identified with underdogs (Gouldner, 1968).

A more radical position—one more consistent with the growing intellectual and political unrest in Western cultures—favoured an approach to sociology devoted to the study of people fighting back against oppressive institutions. In an era marked by countercultural assertions that challenged the establishment and values of the ruling class, the conflict perspective in sociology emerged.

Conflict Theory

By the late 1960s, a social-conflict view of law was beginning to develop in North America in earnest (cf. Chambliss, 1969; Quinney, 1969; Turk, 1969; Cook, 1969). Conflict theorists rejected the liberal notion that law represents the compromise of diverse interests. Rather, some interests are supported at the expense of others, through the coercion of those segments by more powerful groups.

Conflict theorists are divided in their understanding of the nature of the conflict that explains unequal power relations and law-making. The **pluralist perspective** views power as existing in a multitude of bases of authority: government, religion, science, medicine, and other institutional relationships and structures. Marxist conflict theorists, by comparison, are focused on class and power relations based on economic factors. The essential conflict in our capitalist society is understood to be the struggle between the haves and have-nots—that is, the owners and the workers who must sell their labour to the owners to survive.

Pluralist (or liberal conflict) theorists are not ignorant of the central influence of economic power. Indeed, their research and case studies sometimes demonstrate it best. The influence of medical professionals in shaping social attitudes toward drugs, for example, cannot be fully examined separately from interests of corporate elites. Who ultimately benefits from waging a war on drugs? Or, more precisely, waging a war on some drugs?

Who has the most to gain from this particular arrangement? In the context of this book, it is doctors, lawyers, judges, and others with a vested interest—shareholders, for example, or those employed within the system. There are the owners of drug companies, pharmacies, and the producers and suppliers of alcohol and cigarettes on the one hand and the corporate elites who finance building prisons on the other. The pluralist perspective on law-making was rejected by Marxist conflict theorists for its weakened focus on the role of law in serving dominant class interests. As a result, attributing the power to influence law-making to multiple segments of society fell out of favour.

By the mid-1970s, conflict theorists started calling for a new criminology (Taylor et al., 1973). Its primary objective would be to undertake a more critical analysis of crime control in capitalist societies (cf. Chambliss, 1975, 1976; Quinney, 1974, 1975, 1977). This meant embracing a more radical **Marxian perspective** on the role of class interests and power in law-making. There was an apparent loss of interest in crimes against morality in favour of laws serving more clearly evident class interests.

A variety of studies in the United States identified an array of factors that influenced law-making or shaped existing policies on drugs. This research was supportive of a pluralist perspective. Becker's (1963) work shed light on the influence of moral entrepreneurs in pushing for the ban on marijuana. As the Director of the US Federal Bureau of Narcotics in the early 1930s, Harry Anslinger successfully mobilized interracial hostility (see also Bonnie and Whitebread, 1974; Helmer 1975; Musto 1973) and growing fear about the drug's effect on youth.

At a time when few Americans knew anything about cannabis (apart from its association with distrusted Mexican immigrants), Anslinger's campaign against marijuana went unchallenged. His efforts ushered in a ban that, while increasingly contested, still dictates US federal drug policy in Washington today. The entrenchment of an antidrug bureaucracy in the United States, and later on a larger global scale, is another factor cited by observers in explaining the emergence and continuation of the war on marijuana (cf. Dickson, 1968; Reasons, 1974).

The relatively short-lived ban on alcohol, notes Gusfield (1963), during the 1920s Prohibition era, illustrates how **status politics** shaped that campaign and the eventual repeal. Although the drug prohibited ostensibly did not correspond with values of the Protestant elite, the popularity of alcohol was ultimately proven too expansive across classes to prevent or outlaw drinking as a way to keep intemperate Catholics "in their place."

Studies on the origin of narcotics laws in Canada also indicate a multitude of influences, including anti-Asian sentiment and economic interests, which led to the banning of opium (cf. Boyd, 1991; Carstairs, 2006; Cook, 1969). Smoking opium was something the Chinese did. It was a habit they brought with them when large numbers were recruited from China for the construction of the railway—a job deemed too unsafe for white Canadians to do. They eventually settled on the west coast in Vancouver; most survived and Chinese businesses began to thrive.

White Canadians felt threatened. Early labour unions are among the vested interests that sought to put the foreign "invaders" in their place. The ban on opium enacted in 1908 did not apply to opiates like morphine, used as medicine in a variety of forms by white consumers at the time. Physicians, pharmacists, drug companies, police, and parent associations—representing myriad segments of society—are among the many interest groups over the past century that have sought to influence the law-making process that decides how different drugs are viewed and their use defined.

Much like Harry Anslinger in the United States, Canadian magistrate Emily Murphy helped initiate a ban on marijuana possession that has stood for more than 90 years. Using the same themes of unsubstantiated violence, and by provoking interracial fear, this early advocate of voting rights for women actively campaigned for prohibition in a country even less familiar with the drug. Marijuana was successfully depicted as a new menace to Canadian society. The law was introduced in 1923, with no debate in Parliament required. No subsequent enforcement of the law was documented for more than a decade, well into the 1930s. With no reported arrests for the offence until that time, there was little evidence that anyone was actually using marijuana. This legislation is a primary example of the making of a law without a problem (Giffen et al., 1991).

The social history and origins of drug laws in this country are taken up at length in other sources, some of which are overviewed in the next chapter and at various other points throughout this book. For the present purposes, it is sufficient to note that Canadian studies have tended to support a pluralistic view of drug laws. The most comprehensive so far, by Giffen and his colleagues (1991), found no evidence of a powerful business elite bringing about drug laws to serve its own interests. Rather, drug laws are brought about by groups that have the power to influence the law-making process at the expense of relatively powerless groups (Table 2.1).

Claims about the harms of using drugs may be important to justify enactment of a law. From a conflict perspective, however, the law that is created is more of a reaction to the characteristics of those who use the drug than its particular properties or evidence of harm. Support for liberal conflict explanations, which suggest a pluralistic view of drug-related law-making, has coalesced into a broader drug politics perspective

Table 2.1 Labelling and Conflict: Overlapping Concepts

Concept	Definition
Deviance defining process	Emphasizes societal reactions to substance use behaviour and what influence these have upon the user
Liberal conflict	Assumes a pluralistic view of power in society, wherein laws that target drug users reflect a multitude of interests and authorities (government, religion, science, medicine, and others)
Marxist conflict	Assumes a view of power in which the emphasis is squarely on the role of class and economic interests in creating laws that target certain drugs
Master status	Assumes the influence of labels and associated stigma are strong determinants of drug-related problems
Status politics	Assumes that drug laws represent the interests of the powerful, as a way to reinforce the dominant group's interests and the legitimacy of its norms and values

(Himmelstein, 1978). Simultaneously, by the 1970s, the role of collective definition in constructing social problems was attracting significant attention among liberal sociologists.

The emergence of the social constructionist perspective thereby coincided with a growing recognition of the need for more attention to the process of **claims-making** by a variety of interests in drug policy debates. Claims-making is a concept that describes the process of identifying a phenomena as a "social problem," and thereby a matter of societal concern. As we shall see, claims-making is a process that social scientists both study and contribute to. The constructionist perspective that informs the present book is developed in additional detail in the next section. We will look at the key concepts and theoretical assumptions that recommend it as a guiding framework for this book. We will also overview its scope and limitations as a theoretical framework for examining drug problems.

The Constructionist Perspective

The constructionist approach to social problems shifts attention away from the actual societal conditions that occupy the focus of other sociological perspectives. Instead the emphasis is squarely on the collective social processes that determine what conditions are defined as social problems and what types of social problems the claims-makers say they are.

Herbert Blumer (1971) first observed that sociologists tend to focus on describing the conditions that determine social problems. As we saw in the last chapter, for example, sociological perspectives on drug problems emphasize the pathological features of the social environment or setting (versus internal, biological influences). Rather than making claims about particular conditions, however, Blumer argued that the role of sociology was to examine what each and every social problem had in common.

What every different type of social problem has in common is public recognition that there is a so-called problem. At any given time there is a wide array of problems that are not the subject of considerable concern. Numerous potential social problems coexist, but only some are given the required level of attention to be broadly recognized as such. Although many problems have existed throughout history—violence against women, environmental degradation, and the exploitation of children, for example—it has not been until recently, over the past few decades, that these have been publicly identified as problems.

With so many social problems competing for attention, not all of them attract consideration or concern, and those that do are often rather short-lived. Others, like societal concerns about drug problems, appear largely interchangeable, from one substance to another. To illustrate, widespread panic over substance use in North American society has emerged time after time in the past century for almost every drug imaginable—from alcohol and cannabis to heroin and crack, from PCP and LSD to ecstasy and steroids (see Goode and Ben-Yehuda, 1994). Each of these drug panics has subsided, only to be replaced with a more general level of anxiety about the use of certain outlawed drugs.

Often based on the depiction of worse-case scenarios, which may or may not actually exist, the extent of actual harm triggering the drug panics ought not to be our primary concern. The constructionist approach draws attention away from the alleged conditions that characterize the social problem and focuses instead on the collective process of claims-making. Verifying claims about conditions is irrelevant. From a constructionist perspective, the focus of analysis is on the activities of claims-makers who seek to assert their own particular definitions and solutions to the problems.

Strict Constructionism

Early constructionists like Spector and Kitsuse (1977: 72) followed Blumer in calling for a clearer sociological analysis of "how categories of social problems and deviance are produced, and how methods of social control are institutionally established." From a constructionist perspective, social problems are only possible as an assemblage of perspectives and collective definitions. Therefore a clear distinction must be drawn between particular constructions of "the problem"—as a practical accomplishment—and the theoretical project of the sociologist. Social constructionists, accordingly, are careful to focus their analysis on claims about conditions.

Most importantly for **strict constructionists**, one must refrain from giving tacit privilege or weight to one's own opinions about the alleged conditions. Despite its logical consistency, the feasibility of maintaining a purely definitional perspective in practice has been the subject of considerable debate among constructionists. Most constructionists acknowledge that their analyses assume some objective knowledge of the "problem" being studied.

Attempts to bracket off or separate the projects of laypersons (participants involved in the social problems process) from the work of sociologists are not entirely new. Social scientists have long argued that we ought to strive for a value-free position to establish facts objectively. The emphasis on scientific evidence is essential if sociology hopes to attain the same prestige and influence as the natural sciences.

The value-free aim, however, can lead to adoption of different kinds of theoretical commitments. Explaining social facts as pathological, or otherwise, violates the standards of neutrality (by not making any claims about conditions). Remaining value-free means avoiding discussing "facts" to maintain the focus on the ways that social problems are collectively defined.

The goal of being value-free in the social sciences is consistent with the aims of those who view themselves as scientists—i.e., positivists—and with those of some constructionists as well. Strict constructionists maintain that social problems are inseparable from the subjective process of collective definition. But attempting to divorce their own perspectives from the process of sociological inquiry puts the point of view of strict constructionists at odds with other critical developments of the last half-century.

In the 1960s, sociologists increasingly began criticizing their discipline's adherence to objective standards in pursuit of formal scientific knowledge. To describe a finding as valid and reliable may serve to justify a finding as objective, argued Gouldner (1968), but tells us nothing about what objectivity really means. The value commitments of researchers are not only inescapable; values, from his standpoint, are a necessary condition of the pursuit of objective inquiry.

To speak of objectivity or bias in sociology, the sociologist assumes a role analogous in some ways to that of a judge who must do justice according to a stated standard, norm, or value. Objectivity, for Gouldner, is therefore a moral struggle over value commitments—and the grounds for those commitments—that support a certain finding or position. These commitments need to be explained, for we cannot hope to be objective without accepting that such knowledge is always problematic. Science must be understood as little more than a perspective, or way of looking at the world, in which objectivity or fact cannot be separated from our cultural understanding.

Sociology, according to constructionists like Gusfield (1981), holds the promise of becoming a perspective of perspectives. The aim of sociologists should be to render ways of looking at phenomena, ordinarily taken for granted, strange and problematic. To imagine different ways of looking at the world is to imagine that things can be otherwise. Sociological inquiry of this nature is political insofar as it diminishes the power of authority and legitimacy gained by unquestioning belief. When political realities are taken for granted, or understood as matters of technical necessity, the technical language of science serves those in power who are able to conceal from public recognition that moral and political decisions are being made.

For Gusfield, the required role of the sociologist is thereby to be skeptical of every perspective and to foster development of many perspectives. One must stay uncommitted. The strict constructionist does not presume some version of reality, vision, or perspective that is superior to other perspectives. She must strive to maintain distance or detachment from political commitments that betray a partiality of interests. This point of view is inconsistent with Gouldner's earlier position that having ideological commitments is not only unavoidable but actually necessary to the construction of a truly objective understanding of social reality (1968).

Failure to explain one's ideological commitments is arguably injurious. Believing in the myth of value-freedom or neutrality invites complacency among sociologists, states Gouldner, by allowing the unspoken ideologies that inevitably guide us in our research to go unexamined. Writing in the 1960s, Gouldner's aim was to examine the role of power elites and their oppressive institutions; how some "are crushed by certain institutions, and how all alike are subjected to institutions that do not permit them to live as they wish" (1968: 111). He advocated for a stance of objective partisanship, set within a larger framework of humanistic understanding. In keeping with the radical spirit of the era, his main critique was targeted at liberal sociology.

Becker and his followers were, most notably, chided for sympathizing with downtrodden persons, like drug users, in a voyeuristic way that did not directly challenge the institutional arrangements that determined their oppression. Forty-five years later, criticism of so-called liberal sociology has more of a conservative agenda. Rather than allegiance to bureaucratic institutions, liberal academics are more commonly disparaged for the threat they represent to political stability.

Challenges to status quo arrangements, such as drug laws, are ordinarily rejected by authorities as unwanted intrusions into State affairs by liberals playing personal politics. In reality, however, few social scientists spend much time defending or developing the left-liberal assumptions that so often guide our academic work. We will engage with these concerns in the analysis that follows.

The remainder of this chapter is devoted to developing a constructionist perspective that views the study of claims-making and social problems in the context of our surrounding culture. It is generally acknowledged by constructionists that some knowledge of conditions is assumed in their case studies. Despite the aim to foster a strict focus on claims-making, or purely definitional perspective on social problems (see Schneider, 1985; Spector and Kitsuse, 1987), researchers inevitably make assumptions about reality based on their understanding of and experiences with the world (Woolgar and Pawluch, 1985).

Increasingly over the past three decades, constructionists have sought to overcome what Gusfield (1985) called "preoccupation with the logic of theory" at the expense of empirical scrutiny. A more pragmatic reading of the theory is required to answer criticisms that constructionism amounts to mere philosophizing by liberal sociologists. A **contextual constructionist** perspective is needed to move beyond a standpoint of moral relativism and develop the analyses presented in this book.

A Contextual Framework

Best (1989) fittingly cites Becker, who in turn cited Herbert Blumer, in calling for a more pragmatic and strategic framework for sociologists employing a constructionist perspective. Blumer sounds like Gouldner in asserting that sociologists perform a role in research like that of a judge: "The task of social and psychological sciences is to improve human judgment—not to supply fixed rules, laws, or rigid generalizations. There is a need for relevant and usable information—and the cultivation of abilities to use the information intelligently" (cited in Becker, 1988: 21).

Although the process of claims-making ought to be our primary focus, Best argues, we must also seek to situate claims-making within its social context of culture and structure. We must acknowledge that all claims, and any study of claims-making, cannot be separated from the cultural and social realities in which they are produced. Because the meanings of all things are situational, or relative, constructionists must also look beyond claims-making circles to understand what claims mean within their larger social context.

Building on the primary assumption that social problems are the products of a process of collective definition, Blumer argued, we must nonetheless seek knowledge as a way to correct for any ignorance or misinformation about the makeup of the problem (1971). The sociologist must seek empirical knowledge of conditions that help explain why and when certain claims come about, and how social problems emerge. This may mean reporting on discrepancies between existing outside knowledge of the actual conditions and the way claims-makers have defined the situation. This position is in no way inconsistent with the idea that all sources of knowledge are social constructions that ought to be treated as claims in their own right.

It has already been established that scientific evidence—including arguments and studies produced by social scientists—is a part of the claims-makers' efforts to persuade. A contextual constructionist perspective is, accordingly, a useful framework for examining **social problems discourse**. By *discourse* social scientists mean a way of thinking and communicating, through the use of speech or writing, which conveys shared understandings or ideas about the world.

The term *rhetoric* more commonly refers to use of language with the specific objective of having a persuasive effect on its audience. The essential features of claims-making that need to be identified are the argumentative, rhetorical styles of expression. The styles and strategies of claims-making are best assessed through research on the role of discourse and rhetorical activity in the collective process of constructing social problems.

Consistent with a purely definitional perspective, emphasizing rhetoric means focusing on language (Ibarra and Kitsuse, 1993). Despite its logical desirability, however, sustaining the requirements of a strict constructionism is an objective that has not been widely realized in practice. In spite of themselves, sociologists cannot help but bring their interests and professional agendas into their interactions with informants (Sarbin and Kitsuse,

1994). If a value- or assumption-free perspective is unattainable, all constructionist analysis is contextual by default (Best, 1995).

Recognizing the sociocultural context of claims-making helps situate it structurally, and ultimately politically, in a world in which sociologists, like the social groups we study, are free to challenge ideas that many people take for granted. As a pertinent example, 40 years ago Gusfield (1975) made note of a trend in drug policy claims-making toward a more rational style of persuasion. He observed increasing use of science as a method of upholding or legitimating official definitions of the nature of drug problems.

To illustrate, the ban on marijuana has been previously upheld on moralizing grounds, in terms of "reefer madness" (cf. Schlosser, 2004; Starks, 1982). In previous incarnations, claims about the drug have ranged from threats of homicide, communism, and amotivational syndrome, to the idea that use of cannabis leads to use of hard drugs. In the last few decades, the nature of the threat has been increasingly defined in terms of mental illness, which is more consistent with a medical science model (e.g., Arsenault et al., 2004).

Increasingly, claims-making must be put forth in a language suggesting rational analysis, in terms reflecting public as opposed to private interests. The participants must appear objective and informed, and must persuade rather than influence their audience. Experts play a role, as they are assumed to be impartial. The impartiality of experts, much like the claim to objectivity, is of course the subject of considerable debate.

Notwithstanding this objection, knowledge shared in public forums can be subversive, argued Gusfield, as a challenge to the factual basis for official definitions and assumptions. Research by experts in the drug field serves to break down the appearance of consensus, setting limits on public acceptance of particular assumptions about drug use. The expected level of public discourse has presumably shifted to the point that more extreme claims, and depictions of drug users, are no longer accepted as credible arguments.

At the same time, here in Canada and elsewhere, we have seen little change in the direction of drug policy reform. After decades of informed consideration and discussion by experts arguing for changes in the law, perhaps such knowledge makes less difference than we are willing to admit. As Gusfield (1975: 13) readily conceded, it appears that "scientific knowledge is only one of a number of factors that bear upon the symbolic and instrumental character of official public action."

To assess the broader role of discourse in claims-making, Best (1987) explored the ways that values are incorporated when they enter into the social problems process. Previously, constructionists, following Spector and Kitsuse (1977), focused on the organizational process of claims-making activity, rather than the style and content of the claims themselves. Values were regarded as resources for claims-making, a view facilitating a sociological perspective that is focused on the process of collective definition.

Strict constructionists—who focus on the people who make claims, and the organization of the claims-making process—caution against drawing attention to the values of claims-makers when explaining social problems. Contextual constructionists, by comparison, are more explicitly concerned with examining the culture than the organization of claims-making per se. This approach attends to the construction and presentation of claims-making, which determine how social problems become "typified" (see Best, 1995).

Best argued that claims-makers inevitably characterize the nature of the problem in particular ways. They emphasize some aspects over others and promote specific orientations or approaches to the problem, by pointing to particular causes and solutions. Claims are therefore conclusions that need to be established, rather than taken for granted. Best's approach (1987) to analyzing social problems discourse divides statements by claims-makers into grounds, warrants, and conclusions.

Grounds are the foundation for interpreting the problem in a certain way. These kinds of statements establish certain boundaries, and advocate for a particular solution. Grounds statements serve to establish the facts, often through the use of illustrations or analogies selected for their extreme and emotive nature. Once the human side of the problem is established, its full extent and impact on society can be foretold.

After strong grounds have been established, effective **warrants** are essential—statements about warrants justify drawing attention to particular conclusions and solutions. For an argument to be persuasive to an audience, it must be interpreted as valid. The validity of claims is contingent on belonging to a field or discipline that deems the warrant valid, and the level of consensus concerning cultural values.

Depending on the nature of the target audience, it may be strategic to downplay certain warrants or tailor them to those in different fields. Though often kept implicit, or glossed over in discussion, convincing warrants are essential for bridging the gap between established grounds and particular conclusions. Strong warrants justify solutions. Certain values and particular interests also need to be accepted in order for a claim about a social problem to lead to the adoption of a recommended policy.

Claims-making is principally a rhetorical activity that involves selecting from the arguments available those that are persuasive within a certain cultural context. Strict constructionists are cautioned against using the same language or **vernacular resources** employed by the claims-makers, which ought to be considered the central focus of analysis (Ibarra and Kitsuse, 1993). The emphasis on language and the definitions process call for a suspension of the "natural attitude." This means adopting a detached, or theoretically removed, view of how reality is socially constructed and represented in conventional everyday talk. In reality, however, claims-making strategies are naturally highly sensitive to—and therefore inseparable from—context.

Claims-makers and claims-making are inevitably situated in a particular moral universe, time and place, or setting. This shapes every aspect of the social problems process, and our sociological interpretation of events. Decisions to make claims and rhetorical choices emerge from a larger cultural context. Rhetorical work is influenced by the weight assigned to various sorts of evidence and values, existing standards of law-making, and the level of consensus about these kinds of judgments (Best, 1987).

Rhetorical Work

In addition to effective mobilization of resources, **social problems ownership** is critical, Best argues, to establishing a successful claims-making campaign. Well-established social problems are owned by well-established claims-makers. While political insiders have easy access to law-makers, claims-makers on the outside must attempt to reach and persuade the general public to pressure politicians.

The early stages of rhetorical work present demands for change, which call for a new interpretation or different way of looking at a problem. Demands for reinterpretation are often propelled by outrage and directed at a receptive or likewise motivated audience. Because political outsiders must appeal to the people, effective claims are usually straightforward, ordinarily emphasizing moral righteousness or rectitude.

The **rhetoric of rectitude** is arguably ideal for bringing new problems to public attention. Yet experienced claims-makers, as political insiders who hope to redefine a well-established social problem, tend to favour rational styles and strategies of rhetoric that build on principles established in earlier campaigns. Experienced claims-makers in developed social movements operate from a foundation that enables them to have a more detailed agenda for policy changes and a clearer sense of which items ought to be prioritized—whether out of principle or of pragmatism (Best, 1987).

Claims-making is a complex social process that ordinarily incorporates both rational and moral types of themes. Although the values, or warrants, that justify drawing conclusions from grounds are not always explicit, compelling warrants are essential for validating claims. Ibarra and Kitsuse (1993) sought to better understand the moral vocabularies, or distinctive ways, in which the problematic status of conditions is portrayed.

Through the use of themes that give their claims significance, hierarchies of value are established by the claimant. Asserting a need for freedom to win over oppression cannot be disputed, for example, by opposing claims-makers without discrediting themselves. Effective opposition means employing the appropriate vernacular resources to counter the claims-maker.

To redefine the drug problem as the war on drugs, for example, civil libertarians invoked the **rhetoric of entitlement** by asserting rights of drug users to freedom of expression. As a counterargument to the **rhetoric of endangerment** most often used to justify waging a war on drugs, the rhetoric of entitlement is egalitarian. It is adverse to all forms of discrimination, espousing a philosophy of **moral relativism** that emphasizes the pursuit of liberty and justice.

The central features of entitlement include

> lifestyle, diversity, choice, tolerance, empowerment, and so forth. Liberation evokes the value of having the freedom to choose how one might realize one's life... claimants seek to expand the distribution or scope of a good, service, or right. The notion is that the greater the extension of fair play, tolerance, justice, equality before the law, respect for human dignity, etc., into greater spheres of social life, the greater the benefits for all members of the society. (Ibarra and Kitsuse, 1993: 34)

The rhetoric of entitlement is associated with a form of relativism, or "perspectivizing" standpoint, which characterizes claims as mere opinions to which people are certainly entitled, but need not be shared by others. Criticism of this view as morally incompetent opens up the claimant to charges of intolerance. Defining the condition as a "lifestyle," similarly, is a tactic serving to legitimize a behaviour or activity by guaranteeing its propriety.

The use of counter-rhetoric, like moral relativism, is a common strategy for overcoming marginality among participants in social problems discourse. Studying such rhetoric can show how credibility is maintained by being well versed in vernacular resources. In the context of the war on drugs, the rhetoric of endangerment has become more vulnerable to charges of hysteria. Fear-provoking characterizations of drug abuse as epidemic are deproblematized by counterclaims that the exaggeration is based on moral judgment or emotion, as opposed to a sound assessment of the condition under scrutiny (Ibarra and Kitsuse, 1993). This kind of counterclaim is unsympathetic, disapproving of both the characterization of the problem and solutions. Sympathetic counter-rhetorics accept, in part or wholly, the problematic status of conditions, but call for different solutions.

The experienced-insider style of claims-making engages in sympathetic and tactical criticism. One might accept the characterization of conditions being offered, while suggesting that the methods of the claimants might themselves be seen and treated as problems. Opponents perceive a tactical approach to criticism as the least hostile because the counterclaimant sympathizes with the problem as defined by the claims-maker and is willing to discuss the situation in these terms.

The rhetoric of endangerment is increasingly delivered in a scientific style of biomedical reasoning that supports official definitions of drug use as a threat to human health and safety. Endangerment discourse shifts the case for moral urgency from freedom and equality to risks posed by expressive practices and beliefs. Altering one's consciousness with psychoactive substances is perceived as threatening by those who do not use them. It is objectionable to others for a variety of reasons.

The moral value or priority of optimal health and functioning is evoked through positive terms like "*hygiene, prevention, nutritiousness, fitness,* and so on. Negative terms pinpoint the processes that warrant fear: *disease, pathology, epidemic, risk, contamination, health threat,* etc. (Ibarra and Kitsuse, 1993: 35 [italics in the original])." Assuming that the facts are objective and discoverable is not a style or strategy that is necessarily restricted to either side of the drug policy debate.

Increasingly, conflicting claims with their basis in science are used to support both sides of the drug war. They will continue to be sources of endless disagreement. Meanwhile, the debate is still determined by the dominance of certain values and related institutional arrangements. Before moving on, then, there is a need to consider the growth of social movements, related work on politics, and media studies about social problems.

The political context of claims-making belongs to the broader cultural context in which movements, in order to be viable, must learn to mobilize and maintain public support. The political climate or mood of the people (Kingdon, 1995) regarding certain issues influences social movements; each is shaped by constant media activity in turn. Cultural meanings are negotiated through media discourse, through a process in which particular facts in the spotlight take on meaning by being framed in a certain way while other interpretations are ignored (Gamson, 1992).

Media representations of social problems are the central conduit for public information and shape our understanding of the issues represented. Public knowledge about drugs is influenced by media content that—through advertising, news, and entertainment, each serving to reinforce the dominant perspective on the nature of the problem—informs us which drugs are good and which are bad. The influence of **moral panics** on defining social problems brings additional perspective on the role of media, which is germane to sociological discussions about drugs (cf. Goode, 2011; Hathaway and Erickson, 2004).

Perspectives on the Role of Media

The distribution of knowledge, leading to the rational dialogue of an informed public through a diverse media, is a longstanding democratic political ideal. Media studies over the last few decades have raised serious questions, however, about the absence of political dialogue in news media and its role in reproducing the existing power structure (see Ericson et al., 1987). In our increasingly administered society, the media arguably serves to reflect the dominant or official ideology.

Social constructionists have long emphasized the role of media in providing a "symbolic canopy" (Berger and Luckmann, 1966) of consistency and stable ideas in the face of increasing cultural diversity. Sociological studies of deviance also point to the media's role in maintaining the official definition and response to drug use as a social problem. Use of the term *moral panics* (Box 2.2) became popular in the 1990s to explain the cultural context, and the influence of media, in which social problems emerge.

Morality and values are often central to context. But a multitude of interests, including corporate elites who exploit their ownership of media resources, help explain the timing of emerging moral panics (Goode and Ben-Yehuda, 1994). A number of case studies documented use of media to reinforce the status quo on drug control through coverage that borders on outlandish exaggeration and fear mongering (cf. Gusfield, 1981; Reinarman, 1988; Reeves and Campbell, 1994; Reinarman and Levine, 1995).

Box 2.2

Defining Moral Panics

Stanley Cohen was the first sociologist to formally develop the idea of moral panic. He defined the term as follows:

> A condition, episode, person or group of persons emerges to become defined as a threat to societal values and interests; its nature is presented in a stylized and stereotypical fashion by the mass media; the moral barricades are manned by editors, bishops, politicians and other right-thinking people; socially accredited experts pronounce their diagnoses and solutions; ways of coping are evolved or (more often) resorted to; the condition then disappears, submerges or deteriorates and becomes more visible. . . . Sometimes the panic passes over and is forgotten, except in folklore and collective memory; at other times it has more serious and long-lasting repercussions and might produce such changes as those in legal and social policy or even in the way society conceives itself. (1972: 9)

The media plays an active role in labelling individuals or groups considered deviant or deserving condemnation. For Cohen, the news media "is a main source of information about the normative contours of society. It informs us about right and wrong, about the boundaries beyond which one should not venture and about the shapes the devil can assume" (p. 17).

Source: Cohen (1972).

For example, Gusfield examined the construction of the drunk driver in American society. The influence of interest groups, including corporations and the grassroots lobby group Mothers Against Drunk Driving (MADD), served to demonize the act and the actor, and individualized the problem. The individualized construction of the drinking-and-driving problem deflects public attention away from social factors: the role of alcohol producers, alcohol use regulators, and the service industry (not to mention US drinking culture). The crack scare in America, emerging in the 1980s, was similarly driven by demonization of the user as well as the drug in skewed media coverage, which neglected social inequality, discrimination, and the role of prohibition in the creation of the problem.

In addition to its role in misrepresenting social problems and stirring the support of moral panics, the media has contributed to increased lay participation in public policy debates. For a growing segment of the public, the advent of the Internet has led to the explosion of alternative resources and exposure to information that conflicts with official definitions and assumptions about drugs. Our understanding of the world today is multimediated (McRobbie and Thornton, 1995).

Today the marginalized are defended and scorned in equal measure within the same mass media outlets, and diverse lifestyles are increasingly celebrated and promoted through a variety of alternative media resources. Since the 1990s, despite the resilience of panics encouraged by sensationalizing coverage in the media, there is a growing recognition of alternative perspectives. The expansion of the Internet has placed knowledge that conflicts with status quo assumptions at the fingertips of millions. Sociological perspectives on the role of media in designating deviance and defining social problems have been subject to revision in light of these developments.

The reality of dealing with social differences and diversity means that moral panics are not necessarily hegemonic, nor dictated entirely by socially powerful groups. Rather, moral panics are continually contested. With increasing media exposure and literacy, perspectivizing is more common in social problems forums. Claims-making based on values and alternative perspectives on morality, therefore, is viable, and arguably advisable, for challenging assumptions about the nature of drug problems.

Gamson (1992) contends that social movements are founded on cultural themes rather than values. Unlike values, cultural themes are dialectical, which means that for every theme a matching countertheme exists that is adversarial by nature. Counterthemes are used to challenge mainstream cultural assumptions and provide an entry point for collective action. Social movements seeking to redefine behaviour that is widely recognized as deviant or criminal must challenge the predominant view of what is normal.

Since the 1970s, for example, this aim has been explicit in the naming of the lobby group NORML—the National Organization for the Reform of

Marijuana Laws. Its title captures an agenda committed to reforming society in ways that go beyond law-changing. NORML's goals extend to instigating fundamental changes in our cultural understanding of the drug. Political consciousness is forged in the process of collective action. The most likely context in which such action can occur is a threat to the pattern of people's everyday lives.

Drug Politics and Panics

Frames of collective action in social movements are concerned with defining an identity—that is, the construction of a "we" who stand in opposition to those who have different values or interests. The main priority is raising consciousness or agency, and the belief that it is possible to change adverse conditions by mobilizing informed and collective action. A sense of injustice, or moral indignation, is also needed to imply the possibility of change.

Injustice is expressed through the emergence of a political consciousness that supports collective action (Gamson, 1992). The possibility of change may be enhanced through presentation of the issue within a framework that is grounded in both personal experience and broader cultural themes. Media representations of issues are embedded with cultural and personal meaning. Experiential and shared knowledge of what "everybody knows" contribute to framing the issues in a way that may reference both mainstream and alternative perspectives. Oppositional subcultures do not necessarily provide enough support for meaningful collective action.

Collective cynicism about politics encourages mundane forms of resistance that require little planning (and typically involve evasion or deception), as opposed to organized and collective action. Even minimal acceptance of political reality, about our own potential to really "make a difference," is enough to discourage most people from being active participants in the political process (Gamson, 1992). In this cynical political climate, members of the public are reliant on the media to fill in gaps in knowledge and inform their understanding of the issues that concern them.

But public knowledge is not limited to what the media supplies. People round out and evaluate information found in media in light of their past learning to see if it is consistent with their own experiences. Unlike political leaders, the general public has traditionally had only indirect access to expert opinion through media sources. Research 30 years ago found that most reporting on the marijuana issue in the US, for example, relied on information that was channelled through spokespersons (public health administrators), as opposed to experts in this area of research (Shepherd, 1981).

Anyone with access to the Internet today has access to a wide variety of facts and sources of information in this area, compiled by online advocacy groups. However, much of what we learn from mainstream media is channelled through official government spokespersons and authorities. Conventional media reporting tends to favour significant actors or events, as opposed to social contexts. The public focus is directed away from abstract forces toward a concrete target stirring righteous indignation.

Such indignation may indeed sustain collective action. The sensationalism of most mass media, however, promotes fragmented meanings or interpretations that distract us from addressing the underlying structural problems. People's reliance on media framing can vary according to class, noted Gamson (1992). When evaluating social problems, he contended, educated individuals are more likely to attend to media discourse than experiential knowledge or the wisdom of their peers.

Those with more education presumably possess more flexibility or openness to shifting media frames. However, despite the larger social consciousness and platform for activism higher education may provide, educated people tend not to generate the level of indignation needed to spur collective action.

Mass media does not provide the impetus for action. It is more of a vehicle for magnifying social movements. Attracting media attention can be vitally important for political outsiders, who must rely on media to convey a message that mobilizes others to challenge authority (Kingdon, 1995). The consequence of media activity for those inside political circles is less readily apparent—apart from when political scandals draw attention to corruption or support for problems in the system.

Research on the role of media in collective action also shows that there are important cultural differences shaping political characteristics of the social problems process. There is a sharper boundary between society and politics in Canada, Schwartz (1981) argues, than there is in the United States. Canada has fewer social movements. The same stirring of moral indignation that compels political action in the United States has proven less productive here.

Historically, in Canada, there has been less explicit partisanship, or single-mindedness, toward issues and less use of the justice system as a means of political influence. Despite a rise in court cases that challenge Canadian drug laws, these efforts are more likely to be thwarted on the grounds that law reform must take place through the legislative process, instead of legal action in the courts (see Hathaway, 2001).

Interest groups in the United States appear more likely to influence public attitudes and governmental action. Canadian social interest groups more often have sought compromise through direct and orderly contact with the government (Pross, 1975; Schwartz, 1986). Unlike in the United States, where the line is often blurred between society and politics, moral causes tend to be negotiated more within the customary confines of government action (or inaction).

The instruments required for social change have long been recognized as being rather limited within Canadian politics. As compared to US politicians, in particular, individual party members rarely have much influence in shaping the political agenda. Moral causes in Canada are defused, Schwartz argues, by means of referral to governmental agencies that claim to acknowledge the legitimacy of issues.

The drug law controversy has been less of a political symbol here in Canada, where governments tend to use public controversies to avoid seeking legislative solutions (Schwartz, 1981). Whatever the political structure, though, highly politicized moral campaigns create similar problems for policy makers.

The political process, for all its complexity, follows a fairly predictable order. By documenting past events and the participants involved, a better understanding of the social problems process can be gained to offer fuller scopes of explanation.

We need not engage in endless description. Nor must we be obsessed about the logic of our theories. Rather our objective is to document the ways in which social problems are embedded in a larger social context that has both political and cultural dimensions. By attending to this process, sociologists can demonstrate the consequences of political actions and facilitate informed investigation and critique.

Chapter Summary

Departing from the classic sociological perspectives on drug problems overviewed in Chapter 1, the present chapter focused on developing a more critical, contemporary theoretical framework. An understanding of the nature of the social world, which calls for a focus on the ways in which situations are defined, favours a contextual constructionist perspective. The collective process of social problems definition needs to be located, I have argued, in its wider context of culture and social structure.

A contextual constructionist perspective frees researchers to link discursive practices to institutional arrangements. Having value commitments is not only unavoidable but necessary for meaningful critical analysis. The emphasis on claims-making adopted by constructionists is generally consistent with the focus of this book. My aim is to examine different ways we understand drugs. This approach does not assume that it is desirable, nor possible, to be objective simply by being "value-neutral."

This observation may seem obvious, if one favours the constructionist perspective on reality developed in this book. Yet it is a relatively marginal position. Most sociologists in practice are opposed to problematizing reality to the extent suggested by constructionists. To say the world is socially constructed is so self-evident that such a point is scarcely worth asserting.

Moreover, it supports the view of those who might object that sociology is no more than a science of the obvious. Constructionist inquiry is a hindrance, from this standpoint, to advancing sociology as a legitimate science.

I recall a memorable discussion with a student, who remained entirely unconvinced by "silly theories." To paraphrase the argument put forward by the student: reality is plain to see. The truth is something out there. Everybody knows that black is black. And white is white.

Such commonsense reasoning, of course, presents a serious challenge to the abstract logic of constructionist inquiry. Responding to such challenges requires an equally reasonable consideration of the use of problematic language such as "everybody knows" when using terms like *black* and *white*. Any visit to a paint store will reveal that there are dozens of shades of black and white to choose from. How we perceive them may depend on where and who we are.

Social characteristics, like ethnicity and gender, influence the ways people "see" colour. Calling someone black or white conveys a certain meaning about the kind of people they are. But not all blacks are black at all. And few whites are white.

What it means to be black or white (or brown or red or yellow) is entirely a social construction. It shapes everything we know or understand about a person. The designation is therefore integral to who and what we are. Likewise, how we understand drugs and the people who use drugs is entirely socially constructed. This idea is developed in the remainder of this book.

Drawing on primarily Canadian contributions, the insights gained in this chapter will be applied throughout this book. The focus of the next chapters will be on situating the historical and cultural dimensions of Canada's "drug problem." Later chapters are concerned with illustrating different socially constructed definitions that determine the ways in which people understand the use of drugs.

Questions for Critical Thought

1. What are the most important contributions, in your view, to the development of critical sociological perspectives on the use of drugs and their regulation?
2. In your own words, how would you explain the difference between strict and contextual constructionist perspectives on drug problems?
3. In your own experience, how does the media contribute to your understanding of drug problems in society?

Suggested Readings

Adler, P.A., and P. Adler. 2011. *Constructions of Deviance: Social Power, Context, and Interaction*, 7th edn. Stamford, CT: Cengage Learning. This leading textbook on the sociology of deviance includes theoretical analyses and ethnographic illustrations of how deviance is constructed, organized, and managed.

Goode, E. 2011. *Drugs in American Society,* 8th edn. New York: McGraw-Hill. This textbook gives a focused sociological introduction to the use of psychoactive drugs. Emphasizing personal experiences of users, it contrasts the images portrayed in the news media with the reality of people who use illicit drugs.

Goode, E., and N. Ben-Yehuda. 2009. *Moral Panics: The Social Construction of Deviance,* 2nd edn. Malden, MA: Wiley-Blackwell. This textbook explores the emergence and dynamics of documented moral panics, and their impact on societies where they are observed.

Holstein, J.A., and G. Miller. 2007. *Reconsidering Social Constructionism: Debates in Social Problems Theory.* New Brunswick, NJ: Transaction Publishers. This collection of contributions by well-known authors in this area provides an overview of formative discussions and ongoing debates within the constructionist perspective.

Loseke, D.R. 2011. *Thinking About Social Problems: An Introduction to Constructionist Perspectives.* New Brunswick, NJ: Transaction Publishers. This textbook offers an accessible introduction to the study of social problems in American society.

Suggested Websites

heretohelp
www.heretohelp.bc.ca/factsheet/stigma-and-discrimination-around-mental-health-and-substance-use-problems

This website provides information and resources for people experiencing stigma and discrimination due to mental health or substance use disorders.

American Sociological Association: Introduction to Sociology
http://www.asanet.org/introtosociology/studentresources/StudentResourcesContents Page.html#

This website provides learning resources for sociology students and teachers.

The National Organization for the Reform of Marijuana Laws in Canada
www.norml.ca

This is the website for NORML, whose mandate is to eliminate all civil and criminal penalties for private marijuana use through government lobbying, public education, research, and legislative and judicial challenges.

reason.com
www.reason.com/archives/2013/12/26/the-5-best-drug-scares-of-2013

From the reason.com archives, this article provides an overview of recent drug scares, and links for further exploration.

The Media Awareness Project
www.mapinc.org/cmap/dpr.htm

This website lists 50 Canadian drug policy reform organizations, and links to other information about drug policy in Canada.

3 Drugs in Historical Perspective

Learning Objectives

- To better understand the social history of drug use and efforts to control it throughout the Western world.
- To understand the origins of drug control in Canada.
- To recognize the influence of early nation-building processes on current antidrug laws.

Introduction

What we know about drugs is shaped by past experience. Our social history and heritage, our customs and traditions greatly influence our understanding of the world. As the products of collective definition, social problems are subject to ongoing processes of interpretation. This means that despite the tendency to treat the two as distinct in the social sciences and in university curricula, the study of the past is the study of the present. And study of the present requires looking to the past.

By the time you will have finished reading this page, paragraph, or sentence, it will be in the past. As readers, it makes no sense to separate this recent experience from your present consciousness. Likewise, it is difficult, if not impossible, to maintain a meaningful distinction between the past and present with a constructionist analysis of drug use. The threshold between the two is arbitrarily defined and always shifting.

As the future becomes the present and the present becomes the past, our own view of history is collectively transformed. As we get older, our perception of time changes, as does our social outlook. Lengths of time that once seemed like forever now pass quickly. And time frames lengthen and contract depending on the situation all the time. As children, eight weeks away from school over the summertime felt like an eternity. As we get older, time speeds up; now, four months of summer vacation for a university student appears to arrive so slowly and disappear so soon.

From the perspective of a child, the reminiscing of elders of years gone by can feel like ancient history. As time goes by, our sense of time and place in time are altered as the scope of our experience expands. When I was in my teens and early twenties, my peers who were only a little older in age seemed much older (and much wiser) due to those extra years of life experience. From the vantage point of my forties such differences now seem negligible. Although my peer group comprises age groups spanning several decades, most of us seem pretty much the same age, from my standpoint. And in a very real sense, we are all of the "same age."

We may know that time is measured using standard units, with which we mark its passing with remarkable precision. But experience suggests that time is rather more subjective. Kids grow up too fast. Good times go by too quickly. Unhappy times or onerous tasks can sometimes, much like long Canadian winters, seem to drag on or hang around forever.

The way that we perceive time is a relative phenomenon. History, like time itself, requires interpretation through the lens of both collective and personal experiences that shape our understanding of the social world. History certainly represents people or events that previously existed or occurred. But history has no inherent meaning in itself; it is always subject to interpretation.

"History is written by the victors," said Winston Churchill. As something that is always in the process of becoming, what is happening right now will soon be what has happened. What has happened is interpreted in terms of our experiences and our individual or collective interests. The history that matters, as the famous quote suggests, tends to be written from the dominant perspective of the so-called winners, who have the power to shape our understanding of the world.

If history is subject to the bias of historians, and the documented version upholds a dominant world view, it is impossible to maintain an objectivist position on the nature of reality in the social world. The constructionist perspective is imperative for a better understanding of how our history determines our reality.

A contextual constructionist historical analysis must be attentive to the discourse and social circumstances that have shaped the meaning of drug use over time. The historical analysis presented in this chapter is relatively brief and necessarily selective. It draws on numerous book-length contributions to the literature, which provide considerably more detail. Though our focus is primarily on Canadian resources (cf. Boyd, 1991; Blackwell and Erickson, 1988; Carstairs, 2006; Giffen et al., 1991; Grayson, 2008), we begin with a discussion of the larger global history of knowledge about drugs and efforts to regulate or ban their use.

A Brief History of Drugs and Drug Control

All cultures that had access to intoxicating plants have long histories of drug use, often dating back millennia (cf. Levinthal, 2014; Sullivan and Hagan, 2002). Arguably all humans, and some other species, have a natural imperative to alter their own consciousness, often with but sometimes without the use of drugs. The motivation and experience is thereby universal (Weil, 1972). The presumed innocence of children in this pursuit is challenged by the observation of kids twirling in the schoolyard to become disoriented, feel giddy for a short time, and experience the thrill of the whole world spinning.

We have used drugs since ancient times to cope with pain and anguish. Some substances have served symbolic purposes as well, in rituals and celebrations marking significant events. From the otherworldly insights of the shaman or witch doctor, to the ceremonial toast, sacrament, or peace pipe, drugs are used to signify our bonds to one another and to bring us closer to the presence of our gods (McKenna, 1992).

Evidence of fermentation of roots and berries to make alcohol has been found in excavations of the earliest cave dwellings. The motivation to take drugs may not be uniquely human, but it might be linked to the progression of our species from hunters and gatherers to settled farmers. The first settlements provided fruit and grain supplies year-round, which allowed production of more and better alcohol.

The ancient use of cannabis as a herbal remedy is documented by its prominence in a Chinese book of medicine (Curran, 2008), use of which reportedly dates back thousands of years. The milk of the opium poppy is likewise historically revered for its power, so noted Homer, to "quiet all pain and strife, and bring forgetfulness of every ill."

The ancient Greeks were not alone in recognizing the significance of drugs like alcohol and opium as valuable commodities. Nor was that society unique in recognizing drug use as a symbol of disorder, hedonism, and other threats requiring greater scrutiny and control (see Box 3.1). Substance use has long been met with cultural ambivalence (cf. Hathaway et al., 2011; Room, 2006). There have always been good drugs and bad drugs—and good and bad reasons to use them.

While medically approved use of drugs tends to be the most defensible, non-medical consumption of some substances (such as alcohol, caffeine, and tobacco) is generally acceptable and legally approved. One might make the case that, historically, drugs that influence behaviour or alter consciousness dramatically have been the ones most often treated with suspicion. The degree of intensity corresponds with the degree of threat, and the more intoxicating substances require the most control.

In an earlier age of mysticism, "magic potions" containing psychoactive plants may have served a clearer purpose in the hands of wizards,

Box 3.1

The Meanads

In Greek mythology, the maenads were female worshippers of Dionysus, the Greek god of mystery, wine, and intoxication. The word *maenad* literally translates to "raving ones." They were known as wild, insane women who could not be reasoned with. The mysteries of Dionysus inspired the women to ecstatic frenzy; they indulged in copious amounts of violence, bloodletting, sex, self-intoxication, and mutilation. They were usually pictured crowned with vine leaves, clothed in fawn skins, and dancing with wild abandonment, in complete union with primeval nature.

The maenads were also known as Bacchae in Roman mythology, named after Bacchus, god of wine. The maenads vividly depicted the intoxicating effects of alcohol. Their insatiable consumption was often portrayed as the cause of their bizarre behaviour, which could not be explained by any other reason. Wine, like the ambiguous figure of Dionysus himself, was recognized as both a seductive and a destructive force.

Sources: Abel (2006); Cole (2007).

witches, and ancient oracles or seers. An outcome of the **civilizing process** (cf. Elias, 1978, 1982) in the West is the outlaw of intoxicating substances that brought on visions that distorted or transcended one's sense of order. Ironically, throughout the modern era, this process has coincided with the advancement of technology enabling the production of more potent, and potentially more harmful, drug derivatives.

Producing stronger alcohol requires a distillation process to separate components of the liquid; in this way, beer is transformed into whiskey and wine into brandy. In Ireland and Spain, this technique for making liquor has been practised for at least a thousand years. The production of increasingly more potent variations of alcohol and other drugs (see Wilson, 2012), like opium to heroin and coca leaf to crack, appears to have intensified concerns about drug addiction and increased societal anxieties surrounding use of drugs. The presumed power of a substance to enslave its users and the related problems for the user and society may partially determine its social status.

At the same time our response to drugs, as previously noted, cannot necessarily be explained by their chemical properties. Efforts to control or ban the use of certain drugs are more reliably determined by how the act of taking the drug is perceived (e.g., snorting versus injecting) and the social status of the using group. Much like alcohol, mild stimulants like coffee and tobacco—which are legal nearly everywhere and, at one time or another, have been sold as health promoting products—have also met with widespread opposition and outlaw (cf. Hathaway and Sharpley, 2010; Schivelbusch, 1992).

Known as *kahweh,* "that which stimulates," in Middle Eastern countries, coffee has been cultivated, praised, and even outlawed in some places for its excitatory properties for centuries. By the eighteenth century, in Europe, coffee houses were popular establishments, attracting merchants, poets, intellectuals, and artists who were drawn by coffee's capacity to stimulate the mind. Coffee today is as culturally embedded, commoditized, and as valued as the use of alcohol for social relaxation, despite its reputation as a stimulant.

Tea, another ancient beverage with hundreds of varieties, has less caffeine than coffee and a considerably longer history of use for health and mental stimulation. Respective differences in use and reputation compared with coffee are probably more cultural than chemical in nature. Tea's origins in the Far East and its associated rituals imbue it with a sense of calm; it is reputed to aid in contemplation and restore harmony and balance.

The popularity of alcohol for social lubrication is quite different from its early reputation as a medicinal tonic that enhanced one's vitality and vigour. The word *whisky* is derived from Gaelic, meaning the "water of life." Distilled spirits in Europe, since the early fourteenth century, have shared this designation; the Latin term is *aqua vitae.*

Tobacco's social history is also widely varied. It has been a banned substance in some eras and a valuable commodity in others, and a helpful stimulant in still more. It has gone from a symbol of conspicuous consumption, style, rebellion, and sophistication to its present social status as a widely scorned public health pariah. Tobacco use is legal in every corner of the world, despite its status as a threat to public health. It is most often regulated through taxation, age restrictions, and prevention messages for youth.

Drugs that are prohibited often have similar properties to the ones regulated within a legal framework. Banned substances, however, clearly represent a greater threat. The nature of this threat to society, resulting in scrutiny and outlaw of these substances, is primarily a product of conflicting moral values. Although drug laws are often justified in terms of health and safety, certain kinds of drugs have come to signify disorder, deviant behaviour, licentiousness, or flouting of the rules.

The Twentieth Century

An early incidence of drug prohibition, foreshadowing what was to come, occurred in 1798 when Napolean banned cannabis use among his troops after occupying Egypt (Abel, 1980). This first recorded drug ban of the modern era followed an army's exposure to a plant virtually unknown to Western culture (until colonization and wider travel introduced it).

Napolean decreed: "It is forbidden in all of Egypt to use certain Moslem beverages made with hashish or likewise to inhale the smoke from seeds of hashish. Habitual drinkers and smokers of this plant lose their reason and are victims of violent delirium which is the lot of those who give themselves full to excesses of all sorts" (Abel, 1980: 148–9).

Napolean's sentiments are echoed in the legislation that made cannabis and other drugs in Canada banned commodities. They convey a sense of danger, urgency, exaggeration, and moral condemnation. The societal response to drugs like cannabis is shaped by values that legitimate prohibiting intoxicants. A central aspect of the civilizing process, corresponding with processes of **nation-building** described in other sources, has been the diffusion of a **temperance mentality** (Alexander, 1990).

Temperance is defined as moderation in the indulgence of an appetite or passion. The meaning of this virtue has been transformed, however, into abstinence from substance use. Maintaining strict sobriety suggests a far more rigorous level of restraint. Demand for self-control is rooted in religious teachings (such as Protestantism, among others) that deem intoxication or dependence on a drug as an irresponsible indulgence.

Another moral dictate condemns pursuit of pleasure unless achieved through hard work or religious fervour (Becker, 1963). Pursuit of pleasure as a sin is less explicitly presented as the justification for banning drugs today. But desire for self-control is an enduring aspiration. The power of the law, no less today than in the past, is reinforced by moral standards that call for exercising discipline and self-restraint.

To complicate the matter, Western cultural values are not entirely inconsistent with substance use per se. These values in and of themselves cannot account for the distinction made between good and bad drugs in our society and the different treatment of their users under law. The banned drugs are neither more harmful nor more addictive than the others. The ones we regulate less strictly generate enormous profits, including the legal sale of alcohol, tobacco, pharmaceuticals, and coffee.

Meanwhile, illegal drugs are demonized, having gained the reputation of being more dangerous to users and society. To better understand how these distinctions have developed requires examination of the early modern history of drug control in Canada and elsewhere. These early laws are the foundation of more sweeping legislation informing the development of the war on drugs.

The passage of the Poisons Act (1858) in the United Kingdom (see Berridge, 1978) reflected little sense of urgency or moral threat concerning drugs. The purpose of the Act was more pragmatic. It restricted government control to regulating the availability of substances that posed a threat in the hands of criminals with murderous intent (i.e., poisons). Such legislation is analogous to gun control in some ways, targeting drugs that can be lethal if misused. Access to poisons became limited to those working in professions that were licensed to handle them, as a way to regulate their use.

The focus of these laws became quite different in the next century, in that they introduced a broader definition of "dangerous" drugs. In 1920, in the United Kingdom (see Berridge, 1999), the Dangerous Drugs Act was enacted. By this time, the definition had expanded to include opium, cocaine, and cannabis. In 1923 an amendment to the new laws was passed to stiffen penalties and expand police powers.

The intent of legislation was aimed primarily at pharmacists and physicians. The regulations introduced were measures to protect the public. The resulting laws, however, also criminalized drug users, and set the stage for waging a war on drugs. In Britain, it meant that for the first time ever drug policy was more aligned with policing than it was with medicine or health.

The legislative path of the United States is similar (see Musto, 1973). In 1868 the Pharmacy Act was passed. It regulated the sale of poisons as well as opium. Half a century later the Narcotics Act (1914) was passed. It severely restricted the availability of opium and cocaine for all but medicinal use. Sales of these substances were handled by registered purveyors, who were required to keep records and pay taxes.

The Marihuana Tax Act (passed in 1937) later added cannabis to the restricted list (Bonnie and Whitebread, 1974). Rather than an outright ban, the Act allowed for sales within a legal framework. But taxation and bureaucracy also introduced penalties, large fines, and years in prison for unlawful use and distribution of the plant. Strongly influenced by *Reefer Madness* propaganda (cf. Schlosser, 2004; Starks, 1982), the new law built momentum for developing drug policies within a prohibition framework, which has served primarily to punish substance users.

The development of new laws in the United States was strongly influenced by claims that marijuana use resulted in murder, insanity, and death. The origin of this law, in the United States as well as in Canada, is linked to overtly racist ideology. Lurid tales about crazed Mexicans and wild-eyed teens provided sufficient justification. Most Americans, like Canadians, had no personal experience with cannabis themselves, nor knew anyone who used it, and could not contradict these outlandish claims.

The connection between drugs and race in the United States has not significantly wavered in the decades since. The same overtly racist overtones were less apparent in drug policy developments in Britain. In 1924—within a few months of amending the Dangerous Drugs Act to introduce stricter criminal controls—the British government established the Rolleston Committee on Morphine and Heroin Addiction (see Berridge, 1980).

Based on its assessment of their impact and effectiveness, the Rolleston Committee called for a reversal of these laws. The emergence of a medical perspective on addiction was apparent in the Rolleston Report (1926). Its call for treatment of drug problems, as opposed to jailing users, formed the basis for the development of the British system of drug regulation. Under the system, which survived until the 1960s, drugs could be prescribed to addicts by their doctors.

The emergence of the British system marked a sharp divergence from the US style of policing drugs. Regarding drug addicts as criminals, however, would become the predominant policy model. In 1961, a global prohibition framework was introduced. It brought together previous drug treaties under one agreement of the United Nations—the Single Convention on Narcotic Drugs (see Bewley-Taylor and Jelsma, 2012).

This worldwide ban on substances that are still prohibited (i.e., cannabis, opium, cocaine, and their derivatives, and other drugs since outlawed in the last half-century) instituted criminalization as the standard practice. The British system, which prioritized drug treatment, was thereafter inconsistent with the dominant framework. The Canadian drug control model has been influenced by its shared history with Britain and the United States (Table 3.1), and its own unique national history as well. The last century has witnessed a dramatic transformation in the way we understand and regulate drug use.

Canadian drug policies continue to reflect a certain cultural ambivalence concerning substance use. Accommodation and promotion of some drugs have coexisted with a deepening commitment to the prohibition framework. The trend toward further criminalization has not always gone unchallenged. And historically there has been significant support for the addiction-as-disease treatment model, as in Britain. However, prohibition has expanded in a manner that is generally consistent with support for criminalization.

Table 3.1 Milestones in Drug Policy: International Developments

1798	Napolean bans cannabis use among his troops in Egypt—the first drug prohibition of the modern era.
1858	The Poisons Act in the UK restricts access to dangerous drugs—i.e., those that could be lethal if ingested or misused.
1868	The Pharmacy Act in the US regulates the sale of poisons (and of opium).
1914	The Narcotics Act in the US restricts opium and cocaine to medical use only.
1920	The Dangerous Drugs Act in the UK expands the definition of dangerous drugs to include opium, cocaine, and cannabis.
1924	The Rolleston Committee is established in the UK to study the effectiveness of the Dangerous Drugs Act. Its 1926 report calls for the expansion of addiction treatment to replace imprisonment of addicts. Under the resulting British system of drug regulation, drugs like heroin can be prescribed to addicts by their doctors.
1937	The Marihuana Tax Act in the US adds cannabis to the list of drugs that are restricted.
1961	The Single Convention on Narcotic Drugs introduces a global prohibition framework. Quite unlike the British system, it institutes criminalization—or the emerging US-style "war on drugs" approach.

To better understand this history, the focus of this chapter now shifts toward examining Canadian contributions (cf. Blackwell and Erickson, 1988; Boyd, 1991; Carstairs, 2006; Giffen et al., 1991; Grayson, 2008). The literature on **moral regulation** is drawn on in particular to examine the historical construction of drug problems as a process of collective definition. This process is illuminated further by inspecting its connection to the project of Canadian nation-building (cf. Glasbeek, 2006; Hunt, 2009; Valverde, 2008).

Constructing Canada's Drug Problem

The literature on moral regulation brings a sense of historical perspective to the social problems process. It traces the development and origins of social understanding of behaviour, which tends to go unquestioned or is otherwise taken for granted. How is it that we come to accept some acts as natural and others as unnatural or wrong in our society?

We learn from a young age what is expected of us, although we may come to understand by word of mouth, through the media, or through personal experience it is not necessary to conform to these expectations. Notwithstanding exposure to alternative perspectives, what is taken for granted is resistant to change. Moral regulation scholars trace the origins of cultural distinctions—right and wrong and good and bad, natural and unnatural, moral and immoral, and healthy and unhealthy, among others—that shape group behaviour and attitudes toward those who pose a threat to dominant group norms.

The term *moral regulation* is preferred over the traditional focus on social control in criminology. Arguably, the latter contributes to a tendency among criminologists to maintain a false distinction between formal and informal mechanisms of control. The term *regulation* conveys a deeper understanding of the use of power through both coercion and persuasion (see Glasbeek, 2006).

Use of power is understood to be especially productive when its targets see their interests as being consistent with those of the State. Put otherwise, when subjects of authority "buy into" the same ideology or world view, they do not require coercing. We, the subjects, have effectively submitted to preserving the interests and resulting institutional arrangements that maintain the status quo on how we look at drugs.

Power is far-reaching. It is applied through vast collective networks and activities between authorities and subjects. Legal scholars emphasize a top-down point of view, which prioritizes statutes and formal methods of control. A bottom-up perspective prioritizes the informal socialization processes that influence behaviour (cf. Loo and Strange, 1997; Valverde, 2008).

Explanations in the literature on moral regulation tend to be more fluid and more nuanced than those stemming from other criminological perspectives on control. Their aim is to shed light on both the roles and interactions of State and non-State actors reinforcing norms of conduct. Politicians, bureaucrats, professionals of all sorts, corporations, and the media each contribute to constructing ideology through discourse and everyday behaviour as a practical accomplishment.

Viewing power as productive, rather than coercive, is not a positive assessment or endorsement of the value of the outcome or intent of any form of regulation. Nor are researchers prevented from providing their own critical perspective on the nature of the "problem" or the process. The preferred method of analysis, however, is to transcend conflict and consensus explanations of law-making.

The law is neither good nor bad, nor even necessary (depending on the reader's political persuasion). Law represents the exercise of power, as determined by a process of collective definition and behaviour (Loo and Strange, 1997). A variety of interest groups have played a role in shaping, reinforcing, and resisting institutional arrangements that reflect the status quo on drug control in Canada.

The discourse has been influenced by claims-making activities on the part of interest groups for much of the past century. These include religious groups, and medical professionals, law-enforcement bureaucrats, and influential politicians. Whereas the claims and interest groups have shifted over time, the nature of the discourse and values represented appear to have not changed that much at all.

Studying societal constructions of drug problems requires an understanding of the nation-building process. This includes past and present efforts to construct a recognizable Canadian identity, distinct from other national cultures. As a nation with colonial ties to Britain, and a close proximity to the United States, this is an ongoing process.

Canadian identity and culture is in some ways in its adolescence compared with Old-World nations that have social histories that date back to antiquity. The question of Canadian identity is perhaps better understood in terms of what it isn't. Most Canadians agree that we are quite unlike Americans (see Lipset, 1991). But the lack of a consensus over national identity is clearly a concern for those who see this as a weakness.

Others are more positive and point to the uniqueness of Canadian identity, including its formation in reaction to a wide array of outside influences. Consistent with this optimistic outlook, one of Canada's strengths is its commitment to multiculturalism. Conversely, there is a more critical perspective that argues that, in practice, this identity has been more about developing a primarily white culture, which historically has been predominantly British.

Canadians from other racial and ethnic groups are largely seen as the recipients of benevolence and tolerance, graciously extended to them by the host society (Mackey, 2002; Valverde, 2008). The presence of these others is required to reaffirm Canada's self-image as a pluralistic nation. Consistent with this image, the Canadian identity is depicted as different from that of the United States and Britain, with their aggressive militaristic and overtly racist pasts. The generous, longstanding interpretation of Canada's treatment of "outsiders" supports this distinction.

Starting with the systematic extinction, assimilation, and displacement of the native population, the illusion of a cultural mosaic is objectionable. Continuing distortion of the facts is clearly evident. The contradictions and seductions of selective memory, and the ambiguity of past interpretations, suggests a need for more reflection on what it really means for a nation to be tolerant. The realization of a strikingly less flattering portrayal of how we govern differences in Canadian society suggests a definition quite different from one of acceptance.

Tolerance has tended to imply a form of citizenship in which outsiders are considered deficient yet redeemable, and therefore deserving of benevolent attention by their hosts. The nation-building project is about positioning white culture as the ordinary standard from which actions must be judged. What is true or natural or normal must be gathered on the basis of the dominant cultural reference. Our social history of moral regulation of drug use is just as much a story of the present as the past—the product of a process of Canadian nation-building.

The illicit drug problem in Canada officially dates back to 1908 (see Giffen et al., 1991). The ban outlawing the production and sale of opium for recreational smoking was enacted in the aftermath of a riot in Vancouver. The unrest reflected growing anti-Chinese sentiment. The resulting legislation was politically expedient. It was noncontroversial and passed easily in Parliament. Cocaine was banned soon thereafter, and drug possession as an offence was introduced to help police with the enforcement of new laws.

In 1923 cannabis became prohibited by an act of Parliament, with unanimous approval and no debate required in the House of Commons. The apparent ease by which the legislation was enacted sheds little light on the legislative process and fails to indicate the indifference of many politicians at the time. The nature of the discourse in the 1920s era, though, is evident in a series of articles in *Maclean's,* the Canadian then-biweekly news magazine, which stoked a growing fear of non-white citizens in Canada about the rising tide of immigration to the country (Boyd, 1991).

The Murphy Factor

The articles in *Maclean's* were written by Canada's first female magistrate, Emily Murphy. Although her political influence appears to have been largely overstated by drug scholars (Carstairs, 2006), these overtly racist writings went unchallenged at the time. The articles were ultimately published as a collection, *The Black Candle* (1922), in which Murphy warns Canadians about blacks and Orientals attempting "to injure the bright browed races of the world."

Among other claims, she cautioned that cocaine and opium were being used by foreign men to seduce white women. Use of these drugs was linked in public discourse to interracial sexuality, promiscuity, and violence. The perceived threat was enhanced by its connection to young females (symbols of innocence and virtue), which called for greater vigilance in protecting pure white values.

Even more forebodingly, Murphy warned of a conspiracy to enslave the white man by addicting him to opium: "Some of the Negroes coming into Canada—and they are no fiddle-faddle fellows either—have similar ideas, and one of their greatest writers has boasted how ultimately they will control the white men. Many of these Negroes are altogether estimable, but contrariwise, many are obstinately wicked persons, earning their livelihood as free-ranging pedlars of poisonous drugs." For those unfamiliar with the term, a *fiddle-faddle fellow* is another way of saying that someone is a fool.

To ensure her words would not be written off as racist, Murphy noted that black people, as a rule, were friendly people. That said, though not all bad, they were often underestimated. Despite appearances of innocence, there were evil, crafty people hiding among the ranks of the outsiders. The menace posed by drugs, and threat of moral degradation, meant no non-white immigrant should be above suspicion.

The use of opiates and cocaine reportedly produced delusions that made users "insane and dangerous to be at large." Marijuana, likewise, was said to turn its users into "raving maniacs" who were liable to kill or indulge in acts of violence. Murphy (1922) eloquently summarized marijuana's dangers in a six-page chapter (pp. 331–7) of her much longer book. This work is often cited for its evident hyperbole of the drug's effect on users. It is worth examining, however, for the insights it gives into existing themes that have become more nuanced but remain consistent in the current discourse surrounding drug use.

As noted previously, ambivalence about intoxication has been a long-standing Western cultural tradition. A sense of this emerges in Murphy's alluring introduction, to the uninformed white reader, about *cannibis indica,* or *marahuana,* also known "more commonly as Indian hemp. Sometimes it is called hasheesh or hashish." The drug's exotic origins are portrayed as something to be feared, because of the seductive power it has over those who succumb to temptation.

In *The Count of Monte Cristo,* says Murphy, Dumas tells of a "hashish debauch" hosted by Sinbad. This well-known literary character is drawn on to invoke images of Eastern mystic fantasy that conflict with Canadian white values of rationality, lucidity, and temperance. Sinbad describes the green ambrosia, which is said to have been served at the table of Jupiter, as "the hashish of Alexandria—the hashish of Abour-Gour, the celebrated maker, the only man to whom there should be built a palace, inscribed with these words, 'a grateful world to a dealer in happiness.'"

Murphy overlooked more balanced studies about cannabis. At the time, the most extensive research on the subject could be found in the Indian Hemp Commission report (1894). The study was commissioned by the British government in response to growing concern about the widespread use of cannabis in India to examine its effects on the physical, mental, and moral health of users. The report produced was comprehensive. It concluded that use in moderation had no injurious effects on the user whatsoever, and that such use may even be medically beneficial.

Far more provocative depictions were available in earlier portrayals of the use of cannabis by literary figures. Nineteenth-century Hashish Club notables in Paris—who included Dumas, Baudelaire, and Hugo—described fantastic visions and dramatic flights of fancy at parties devoted to ingesting massive doses of hashish. Their transcendent journeys of the self "in all directions" are articulated as a kind of "wonderful debauchery" (Baudelaire, [1860] 1971), experienced along with deeper feelings of benevolence.

Yet Baudelaire described it as an "Artificial Paradise." This fantastic God-like state demanded heavy payment—lethargy and discomfort after the intoxication ended, and a troubling surrender of the will to substance use. The rapturous heights attained, for Baudelaire, were an affliction, marked by equal lows and an intense habituation after failure to reach the high through other pleasurable pursuits. His view exemplifies a wider and ongoing fascination that seems to coexist with an altogether different cultural aversion to pursuing altered states.

It is unclear whether Murphy was aware of the more balanced conclusions of the Indian Hemp Commission. Instead of citing studies about ordinary users, who used in moderation with no injurious effects, her review of evidence is rather more consistent with the depictions of excess by avant-garde French writers. Cautionary tales of seeking said artificial paradise with exotic substances are quite consistent with Napolean's earlier indictment.

Most importantly, it was Murphy's duty to establish that users of these substances were morally inferior outsiders requiring condemnation and control. She cited experiments by eminent medical doctors in Calcutta who discovered that cannabis induced trance-like symptoms. A truly sinister portrayal of the habit was supported with reference to "fakers" who, through the agency of this drug, submitted to being buried alive and later resurrected.

In addition to a sacrament for zombie cults in India, Murphy notes that *hashish* or *hasheesh* is the Arabic name from which the English word *assassin* is derived. There is cause for much concern in North America, she continues, according to US authorities: "This Indian hemp is used chiefly in Asia Minor, India, Persia and Egypt, but is being increasingly used on this continent, particularly by Mexicans. . . . The addict loses all sense of moral responsibility . . . liable to kill or indulge in any form of violence to other persons, using the most savage methods of cruelty. . . .”

Distorted images of violence and insanity compete to present a highly menacing portrayal of the user as a creature out of control. “When coming from under the influence of this narcotic, these victims present the most horrible condition imaginable. They are dispossessed of their natural and normal will power, and their mentality is that of idiots. If this drug is engaged in to any great extent, it ends in the untimely death of its addict.”

The real and symbolic threat posed by this foreign enemy is bolstered by the story of a weed-maddened Mexican, shot at the US southern border after taking “marihuana” and attempting to invade the country on his own. Cannabis was reportedly also routinely used “for the purpose of inducing pleasurable motor excitement and hallucinations which are commonly sexual in character among Eastern races.”

Disturbing images of sex, death, violence, and madness are followed by less vivid descriptions of effects. While these claims are often contradictory, they are surprisingly consistent with a discourse, which is albeit less overtly racist, about the use of certain drugs today. In addition to some acute physical effects like numbness, intoxication is said to be “characterized by sleepiness and ‘a certain impudent, dare-devil demeanor.’ As in intoxication from alcohol, the gait is staggering. The addict has delusions of persecution or of measureless grandeur.”

The effects of hasheesh can reportedly vary from “a mild, short attack of excitement to a prolonged attack of furious mania, ending in exhaustion or even death.” Hasheesh users are described as “good-for-nothing lazy fellows who live by begging or stealing, and pester their relations for money to buy the hasheesh, often assaulting them when they refuse the demands. The moral degradation of these cases is their most salient symptom; loss of social position, shamelessness, addiction to lying and theft, and a loose, irregular life makes them a curse to their families.”

In concluding her short chapter on the effects of the drug, Murphy returns to the Eastern visions of fantasia she began with. Having fostered a description and associated discourse of the marijuana user, which continues to this day, she ends with a strong warning for future apologists who are certain to be tempted and fooled by false promises. Murphy tells of nineteenth-century well-born intellectuals Thomas De Quincey and Fitz-Hugh Ludlow, who dabbled in Oriental drugs (i.e., opium and hasheesh). They wrote of “unimaginable horrors” and “hellish agonies” of addiction, a life spent as “an outcast from man’s league with God.” Should whites believe that this “weed of madness” is an affliction only found in other races, they must be made aware “of the sharp danger that lies in even curiously tasting poisons which have been inhibited, or which are habit-forming.” The innocently curious and morally inferior, and those who might object to the preceding characterization based on their own personal experience with drugs, are all blameworthy as devils and fools.

As Murphy writes, "There are plenty of folk who pretend to themselves that they yield to narcotic enchantment in a desire for research and not for sensual gratification, and they inure their friends to its effects for the same reason, but, however kindly in judgment, one finds these statements hard to credit, and even if credited, only demonstrates these persons as rascals-manifest."

Despite the credibility of differing conclusions, such as those arrived at by the Indian Hemp Commission, Murphy's claims went widely unchallenged at the time. While most people today would recognize her statements as outrageous, cannabis was largely unknown to Canadians at that time. History gives little indication as to whether such ignorant and misinformed opinions in the decades since have entirely given way to an educated view.

By 1923, the use of opium and cocaine and cannabis in Canada had become a social problem that demanded severe penalties. Use of these drugs had been effectively transformed from a matter of private indulgence to a matter of public evil (Boyd, 1991). This new class of crime would go unchallenged for another fifty years, when a government commission of inquiry first recommended that criminal penalties for cannabis possession be removed (LeDain, 1972).

With the passing of nearly another half-century, far from showing progress after the drug war that resulted, the evolution of these laws has only made the problems worse. There is more to tell about how the discourse of that era continues to shape arguments and policy today.

The final section of this chapter draws on other contributions that further illustrate the historical transformation of the moral regulation of the use of certain drugs. This social history is chronicled in more detail below.

Origins of Drug Law

As noted previously, there has been a dramatic transformation in Western cultural perceptions of the use of certain drugs. Before the twentieth century, banning these commodities was not a course of action of much interest to Canadians. Opium was widely viewed as a useful medicine. It was deemed so valuable to the British government that two wars were fought with China to protect the trade in opium.

British business interests in this drug are said to have been on par with profiteering from the cannabis trade in India. The Opium Wars (1839–42 and 1856–60) resulted from attempts by Chinese rulers to shut down supply routes due to concerns about addiction. Similar concerns in the United Kingdom a few years later gained a foothold, prompting more restrictive legislation. Restriction of opium under the Pharmacy Act (1868) is noted to have emerged in an era of unscrupulous promotion and unregulated access to the drug (see Berridge, 1999). Used as a medicine to treat a wide variety of ailments, many tonics at the time included alcohol as well. Drinking these concoctions relieved a variety of symptoms, but because they were habituating, patrons often required more and more to achieve the desired effects (which was also good for business).

Recreational use of opium later led to rising fears about its use by Chinese immigrants and working-class whites. Thus the nineteenth century in Britain saw a dramatically changing view of opium, from accepted medical habit to a sickness or disease necessitating treatment.

Canada initially saw no such opposition of the kind that was observed in Britain (and in China). At the frontier of a new nation in the 1860s, the dangers of habituating substances and tonics appear not to have generated all that much concern. The emergence of opium dens in Chinese-populated areas had not been cause for widespread panic either (Boyd, 1991). It is improbable that these had looked like anything resembling the pits of sorrow and debauchery they were later claimed to be.

Boyd cites Somerset Maugham's account. After visiting an opium den in China decades earlier, Maugham recalled it as a cheerful spot, comfortable and cozy. The one he visited was likened to the intimate beer houses familiar to Europeans, where the tired working man could go and spend a peaceful hour.

There is no documented widespread disapproval of the practice of smoking opium before the twentieth century in Canada (cf. Blackwell and Erickson, 1988; Carstairs, 2006; Giffen et al., 1991; Grayson, 2008). It was produced in factories and sold in British Columbia from the early 1870s until the trade was outlawed (Box 3.2). At the time of the ban, amounts purchased by whites equalled those sold to the Chinese. Although, as we shall see later, some Chinese were also against opium for moral reasons, the association of the habit with the growing **yellow peril** served both racist and economic interests, contributing to support for halting immigration of non-whites into Canada.

It was in this fervent social context from which disorder ultimately erupted in a 1907 riot that targeted Chinese business owners in Vancouver. William Lyon Mackenzie King, who would later be prime minister, was dispatched to settle claims for damages by Chinese businesses (including a company that supplied opium). Though his initial stance had been that legal sales should be continued, a delegation of Chinese Christian clergymen and merchants is believed to have convinced him that an outright ban was needed. Consistent with the literature on moral regulation, therefore, the legislation that resulted was neither entirely coercive nor forced upon an outside group without inside support. The 1908 ban on smoking opium provided up to three months in prison for its sale or manufacture; merchants were given six months to sell off all supplies. In the same year, an agreement between the British government and China called for lowering production by 10 per cent per year over the next decade, until the trade was phased out and abolished altogether.

Box 3.2

Early History of Canadian Drug Laws—Key Events

1850s	Chinese immigrants brought to western Canada to fill labour shortages.
1870	First opium den opens in Vancouver.
1876–1908	Thousands of pounds of opium imported into Canada.
1880	Chinese immigrants constitute 20% of the population of British Columbia.
1883	Three opium-production factories are operating in Victoria.
1891	More than 10 opium dens estimated to be operating in the Canadian west.
1907	Anti-Asian riot in Vancouver.
1908	Canada passes the Anti-Opium Act, which prohibits the importation of opium without proper authorization; limits use of opium to medicinal purposes; sets a maximum prison term of three years and/or a $1000 fine.
	Propriety or Patent Medicine Act is passed.
1911	Canada passes the Opium and Narcotic Drug Act, restricting morphine and cocaine use, giving police new search and seizure powers, and placing the burden of proof (guilty until proven innocent) on those accused of drug possession.
1912	International Opium Convention signed by Canada.
1921	Amendments to the 1911 Opium and Narcotic Drug Act bring tougher sentencing provisions.
1922	Further amendments to the 1911 Act increase police authority over search and seizure, add whipping as a penalty, and deportation for immigrants charged with drug offences.
	From 1922 to 1930, 7096 persons are convicted under the Act, 69% of whom are Chinese Canadians.

With the diminishing supply of opium came rising prices, growing profits, and the proliferation of an underground black market. In a social climate in which foreign drugs and their users were portrayed as a kind of cultural poison, harsher penalties soon followed. There is no documented outcry against the quick progression from regulating trade to criminalization. The new laws introduced first targeted suppliers then smugglers of illegal drugs, and next the substance user.

1923	Marijuana is added to the list of prohibited drugs. Police search and seizure powers are extended further.
1929	Police officers are issued lifetime writs of assistance, allowing them to enter private dwellings suspected of containing drugs without a warrant.
1932	Medicines are permitted to include small amounts of certain prohibited substances. Ten more psychoactive substances are added to the schedule, including coca leaf and synthetic drugs.
1954	Possession for the purposes of drug trafficking is defined so that the burden of proof falls on the accused. The maximum prison sentence is increased from 7 to 14 years. Whipping and deportation are still among the punishment options.
1955	The Special Committee of the Senate on the Traffic in Narcotic Drugs is created. The Committee concludes that drug addiction is a symptom of individual character weaknesses that lead to criminality. Tougher sentencing provisions are recommended. Treatment options are rejected; instead, it is suggested that incarcerated addicts be segregated from the general prison population.
1961	The Narcotic Control Act replaces the Opium and Narcotic Act. The new Act repeals the whipping punishment. Importing and exporting prohibited drugs is now subject to a minimum sentence of 7 years, up to a maximum of 25 years imprisonment. The trafficking penalty is raised from 14 to 25 years. The schedule of banned substances now comprises 92 different drugs and drug derivatives. The Food and Drug Act is passed to regulate the distribution and use of barbiturates and amphetamines. The Single Convention on Narcotic Drugs is established, to usher in the modern era of international drug control.

Source: Adapted from Grayson (2008).

Within two decades, by the end of the 1920s, drug laws imposed sentences of up to seven years imprisonment for trafficking—and a mandatory minimum of two months in prison, plus a flogging, for those found guilty of possession. Concern for public health was not a motivating factor. Mackenzie King himself had been aware that use of opium in moderation was a habit not unlike cigar smoking, and no more injurious to the user's health. He was informed as well of adverse outcomes of the ban.

These laws prompted the production of more concentrated opiates, first morphine and later heroin, that could be more easily transported by suppliers. Once a relatively harmless foreign habit had been outlawed, it was soon replaced by the use of substances with much higher potency and potential for abuse. In the decades since this legislation was enacted, it has been increasingly observed that prohibition contributes to, and indeed creates, the circumstances that motivate calls for harsher drug laws.

Parliamentary debates in 1960 indicate that there was support for the execution of drug traffickers. With the repeal of the death penalty in 1976 (though there have no executions since 1962), this fate for drug offenders has not come to pass. But much like the demand for a return to capital punishment, the scourge of those who deal in drugs continues to elicit widespread condemnation in contemporary Canada.

The social history of cocaine in the Canadian experience is not unlike the history of opium. It was hailed as a wonder drug for nearly half a century, after its discovery in the 1860s as a powdered extract of the coca plant. Cocaine was prescribed by medical professionals and even used for treatment of opiate dependence. But by the twentieth century, it was increasingly observed that there were some serious physical and mental health problems linked to stimulant abuse.

The Opium and Narcotic Drug Act of 1911 added cocaine to the list of banned drugs. Once again, public health concerns do not appear to be the primary motivation for expansion of the drug laws. The moral threat presented by another foreign drug is unmistakable in later propaganda like *The Black Candle* (1922), in which Murphy claimed that black men peddling cocaine encouraged interracial sex, sexual promiscuity, and propensity for violence. Such claims clearly justified harsh treatment under law.

Early narcotics legislation was also influenced by licensed pharmacists and doctors who were threatened economically by an unregulated, thriving patent medicine industry. Coinciding with the Opium Act of 1908, the Proprietary or Patent Medicine Act restricted the sale of drugs to licensed pharmacists and doctors. At that time, more people were reportedly addicted to opiates from using patent medicines than from smoking opium (Solomon and Green, 1982).

Not unlike caffeine today, cocaine was widely recognized as an effective pick-me-up (Murray, 1987). It was a popular ingredient in patent medicines and tonics sold in an unregulated market until a century ago. Under the new drug laws, though, social attitudes transformed. Politicians and police were in agreement with physicians, who characterized cocaine as a threat to public safety even more serious than opium. The drug was also banned in Britain after stories of crazed soldiers who took cocaine in Europe during World War I.

By the 1920s, cocaine use in Canada was understood as threatening to decency and order. Another 50 years would pass before it became popular in the 1970s as both a party drug and an alluring status symbol among certain segments of society. It would be demonized again: crack cocaine became a symbol of degradation and drug problems in the 1980s (cf. Reinarman and Levine, 1995, 1997).

Drug Use–Related Discourse

The drug wars of the past four decades were initiated by a legislative process and transformation of public opinion that began over a century ago. Drugs that were considered morally neutral by most people became "monstrous" vices at once identified as criminal (Blackwell, 1988; Boyd, 1991). By definition, criminals used these drugs for pleasure rather than for coping or self-medication.

Although concern for medical and moral health has long been evident in policy discussions about drugs, these explanations rarely shed much light on the target or rationale for the resulting legislation. An earlier proposed ban on tobacco, for example, failed to pass despite debate about smoking's detrimental impact on the physical, mental, and moral health of Canadian youth. Just two measures were enacted—one intended to assist domestic growers of tobacco compete with foreign producers and the other a $10 maximum fine for those caught selling it to minors.

The Patent Medicine Act (1908) also sought to safeguard both business and public interests. The legislation regulated, rather than prohibited, the non-medical use of patent medications. The Act banned use of cocaine additives and excessive amounts of alcohol, and required producers to be registered with the government and to label products containing scheduled drugs. Although at the time heroin was included on the schedule, opium and morphine were not. The maximum penalty for violation of this section was a $50 fine for a first offence, and $100 for subsequent offences (Solomon and Green, 1982).

The success of the campaign against opium smoking—followed by cocaine, and soon thereafter cannabis—is more of a reflection of racial, economic, and political factors than drug properties per se (cf. Blackwell and Erickson, 1988; Cook, 1969; Giffen et al., 1991). The legislation enacted in 1908 protected white professional and business interests in the patent medicine and tobacco industries, while sacrificing Chinese business interests. This pattern of criminalizing certain substances—and groups—while accommodating others has steadily persisted ever since.

The early twentieth century is characterized by growth of international commitments, largely spurred on by the United States, to increase the penalties for drug crimes. In addition to the introduction of restrictions for enforcing global prohibition, it is also marked by the expansion of a federal law enforcement bureaucracy to uphold the ban on drugs.

It was not until the 1950s that alternative punishments for addicts became prominently discussed (see Carstairs, 2006; Grayson, 2008). Growing discontent with the impact of criminalizing drug-related problems is even more in evidence today. At the same time, much like in the middle of last century, policing priorities dominate drug policy debates.

In 1955, a Senate Committee held hearings on the Traffic in Narcotic Drugs in Canada. Testimony was received from concerned citizens and experts, including medical doctors, drug researchers, and police. Among the law-enforcement representatives consulted was Harry Anslinger, then commissioner of the US Bureau of Narcotics. Police officials argued forcefully for strengthening the drug laws to stop the flow of drugs into Canadian society. Law enforcement witnesses definitively rejected recommendations for expansion of treatment facilities. They opposed well-meaning doctors and academics who admired the British system, which medicalized opiate addiction by diverting addicts into maintenance clinics. These services allegedly caused problems for police on account of the growing trend of narcotics sold as street drugs (Grayson, 2008). Medical availability of dangerous narcotics would only raise addiction rates by encouraging more drug use.

Drug addicts were depicted as immoral and unprincipled criminals, neither to be pitied nor treated as victims. Police officials testified that demand for drugs must be reduced through more aggressive enforcement of the laws against possession. Rather than supplying drugs to addicts, what was needed was the removal of the addict from society entirely.

To ensure the full rehabilitation of the addict, longer prison sentences were thereby justifiable. The testimony of the law enforcement representatives was accepted at these hearings almost without question. Their opinions are consistent with the discourse of Emily Murphy's era; in fact, she had once proposed building remote "drug treatment prisons" to remove threats posed by addicts.

The preference for policing priorities was reflected in the Narcotic Control Act (NCA) of 1961. Initial drafts of the Act included a provision for custodial drug treatment and "preventive detention" for those convicted of drug crimes. This was not enacted into law—and some of the harsher features of existing legislation at the time, such as whipping drug offenders, were repealed.

Under the NCA, however, maximum penalties were raised from 14 years to life imprisonment for importing, exporting, or trafficking narcotics, and for possession of narcotics for the purpose of trafficking. Conviction for importing or exporting drugs required a mandatory minimum of seven years in prison. No criminal offence apart from murder and treason carried so lengthy a minimum term.

The NCA reflects a contempt for users and suppliers that is still in evidence today. It is noteworthy that lawmakers, in the name of treatment, have been and continue to impose sentences on addicts that at one time were reserved for violent criminals (Solomon and Murray, 1982). There has been little deviation from that era to the present in the evolution of Canadian drug laws.

Subsequent commissions and parliamentary debates in the decades since the 1960s do, however, show more balance, moderation, and respect for the opinions of reformers over time (cf. Erickson, 1992; Fischer, 1994). Removing criminal penalties for cannabis possession are among the options most prominently discussed. Challenges to drug-war-style enforcement for more dangerous illicit drugs have also gained support.

Forcing treatment on drug addicts through incarceration has been increasingly challenged by critics. Many favour harm reduction, an emerging evidence-based, public health approach to substance use. Yet, despite the discontent and evidence in favour of law reform, the efforts of reformers have been stymied. Building on the history presented in this chapter, Chapter 4 provides a more contemporary overview of drug politics and policy developments in Canada.

Chapter Summary

The history of substance use and efforts to control drugs in Canada and elsewhere has been the focus of this chapter. Human interest in, and experience with, intoxicating substances has been observed for several thousand years. The present overview was brief and necessarily selective, putting emphasis on Western cultural perceptions, societal responses in the past few centuries, and relatively recent Canadian experiences.

The constructionist perspective was augmented here with reference to moral regulation. This explanatory framework points to the emergence and persistence of legislation meant to reaffirm white values as the predominant source of identity in Canada. Societal reactions to the use of drugs are thereby better understood in terms of nation-building processes than drug properties or health and behavioural effects.

Canadian antidrug legislation has its origins in a social context in which "foreign" drugs were demonized for their association with non-whites. These drugs, and those who used them, were perceived as threatening to influential interest groups. A variety of racial, economic, and political interests are reflected in the resulting legislation.

Despite our preference today that Canadian nation-building be touted as that which results in a **cultural mosaic**, this multicultural identity is severely challenged by the documented history and origins of drug law. Addicts have been depicted as both sinners and sick people who require drug treatment. This contradiction has not restricted the expansion of a legislative framework predicated on the notion of eliminating certain kinds of drugs and those who use them.

The growing call for public health approaches, evident in drug policy discussions of the past half-century, has ushered in an era in which punishment and treatment discourses have been merged or coexist. Drug use is understood as both a crime and as a sickness. Among other implications, merging discourses have led to laws that curiously force addicts into custody for "treatment." The philosophical development and political implications of drug policy discourses are discussed in the next chapter.

Questions for Critical Thought

1. Who have been the most influential claims-makers in the documented history of drug control in Canada? What interests were they seeking to promote or preserve?
2. What specific interests, from a nation-building standpoint, have been served by Canada's approach to drug control?
3. In your view, are the origins of Canada's drug laws racist, or are there other explanations worth examining as well? Which of these explanations are still in evidence today?

Suggested Readings

Belenko, S.R. 2000. *Drugs and Drug Policy in America: A Documentary History.* Westport, CT: Greenwood. This textbook traces the origins and nature of drug use and abuse, and control efforts in America. It charts the evolution of ever-stricter policies, and reactions to them, through primary documents, including court cases, speeches, laws, and opinion pieces that illuminate this history.

Carstairs, C. 2006. *Jailed for Possession: Illegal Drug Use, Regulation, and Power in Canada, 1920–1961.* Toronto: University of Toronto Press. This social history of drug use in Canada examines the regulation of drug users by physicians, social workers, and police. The book illustrates the impact of drug laws on users' health, work lives, and relationships in the middle of the century.

McKenna, T. 1992. *Food of the Gods: The Search for the Original Tree of Knowledge. A Radical History of Plants, Drugs, and Human Evolution.* New York: Bantam. This book provides a detailed history of human desire to alter consciousness, and our complex relationship with psychoactive plants.

Suggested Websites

The Fix

www.thefix.com/content/drugs-addiction-history-alcohol9605

This website provides a brief slideshow through time of the world's most popular psychoactive drugs.

Canadian Drug Policy Coalition

www.drugpolicy.ca/progress/timeline/

This website provides an interactive timeline of the origins and history of Canadian drug policy.

The International Network of People Who Use Drugs

www.inpud.wordpress.com/timeline-of-events-in-the-history-of-drugs/

This website provides a comprehensive timeline of events in the history of drugs around the world.

4 Drug Policy Perspectives

Learning Objectives

- To recognize connections between classic philosophical perspectives on the role of law in regulating morals and contemporary Canadian drug policy debates.
- To understand the basis of rights-based and harm reduction arguments for implementing policy reform.
- To critically evaluate drug policy in Canada in terms of fundamental moral principles and values.

Introduction

In Chapter 3, the origins of Canadian antidrug laws were traced to bans on opium (1908), cocaine (1911), and cannabis (1923) in the early decades of the twentieth century. For the next few decades, up until the 1960s, the enforcement and development of drug laws focused primarily on heroin possession. Throughout this period, this crime accounted for about half of all drug convictions.

By the 1950s, health experts favouring medicalization over criminalization began calling for expansion of addiction treatment services and methadone maintenance programs (see Carstairs, 2006; Giffen et al., 1991). Access to these services and programs nonetheless remained severely limited until the 1990s. Over the last 25 years, concerns about injection drug deaths due to overdose and HIV transmission have forced increased attention to pragmatic interventions, and new interpretations of existing laws.

This chapter traces the development of Canadian drug policy since the public health perspective—widely known as the "harm reduction" approach—first entered the discussion a quarter-century ago. Continuing commitment to more punitive approaches is reflected in our drug laws' resistance to reform. Drug prohibition is resilient, despite support for harm reduction among experts, informed members of the public, and police.

Since the later 1980s, Canada's national drug strategy has officially sought to strike a balance between policing, treatment, education, and prevention. This era witnessed the emergence of a public health perspective on drugs in widespread use, as well as those with lower use rates. In addition to injection drugs, it is applied to cannabis, alcohol, tobacco, and other regulated substances. However, we have seen few changes in the laws concerning cannabis—the most widely used illicit drug—that would indicate commitment to significant reform.

Chapter 4 continues where Chapter 3 left off. Its aim is to develop a contemporary outlook on drug policy perspectives in Canada today. The recent history of legislative action (and inaction) and discussion will be augmented by examining the values represented at the centre of drug policy debates. We begin by overviewing drug use trends and social factors that influenced the call for action and resulting legislation that defines Canadian drug policy today.

Drug Use Trends and Policy Activities

Relying on official surveys and statistics to chart the prevalence of drug use is problematic (Blackwell, 1988). These may tell us something about changes over time, assuming that the methods and measures used are consistent. Population surveys and reported police activity (Figure 4.1) do provide some insight into the emerging trends.

But there are also limitations to relying on these data. Police statistics, for example, often tell us more about policing priorities and patterns of enforcement than the rate of substance use (Blackwell and Erickson, 1988; Kitsuse and Cicourel, 1963). Aggressive law enforcement inflates arrest statistics and encounters with drug users reported by police.

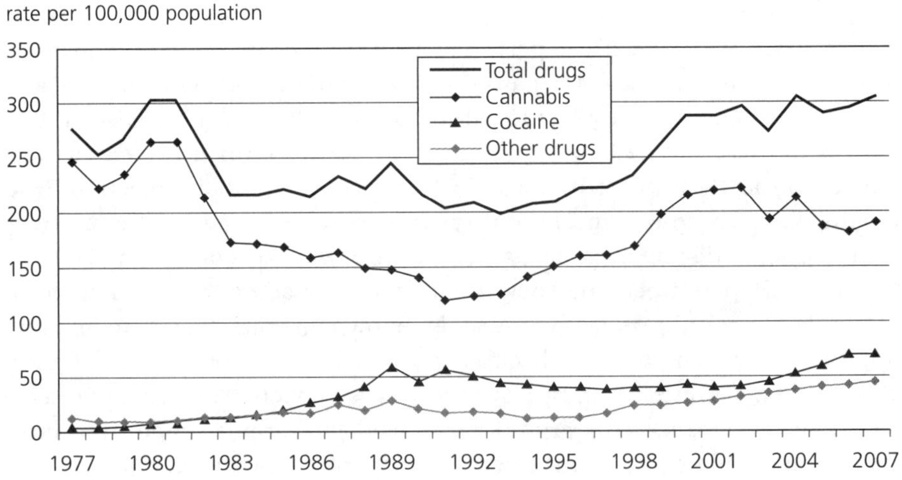

Figure 4.1 Police-Reported Drug Offence Rates in Canada, 1977–2007
Source: Dauvergne (2009).

Perceptions of a growing "epidemic" can be triggered by police activity and media attention, which in turn alerts the general public to the problem. This increased exposure may result in a drug panic that manifests itself in more support for harsher penalties. Public perceptions and enforcement priorities are, accordingly, inseparable from official crime statistics.

Although population surveys are informative as well, they are also vulnerable to certain forms of bias. The reliability of estimates produced are subject to exaggeration—for example, in the case of those who might admit to using a drug they have not taken owing to its perceived "cool factor" among peers. The prevalence of drug use in the general population is probably more often underestimated, as respondents may be wary of talking to researchers about any personal involvement in a criminal activity.

Because these sorts of biases need not be systematic or consistent from one survey to another, we must exercise due caution when interpreting results. Despite the limitations of these methods, Blackwell's research (1988) indicates a rapid increase in use upon the introduction of new substances in most cases. Declining rates of use, and long-term relative stability at a lower rate thereafter, typically follows this initial rise.

Dramatic increases in use rates, followed by a sharp decline, appear particularly common in populations of drug users whose habits are considered risky in their community of peers. Dangerous drug preferences and practices are thereby largely self-contained. Rarely do they spread too far beyond initial outbreaks owing to social learning in drug using groups.

Most so-called epidemics really represent a minor deviation in drug prevalence. Statistically significant increases in small segments of the drug-using population are not necessarily practically significant. Yet worst case scenarios based on presumed "alarming" trends have often been sensationalized by media, whose observations, which prompt disproportionate concern, are also used to justify resistance to reform.

Estimates of drug use in the early twentieth century tell us little of value in explaining the emergence of increasingly restrictive legislation at the time. By 1900, medical use of opiates was declining, while public health improvements and medical advances were beginning to reduce the incidence of illness. Illicit use of opium, morphine, and eventually heroin occurred in an increasingly large segment of the opiate addict population.

Rates of use reportedly remained fairly stable, declining in the war years in most places, though convictions began to rise in large cities starting in the 1930s. By the 1950s, it is estimated that there were about 2000 heroin users in the country (Blackwell, 1988; Carstairs, 2006).

Neither cannabis nor cocaine was known to most Canadians, despite campaigns against them in the early twentieth century. Before the Second World War, however, powerful synthetic drugs (e.g., amphetamines, barbiturates) were introduced in medicine, and became increasingly exploited for non-medical consumption.

When illicit drugs were scarce during the war years, these alternatives were discovered and co-opted by recreational consumers—much like intoxicating patent medicines decades earlier. Unlike in the United States, Canadian research shows that in the post-war era heroin users were mostly white and had not grown up in greatly impoverished circumstances. The most important factor contributing to their involvement with the drug was their association with other heroin users. Heroin addicts were discovered to be rather unremarkable, possessing fewer neurotic features than the researchers themselves (Stevenson et al., 1956). Despite such findings, which favour a public health perspective on opiate addiction, addicts were still treated primarily like criminals. Heroin addiction, and crack and meth addiction later, was reviled.

Other drugs, like cannabis and LSD, continued to be associated with the fringes of society—at least until the arrival of the psychedelic era. Also known as "acid," LSD was invented in the 1940s. Much like MDMA, or ecstasy, a generation later, it soon gained a following after its discovery as a potential adjunct to psychiatric treatment.

Increased experimentation with LSD and other hallucinogens was also spurred on by government restrictions. New controls to stem the use of these drugs subsequently enhanced the notoriety of previously unknown drugs, increasing profit margins and unlawful production for non-therapeutic use. Following in this path, from the mid-1960s onward, an array of substances (either derived from natural plants or man-made) has been rediscovered or produced.

While tastes for certain drugs change with the times, most illegal substances are consumed by a small fraction of the general population. The one exception has been cannabis, which has charted a more vigorous and sustained intrusion from the margins to the mainstream.

By the 1970s, estimates suggest that as many as one million Canadians had tried cannabis. Use rates increased throughout the decade, before declining somewhat in the 1980s. Rates of use, then and now, were higher among youth. Student surveys in Toronto indicate that, at their peak, in 1979 about one-third of students aged 12 years and older had used marijuana during the past year. About half of high school students 16 to 17 years old identified as being current users. Nearly one in five adults reported having tried it, and 10 per cent had done so in the previous 12 months.

Estimated rates of other drug use are much lower, and appear to have peaked sooner, with the declining cultural influence of the psychedelic era. Nonetheless, by the early 1970s, there was increasing societal anxiety about a drug use epidemic. Apart from the dramatic rise in cannabis consumption—and subsequent convictions of middle-class, white youth—drug use does not appear to have been any more epidemic in this period than in others.

Although rates of substance use were certainly increasing after the 1960s advent of a burgeoning drug culture, the actual prevalence of drug use remained relatively low. In 1973, for example, an estimated 3 per cent of Canadians older than the age of 12 had taken LSD or similar hallucinogens. Heroin use in Canada also peaked around that time, at an estimated 50,000 occasional users, 15,000 regular users, and about 7000 addicts.

Cocaine use was negligible, and remained as such despite related drug panics. Even in the 1980s, at its peak of popularity, only about 3 per cent of Canadians had ever tried cocaine, with maybe one-third of this group having used in the past year (Blackwell, 1982).

The earlier scarcity of cocaine, much like opium before it, led to more experimentation with other stimulants that often had more dangerous effects. The drug scene of the 1960s, for example, saw increasing amphetamine injection and combination use of different drugs. The emergence of the "speed freak" (like the "junkie" and the "crackhead") led to broad perception of a fearsome epidemic.

Amphetamine abuse has clearly recognizable behavioural and health effects that appear to be self-limiting. High rates of overdose, infection, death, and psychiatric problems deterred potential users, reinforcing negative attitudes and controls within drug-using communities. At its peak in 1970, high-dose injection of amphetamines was something practised regularly by about 3000 users. Though prevalence rose rapidly in a relatively short period, in retrospect the practice, like past and subsequent drug panics, was epidemic in only a very limited sense.

In sum, Blackwell's observations put so-called drug problems into perspective, particularly in terms of the drug culture's wave of influence on youth. The rising prevalence of substance use (particularly marijuana), along with the involvement of young (white) people with the legal system, however, led to calls for action. These societal developments resulted in formation of a government committee—the Le Dain Commission of Inquiry into the Non-Medical Use of Drugs.

The Le Dain Report

The final report of the Le Dain Commission (1972), so named after its chair, Gerald Le Dain, had a significant impact on drug policy discussions (Grayson, 2008). Most significantly, it represented the first challenge to law enforcement's unquestioned jurisdiction over policy decisions. The commission's recommendations marked the beginning of a shift toward more balanced discourse informed by medical authorities, with claims about addiction based on scientific evidence.

Among other notable changes in the nature of the discourse, the conventional term *addict,* applied to users of banned substances, was replaced by less judgmental language. Although largely opposed by law enforcement representatives—and, ultimately, rejected by Canadian lawmakers—the committee's recommendations were groundbreaking in their scope. Most significantly, the committee recommended a gradual withdrawal from the use of criminal penalties for illicit drug possession, phasing out incarceration in favour of medical treatment.

Occasional use of drugs with low-dependency potential was exempted from compulsory treatment criteria. More and better research on illicit drugs was called for, including greater access for the purposes of research, improved data gathering, and use of government statistics. The distinction between legal and illegal drugs was also scrutinized, resulting in a call for greater balance in their treatment—including strict controls on alcohol and tobacco advertising.

The committee's recommendations would ultimately prove prophetic, as public health restrictions of this nature have become increasingly more commonplace in Canada today. Closer monitoring of prescription drugs was also called for to address any overlooked potential for abuse. The Le Dain report, accordingly, foreshadowed the emergence of a public health perspective with the goal of harm reduction. In calling for a shift away from law enforcement measures, it also recommended more attention to the principles that underlie drug policy debates (see Hathaway, 2001a).

The Le Dain committee comprised five commissioners. Each committee member was to reach his or her own conclusions based on the evidence presented over four years of research. Reaching a majority consensus, the committee recommended a combination of punishment and treatment options for the use of "harder" drugs. Due to its low toxicity (see Figure 4.2), the majority proposed that cannabis be decriminalized. For cases of simple possession, the favoured measure was to retain a small fine, indicating both disapproval and consequences for illegal activity (much like a parking ticket), while removing the threat of jail time, and therefore a criminal record.

The legalization option—removing penalties entirely in favour of a regulated system of supply—was rejected as too liberal. Legalizing cannabis possession, it was argued, implied a higher level of acceptance, which would likely encourage young people to take up the habit.

The view endorsed by three of five commissioners was that the law is meant to serve a paternalistic function, in which the State fulfills a role analogous to parenting. The State is justified, they reasoned, in restricting certain rights to protect Canadians, particularly young people, from harms they are apt to inflict on themselves. Access to drugs is reasonably restricted by the government to maintain social order and prevent drug harm.

The paternalistic view of the majority was offset by the opposing viewpoints of two Le Dain commissioners, who put forward sharply contrasting

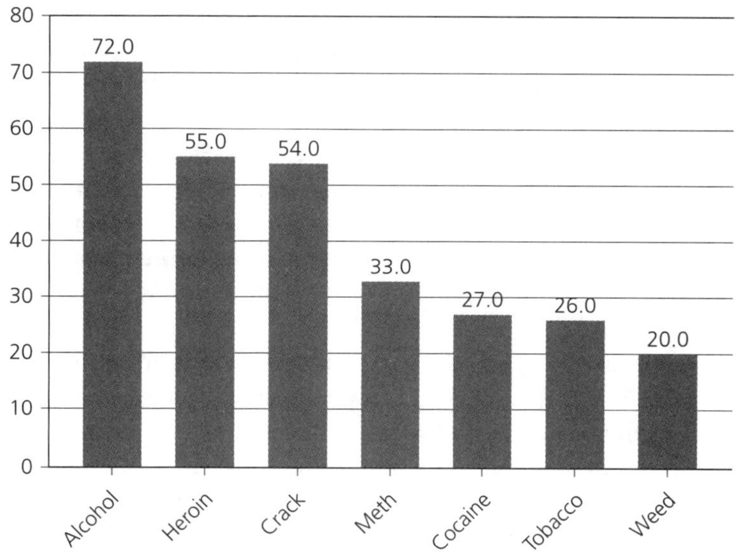

Figure 4.2 Total Harm Scores for Various Drugs
Source: Adapted from Nutt et al. (2010).

moral arguments. One sought to uphold the status quo on prohibition. The other held a moral view that prioritized rights. The more conservative perspective was that of Ian Campbell. He contended that the government must safeguard public order, and seek to maintain existing moral standards. Drug use, viewed as offensive or disturbing from this standpoint, should be properly prohibited by law. This response is justified whether or not drug use is actually injurious to others.

Whereas harder drugs like heroin and cocaine indisputably appear to meet the threshold for restrictions under law, the status of cannabis was somewhat more contentious. Even Campbell, for example, concurred with the majority opinion that the punishment for cannabis possession was disproportionate to the harms caused by use of the drug. He supported penalty reduction, while maintaining that removing criminal penalties entirely would send youth the wrong message. Decriminalizing cannabis, he argued, went too far by neglecting the law's role to enforce morality, regardless of actual harm.

What is meant by "harm" is divisive when debating the proper role of law in the development of policy. Does the alleged harm refer to health or to morality, or to both? In this respect, the findings of the Le Dain Commission echoed the benign view of the Indian Hemp Committee three-quarters of a century before. The growing prevalence of marijuana use among young people, however, clearly tested the boundaries of social tolerance. In so doing, cannabis brought conflicting cultural values to the forefront of Canadian drug policy debates.

In retrospect, it seems that Campbell's moderate proposal to reduce the penalties for cannabis possession was actually quite liberal. Indeed, the decades following Le Dain's report have witnessed even more oppressive laws and law enforcement practices, premised on the punishment of users in the name of maintaining public order and upholding traditional values (Beauchesne, 1991).

Before continuing, we shall briefly return to the position of the fifth Le Dain commissioner. In opposing Campbell, and the rest of the committee, Marie-Andre Bertrand took a more liberal position on the role of law in regulating moral conduct. The only time intervention is warranted, she argued, is when substance use threatens public security. Therefore, the sale of impure drugs, which are mixed with unknown additives, justify restrictions or intervention by the State. Any more extensive State intrusion into drug use is deemed a violation of the human rights of users. The ban on marijuana in particular, stated Bertrand, represents a blatant abuse of the State powers bestowed on government authorities by the Canadian people. Cannabis must be legalized, therefore, because the laws against it are not proportional to the harms they are seeking to prevent.

State intrusions are not justified to protect society, from neither a moral standpoint nor for paternalistic reasons. For Bertrand, freedom of drug choice should not depend on proof of harmlessness (see also Mitchell, 1990). Applying harm criteria consistently and fairly, however, helps put drug use in perspective as but one of many risk activities that people choose to do. Driving, sex, sky diving, and other extreme sports, although often dangerous, are not outlawed by the government, nor even necessarily discouraged.

Legal fairness calls for equal treatment of all drug use. Therefore, restrictions based on risk or harm ought to be consistent. Because alcohol, tobacco, and prescription drugs are not subject to the same system of control, this principle of justice has not been demonstrated. Adherence to the principles of fairness and consistency could mean that now-legal substances might be prohibited as well.

From a legal standpoint, stricter measures might be considered just as fair, and equally justified as moving toward removal of the ban on outlawed drugs. A commitment to ensuring proportionality and fairness would encourage law-makers and enforcers to consider their own legal substance use, and other risk activities, when deliberating and enacting new drug policies. But considering that not even the more moderate recommendations of the Le Dain majority were implemented, the liberal position of Bertrand appears quite "radical." Despite their grounding in well-recognized principles of justice, her views were not accepted; this continues to be the case.

In both principle and practice, drug-law enactment and enforcement continues to reflect a morally conservative interpretation of the function of the legal system. In responding to Le Dain's call for alternatives to punishment and support for marijuana law reform, police and government officials reframed their arguments accordingly, and brought in new evidence from quasi-scientific studies. This evidence included claims that marijuana was a "gateway" to heroin and the cause of severe apathy, both of which were widely publicized by government authorities in the years directly following the Le Dain report (Grayson, 2008).

Law enforcement representatives were able to co-opt medical discourse to regain a position of authority in policy debates. The adoption of a medical model made it possible for drugs to be portrayed as multidimensional, presenting both a criminal and a health threat to Canadians. Many drug treatment programs were located in prisons and resources earmarked for drug research were routinely used for the production of antidrug materials (Giffen et al., 1991; Grayson, 2008).

The most substantial law reforms concerning marijuana occurred during the timeframe of the Le Dain inquiry. In 1969, fines were established as an option, or as an alternative to prison, for those convicted for possession. This amendment was enacted to alleviate the burden and severity of punishment for youth who had no other indications of involvement with criminal activity.

In 1972, the Narcotics Control Act was amended to allow for a guilty verdict without conviction in cases of simple marijuana possession. It might be argued that these changes, which acknowledged the harms or hardship brought upon individuals after conviction for possession, were enacted so significant reforms could be avoided. Downgrading penalties for cannabis offenders has, put otherwise, enabled more efficient use of police and court resources—to facilitate the processing of more drug possession cases within the legal system.

More substantial penalty reduction, in response to continued calls to decriminalize possession of cannabis, has been rejected outright by lawmakers ever since (see Erickson, 1998). Convictions for possession of marijuana increased dramatically throughout the 1970s and 1980s. In addition to neglect of the inquiry's recommendations, the decades since the Le Dain report have seen a resurgence of intensified conservative perspectives on drug policy in Canada.

At the same time, the more liberal opinion of Bertrand has anticipated arguments that challenge state authorities to justify their intrusions into substance use behaviour. The types of claims put forward by proponents of Bertrand's view are self-consciously political as opposed to scientific. However, this perspective can be powerfully persuasive, considering that courts and legislators are accustomed to evaluating claims derived from rights-based arguments (Mitchell, 1988). Recognizing the potential of pursuing rights-based discourse as a strategy for policy reform most notably required the enactment of the Canadian Charter of Rights and Freedoms in 1982.

Today, more than 30 years after the Charter was enacted (about a decade after the Le Dain report was tabled), its impact on drug policy has been similarly modest. However, its potential to transform the drugs debate warrants our attention as a critical drug policy development in Canada. Upholding freedom to use drugs as an individual right worthy of protection by courts and legislatures was a significant departure from use of evidence-based arguments emphasizing reduction of drug-related harms. The impact of the Charter is discussed in the next section as a key development and resource for reform.

On Charter Rights

Proclaimed in 1982, the Canadian Charter of Rights and Freedoms states that everybody has the fundamental right to freedom of conscience and religion, thought, belief, opinion, and expression. Section 7 of the Charter guarantees all individuals the right to life and liberty, and security as a person. The right or freedom to use drugs is not specifically protected. To make this argument requires successful establishment that a pre-existing right (such as the right to liberty or freedom of expression) extends far enough to include substance use (Mitchell, 1988). Canadian courts, to date, have not responded very favourably to calls for liberalizing drug laws that rely on rights-based claims.

Three decades after the enactment of the Charter it is evident that incremental, gradual reform is far more likely than a sudden transformation of drug laws in the courtroom. Interpretations and decisions from accumulating case law involve a long-term process, taking years or even decades, and are not deemed conclusive unless favourably received and proclaimed by the Supreme Court of Canada.

Nonetheless, regardless of the outcome, the Charter focuses attention on, and demands consideration of, whether rights and freedoms have been adequately protected or whether they have been violated by the actions and requirements of the State. Drug enforcement policies and practices, since the Charter, have been openly discussed and scrutinized in open court. This has led to changes in questionable police practices, and those of prosecutors in drug cases—for example, to avoid attracting a constitutional challenge.

Court challenges have occasionally succeeded in striking down or limiting excessive drug enforcement tactics, powers of arrest, and search and seizure. Changes in the law facilitated by the Charter include banning the use of chokeholds (to prevent suspected drug users from swallowing the evidence) and more police accountability when carrying out search warrants (Solomon, 1988). Police powers of search, arrest, and seizure for drug offences were deemed disproportionate to other types of crime.

For drug-related crimes, it was acknowledged for the first time that enforcement powers over suspects had exceeded even those for violent crimes, including rape and murder. Challenging these practices on Charter grounds put limits on invasive practices like searching body cavities, and forced observance of due process when searching private dwellings. While it is arguable that enforcement is inevitably intrusive, and difficult to justify for drug-related crimes, successful legal challenges have made police increasingly accountable to a higher authority in law.

Charter challenges have raised awareness of existing enforcement policies and practices among the general public. In addition to debate in public forums and in media, such scrutiny encourages law-makers to consider the rights and freedoms of Canadians that have led to actual changes in the law when examining drug policy.

The most significant court challenges in recent years have been predominantly cannabis-related (see Hathaway, 2001a). Beginning in the 1990s, marijuana laws began to attract attention in the courts as being an unjustified intrusion into an activity widely recognize as harmless. Building on the earlier conclusions of the Le Dain report, scientific arguments for loosening restrictions on cannabis possession have met with little opposition. With the exception of allowances for medical consumption, however, court decisions have upheld the constitutionality of the ban on cannabis to date.

Although it may be recognized as relatively harmless, and support for law reform continues to expand, marijuana use has not been deemed a right deserving constitutional protection by the courts. If such a case can be established, as a matter of public policy, it is contingent on the government to introduce new legislation through the democratic process—not a judgment rendered in the courts (see Box 4.1).

The Clay decision represented a continuation of the legal–political stalemate around cannabis, which has been apparent since the tabling of the Le Dain report. The scientific evidence for law reform is growing; there is decreasing weight attached to opposition based on moral arguments alone. Nonetheless, resistance remains steady. Law reform has been a "hot potato" that for decades has been passed back and forth between the courts and Parliament, only to be dropped when an election comes around.

Employing rights-based discourse to argue for reform has weaknesses as well. Drawing on abstract principles does not shed much light on the interpretation of these principles. For example, what exactly does "fundamental right" mean? Asserting that we have the right to use drugs still requires explaining the Charter in a way that is contestable, regardless of the strength of evidence presented.

Box 4.1 R. v. Clay

In May of 1995, hemp-shop proprietor Chris Clay was arrested and charged with cultivation and possession for the purpose of trafficking after selling small cannabis plant cuttings in his London, Ontario, store. Although he had operated Canada's first "Hemporium" since 1993—openly selling marijuana seeds, water pipes, and other paraphernalia—local police decided he had pushed the limits of tolerance too far and laid down a number of charges. After enlisting the counsel of constitutional lawyer Alan Young, who in 1994 had fought successfully to strike down the section of the Criminal Code prohibiting promotion or sale of illicit drug literature, Clay launched a new challenge of Canada's drug laws. Raising funds collected through donations to his website, Clay was able to bring in more than a dozen expert witnesses from across North America. For three weeks during the spring of 1997, the court heard testimony from a variety of experts.

The challenge launched by Clay before the Ontario Court of Justice sought to establish that the charges brought against him violated Section 7 of the Canadian Charter of Rights and Freedoms. The burden of proof was on the applicants to demonstrate a violation of the principles of fundamental justice. A central matter for the court to deliberate was whether Parliament is justified in prohibiting behaviour that is relatively harmless. Or does the ban on cannabis interfere with Charter rights to make autonomous decisions in the absence of compelling reasons? In his factual assessment of the arguments presented, the presiding judge agreed with the general consensus among experts that moderate use of cannabis is unlikely to cause harm to the user or society. Citing support for law reform among the majority of Canadians, and more liberal drug policies in Europe and Australia, he also noted that the drug laws in North America appeared "somewhat out of step with most of the rest of the western world" (Hathaway, 2001a).

The constitutional assessment of the arguments presented for striking down the marijuana law was less sympathetic. Despite support for law reform, and an easing of restrictions found in other jurisdictions, it was noted that possession of the drug remained illegal in most countries. Where marijuana was decriminalized, in the Netherlands and elsewhere, these had been legislative (not court-imposed) initiatives. Therefore, the challenge constituted an "unwarranted intrusion into the legislative domain." Furthermore, although "relatively harmless," the use of cannabis was ruled to cause sufficient harm to justify the ban. Whereas the right to liberty grants a degree of autonomy in making decisions of fundamental personal importance, it was argued, individual freedom must also be subjected to numerous constraints for the **common good**. Since cannabis is used primarily for recreation, the ban against it represents a trivial limitation of individual rights to personal autonomy.

Source: Adapted from Hathaway (2001a).

As a test case for the limits of state tolerance, marijuana may be relatively harmless. Yet so far this argument has failed to pass the threshold that is needed to incite action. In the contemporary context of continuing debate, harm arguments are easily refuted by opponents who respond with claims of greater harm. The kinds of harm behind the claims are interchangeable as well. Cannabis now allegedly causes schizophrenia, for example, as opposed to heroin addiction, amotivation, or other earlier common concerns about the drug.

Although the harm claims may have changed, the onus is still clearly on drug policy reformers to make the case for changes in the law. To be conclusively persuasive, rights-based arguments must ultimately put the onus on lawmakers to justify intrusion into the private lives of people who use drugs. This interpretation of the Charter draws upon a Western liberal tradition passed on from notable philosophers like Immanuel Kant and J.S. Mill. Invoking the spirit of liberalism—as like-minded politicians, academics, and law reformers often do—means engaging with a living, evolving tradition of moral contemplation and political thought (see Hathaway, 2002).

The pursuit of individual freedom is a core value that has guided constitutional democracy's development in Western culture and society for centuries. Given the neglect of guiding principles in practice, in the bureaucratic context of drug policy today, engaging with core values is essential to the process of challenging restrictive legislation.

From Le Dain's revisitation of the proper role of government to more recent legal challenges facilitated by the Charter, the liberal tradition is evidently a contentious feature of Canadian drug policy debates. Before moving on to other policy activities and developments in discourse from the 1990s onward, a brief overview of the origins of modern liberalism's philosophical foundations follows next.

A Philosophical Perspective

Modern liberal philosophy emerged from the Enlightenment period in the eighteenth century, wherein humanistic reason was seen as the way forward out of the dark ages. Kant and other early liberal philosophers (Table 4.1) called for the pursuit of self-actualization and humanity as valued moral ends. They rejected then-traditional philosophies of living, which promoted certain virtues or prosocial characteristics to further the collective common good.

Two centuries removed from the Enlightenment, one might argue, most Westerners no longer see themselves as necessarily determined by the

Table 4.1 Famous Liberal Philosophers

John Locke (UK, 1632–1704)	"All mankind... being all equal and independent, no one ought to harm another in his life, health, liberty or possessions."
Jean-Jacques Rousseau (Switzerland, 1712–1778)	"I prefer liberty with danger to peace with slavery."
Immanuel Kant (Germany, 1724–1804)	"The death of dogma is the birth of morality."
Thomas Paine (US/UK, 1737–1809)	"Government, even in its best state, is but a necessary evil; in its worst state, an intolerable one."
Thomas Jefferson (US, 1743–1826)	"No man has a natural right to commit aggression on the equal rights of another, and this is all from which the laws ought to restrain him."
Jeremy Bentham (UK, 1748–1832)	"Every law is an infraction of liberty."
John Stuart Mill (UK, 1806–1873)	"But was there ever any domination which did not appear natural to those who possessed it?"
Isaiah Berlin (Latvia/UK, 1909–1997)	"All forms of tampering with human beings, getting at them, shaping them against their will to your own pattern, all thought control and conditioning is... a denial of that in men which makes them men...."
John Rawls (US, 1921–2002)	"Each person possesses an inviolability founded on justice that even the welfare of society as a whole cannot override. For this reason, justice denies that the loss of freedom for some is made right by a greater good shared by others...."

roles and expectations of tradition or community. More emphasis is put on people's individual rights, including freedom and equality, and what each is entitled to claim from other members of society. The birth of the individual ushered in the modern era, and a rights-based vision of morality and justice.

Whereas conflict arises between groups and individuals in exercising preferences or rights, resolutions require making difficult decisions about what kinds of rights or preferences have priority over others. To justify that order requires debate about the principles of justice that are guiding the decision. Like morality, these principles are thought to be evolving. This means such debates are necessarily continuous, and should never be considered entirely conclusive.

Whereas fundamental principles of justice are evolving, there is a general agreement among liberal theorists on what justice ought to achieve. A primary concern is that any inequality in the treatment of individuals must be justifiable. Accusations of injustice are referred to formal rules and processes in a legal system that functions to sustain the social order.

Regard for individual freedom is a pervasive Western value, and respect for life and liberty is central to democracy. Rather than a common good defined in terms of group morality the essence of the system is to find the common good in doing right by individuals. Because democracy is sensitive to the whims of the majority, it provides no guarantee of a right to be different (Ignatieff, 2001). Nonetheless, the spirit of the liberal tradition is reflected in associated principles of justice.

The fundamental tenets of modern liberalism include respect for personal autonomy, social tolerance of others, the recognition of diversity and moral relativity. Morality is recognized as a social construct, which is constantly evolving in response to peoples' need to resolve interpersonal conflict (Wong, 1984). Conflicting lifestyles are increasingly the norm in Western culture. In diverse nations such as Canada, one will often interact with people with different values hailing from a wide variety of backgrounds.

In this pluralistic context of social interaction, we may have cause to question our own moral standpoint and, after reflection, make occasional adjustments. In this light, it is not obvious that absolutes are needed to determine right and wrong in every moral disagreement. Regard for moral relativity reflects the adaptability of human nature and society in response to changing needs of conflict resolution.

The practical requirement of maintaining social order suggests that tolerance of others with different ways of living is a complementary fundamental value. As Kant said, one should refrain from interfering with the ends of others, unless the interference can be justified. Because people are rational beings, with the capacity to reflect on how they live their lives, their personal autonomy ought to be protected, unless it interferes with the autonomy of others (Richards, 1982).

Liberalism frees the individual to pursue autonomy by fostering self-critical reflection. Rights within this framework mark the boundary of constraints within which we are free to define our own understanding of "good." A human rights–based argument for freedom to use drugs builds directly on the Kantian liberal tradition of the need to treat individuals as equals by virtue of their personal autonomy.

For J.S. Mill (1901), protection of autonomy required that the coercive power of government over individuals be restricted to preventing a demonstrated harm. There is no justification for State interference, other than that exercised on grounds of the prevention of harm to other persons. Any intervention for the sake of protecting the individual from self-inflicted harm is not only ineffective but also counterproductive. Banning use of (some) drugs, from this standpoint, is a blatant violation of the right to personal autonomy.

Marijuana prohibition is the most prominent example of what Richards (1982) has termed **overcriminalization**. The law's intrusion into relatively harmless lifestyle choices and consensual activities, from a liberal perspective, represents a greater harm to Canadian society than the behaviour that the law is seeking to prevent. Such intervention is also wasteful of resources, which ought to be devoted to policing more injurious, violent, and predatory crimes.

Forcing drug activity onto the "black market" invites involvement into the trade by ruthless criminals, who often resort to violence to further business interests. This scenario facilitates more dangerous drug taking. It also breeds distrust of the authorities among those who have been criminalized, as well as others in society, which ultimately threatens the legitimacy of government.

People must be granted moral freedom to decide how they exercise their rights to individual autonomy. The existence of a right does not require that it be exercised, and the exercise of rights is subject to mistakes. Respect for rights does not mean that criticism is unjustified. While coercive interference is almost never justifiable, people are free to criticize the exercise of rights.

Whether based on moral claims, or scientific evidence, or appeals to simple common sense, the availability of outside criticism allows protected rights to be more critically informed. The exercise of rights is not infallible, but rather something that is malleable, or to be cultivated through self-critical assessment of social criticism. Criticism aimed at others should be limited, however, due to the strong likelihood of mistaken judgments.

The moral criticism that is evident in drug laws, for example, like these laws themselves, suggests a lack of understanding of the ends and circumstances of illicit-substance users. Forced treatment of drug addicts, or any other intervention that adopts a punitive approach to substance use, is unjustifiably coercive from a liberal perspective centred on respect for human rights.

Rights-based discourse in the Charter is derived from long-established principles of justice and constitutional democracy. Despite its evident potential to influence drug policy, this claims-making strategy has so far had a modest impact in compelling law reform. Successes have primarily been limited to legal challenges that led to striking down the most egregious policing practices and harsh punishment for drug crimes.

To date, reform arguments drawing on the Charter have not initiated sweeping changes in the law. Penalties and incarceration rates for drug offenses were not significantly reduced by these court challenges and rulings.

The Harm Reduction Movement

Courts and government authorities have increasingly acknowledged that drug laws are ineffective and excessive in proportion to the harms inflicted by the use of drugs. In the last quarter-century, however, the harm reduction movement has largely overshadowed rights-based discourse as the primary vehicle for policy reform.

By the late 1980s, recognition of the problems caused by prohibition gained significant momentum. Fifteen years after the Le Dain report, the call for changes in priorities—away from punishment to treatment and harm reduction—was not new. The launch of Canada's Drug Strategy in 1987 was nonetheless significant drug policy activity, which went another step beyond striking a committee and producing an official report.

The announcement of the strategy signalled monumental changes in the language of drug policy discussion. From this moment onward, it is evident that medical discourses and principles of public health were gaining jurisdiction as the predominant authority in shaping reform arguments. This is a trend consistent with a broader transition observed: the shift away from viewing criminals as sinners, in need of punishment, toward seeing them as sick (see Conrad and Schneider, 1992).

Medicalizing crime or other deviant behaviour does not necessarily ensure respect for rights. More accurately, it substitutes one form of authority or jurisdiction for another. From a public health perspective, for example, priority is given to the protection of society. This obligation necessarily outweighs respect for rights, including the right to alter consciousness or freedom to use drugs.

The rights and freedoms of drug users may be inconsistent with public health priorities of harm reduction advocates who favour a transition from punishment to treatment goals. The political expediency of harm reduction arguments, which rely on scientific reasoning and evidence, might thereby be shortsighted from the standpoint of reformers seeking to initiate more meaningful reform.

In this light, the remainder of the chapter is devoted to examining the progress of the harm reduction movement. The illustrations offered also demonstrate the evident resilience of official definitions and discourses that continue to legitimate the war on (certain) drugs.

Canada's Drug Strategy

The specific aim of Canada's Drug Strategy (1987) was to reduce harm among individuals, families, and communities caused by the abuse of drugs. Recognizing that enforcement had limited effectiveness, its emphasis was on developing a more balanced approach. Covering the full spectrum of non-medical drug use, drug abuse was recognized as including both illegal and legal drugs—including alcohol, prescription drugs, and even solvents.

More than merely offering a set of recommendations, the strategy set out to take Canadian drug policy in a bold, progressive new direction in its departure from adherence to a war-on-drugs approach. It allocated millions of dollars in new funding, most of which was to be spent on treatment and prevention, with a smaller portion (30 per cent) devoted to enforcement. Officially, therefore, the focus of drug policy had shifted from supply reduction to "demand reduction"—better educating young people to prevent abuse, and treatment to help those with serious drug problems.

The largest portion of the budget (38 per cent, or about $100 million) was earmarked for funding new drug treatment programs. But the actual implementation of Canada's Drug Strategy was severely limited owing to bureaucratic challenges. Fischer (1994) notes that because drug treatment is a provincial responsibility, federal funding for new programs was devised as a cost-sharing agreement with the provinces. Half the total costs invested in each province, up to a predetermined maximum, would be reimbursed.

Over the five-year time frame of the initial strategy, just one provincial jurisdiction secured the full amount; four others received nothing, and less than half of the funds available ($48.2 million) were spent in total. The other targets of demand-reduction, drug education and prevention, accounted for one-third of the total budget. As an indicator of funds spent, it was reported that several hundred Community Action Programs across the country were established to design and deliver local prevention programs.

These initiatives were never systematically assessed, nor were they required to meet any measurable objectives (Single et al., 1992). At the same time, it is evident that emphasis was clearly on prevention messages, as opposed to education, in the demand-reduction programming delivered. Indeed, in actuality, most of the funding went to police-controlled drug education programs. These were modeled on the DARE (Drug Abuse Resistance Education) or "just say no" programs that were used in the United States.

Meanwhile, the RCMP (Royal Canadian Mounted Police) claimed funds sufficient to create 32 new drug education coordinator positions. Accordingly, unlike drug-treatment service providers, law enforcement bureaucrats were evidently able to respond in time to take advantage of new funding. In 1992, when the strategy was renewed, the government declared, as a sure marker of success, that Canada now led the Western world in police-delivered drug prevention messages to youth (Erickson, 1992).

With regard to seeking balance, there is little indication of concern for harm reduction or the new priorities in practice. Drug-related charges continued to increase, with charges for possession accounting for two-thirds (and cannabis for half) of all convictions. From 1987 to 1991, the proportion of inmates in Canadian prisons for drug offences increased significantly, from 9 to 14 per cent.

With surveys showing drug use rates declined into the 1990s, police were not responding to another so-called epidemic (Erickson, 1992). Adopting the new language, however, law enforcers were able to contend that, by arresting substance users, they too were contributing to harm reduction efforts. Clearly, the balance was still weighted on the side of policing, despite the wealth of evidence about its limitations and claims to the contrary by governing authorities.

In the second five-year phase of Canada's Drug Strategy, attention shifted to developing a new set of drug laws to replace the existing Narcotic Control Act (NCA). Some of the more severe sentencing provisions, such as life imprisonment for trafficking narcotics and a mandatory minimum of seven years for importing, had been struck down or withdrawn since introduction of the Charter (1982).

Other legal changes that protected rights of users, from excessive punishment and policing practices, had not been informed by harm reduction measures either, but rather by Charter guarantees of fair and equal treatment. With incarceration rates and penalties for drug crimes at high levels, it became increasingly apparent that a whole new act of legislation was required to shift the focus to reducing drug-related harm. The legislation that resulted from this reform momentum, in the 1990s, has been ruefully described as a lost opportunity to rewrite the drug laws.

Although it was allegedly informed by harm reduction, the Controlled Drugs and Substances Act (1996) was largely a revamped NCA. Significantly, the act included a vaguely phrased provision allowing judicial discretion during sentencing and made mention of diverting drug offenders into treatment programs. Apart from these concessions, however, its central feature was giving greater powers to police and prosecutors to facilitate more efficient processing of drug crimes (Fischer et al., 1996).

Whereas the name of the act suggested a more accurate and sophisticated understanding of drug issues, the tradition of irrational drug scheduling continued. Banned substances (like amphetamines, heroin, and cocaine) and punishments—up to seven years in prison for possession, and life for trafficking—are grouped together indiscriminately, with no recognized distinctions based on quantity or potency of the substance in question.

Despite some indication of growing rights protections for drug users and sellers, police were re-granted previously held powers of enforcement that were not allowed for other types of criminal investigations. The need to obtain a search warrant was waived, for example, "if it would be impractical to obtain one." Police had lost these powers when a Charter challenge had struck down the writ of assistance. Once issued by a judge, a writ gave privileges to specified drug enforcement officers for an indefinite time period, which was sometimes known to span one's entire career.

Clearly, commitment to reduction of enforcement activity was not a characteristic of the Controlled Drugs and Substances Act (CDSA). There is little evidence of leniency for cannabis, nor toward offenders who used more addictive drugs. Penalties for cannabis possession remained the same under the new act—up to a maximum fine of $1000, and six months imprisonment for a first offence.

The only benefit for users arrested for possession was the creation of a separate summary offence—for those caught with less than 30 grams (about one ounce) of marijuana, and less than one gram of hashish. This reform, however, merely reflected actual practice in many courts before the act (Erickson, 2000). The preferred sentencing option for small amounts of marijuana—a charge accounting for the lion's share of all drug offences—was already discharges and fines.

The fine-only option had been available since the NCA of 1969. It was the most popular sentencing option for charges of possession, employed in about two-thirds of all cases. Although 5 per cent of those charged with possession were imprisoned, this occurred primarily for nonpayment of fines.

Cannabis-related charges, mostly for possession, continued at high levels throughout the 1990s, averaging more than 30,000 charges annually. Instead of penalty reduction, the primary purpose and result of new legislation was improving the efficiency of an overburdened criminal justice system. The downgrade in penalties for designating marijuana as a separate summary offence also meant that people charged with possession of small amounts of cannabis forwent the option of a (costly, time-consuming) jury trial.

Undoubtedly this change made the system more efficient, easing congestion in the courts as the arrest rates remained high. To date, accommodating higher numbers of offenders in the system has been accomplished by imposing a net-widening effect, which sacrifices due process in exchange for lower penalties. Considering fines and discharges for possession were already fairly standard practice in the 1990s era, no significant reform for marijuana was forthcoming under the CDSA.

In 1998, another move toward greater leniency was introduced under the auspices of a new federal diversion policy. This initiative enabled eligible cannabis offenders to avoid the burden of a criminal record entirely by doing community service. Such options for diversion of drug criminals employ greater variation in the use of State resources, and are consistent with the trends observed in literature describing moral regulation as a method of control.

Such measures institute in policy what judges and police, and others in positions of authority, have often done in practice: exercise discretion to reduce the impact of the law on drug offenders. These practices fall short of demonstrating a commitment to the goal of harm reduction in Canadian drug policy. Diversion, for example, still invokes a criminal process that has been unevenly applied. And as with any other drug court, which allows the option of attending treatment versus prison, drug offenders ordinarily view it with resentment.

When there is disrespect for law, a change in law is needed to succeed in the reduction of drug-related harm. On the contrary, however, the most noteworthy development of the new millennium has been a recommitment to an antidrug agenda that is anti–harm reduction. Tracing the rise and fall of harm reduction in drug policy (Table 4.2), therefore, suggests a need for more reflection on the matter of what we mean when we say "harm reduction."

Table 4.2 Contemporary Drug Policy Activities in Canada

Le Dain Commission Report (1972)	Recommends a shift from punishment to public health as the guiding principle of Canadian drug policy and foreshadows the emergence, in the late 1980s, of the harm reduction movement and Canada's Drug Strategy.
Introduction of the Canadian Charter of Rights and Freedoms (1982)	Established constitutional protection that effectively put the onus on the state to justify interfering with individual rights and freedoms. It thereby serves as the foundation for court challenges protesting the constitutionality of laws that criminalize the use of drugs.
Canada's Drug Strategy (1987)	Officially establishes demand reduction as the primary drug policy objective. Calling for greater balance between public health and law enforcement, it devotes new resources to treatment and prevention.
Controlled Drugs and Substances Act (1996)	Reaffirms the government's commitment to enforcement as the primary priority of Canadian drug policy. A generation after the Le Dain report was tabled, the CDSA demonstrates a resistance to reform that continues in drug policy today.

Redefining Harm Reduction

What does harm reduction really mean? Since its introduction in the 1980s, there has been considerable debate among drug experts about the proper use of the term (see Hathaway, 2001b). It is generally agreed that the role of harm reduction is to provide a comprehensive public health framework that falls between prohibiting and legalizing drug use. In so doing, it is able to find some common ground between proponents of more liberal drug policies and those opposed to policy reform.

Harm reduction remains neutral on long-term goals of intervention—unlike strategies that target cutting off supply, or treatment programs that require strict abstinence from drugs. Short-term, realizable goals are prioritized instead. The aim is to reduce drug harm while substance use continues—at least for the time being (Single, 1995).

In the early days of the harm reduction movement, which emerged in the wake of the AIDS epidemic, this definition served to differentiate it from abstinence-based policies and programs. Its basic principles belong to a public health perspective, with deeper roots in humanism and modern liberal philosophy. Focusing on harms, not necessarily use, is a pragmatic response that recognizes drugs are a continuing and inevitable presence in society.

Harm reduction's hierarchy of goals prioritizes realistic steps instead of moral absolutes. In this respect, it is analogous to educating youth about the risks of sexual behaviour, providing access to condoms and information so they can protect themselves. While abstinence is arguably the most effective method of achieving harm (or risk) reduction, in practice it is often an unrealistic goal.

Respect for individual autonomy means drug users must be treated with dignity as normal human beings. Each individual has the right to choose or not choose drug use. We are ultimately responsible for our own behaviour.

Some of the humanistic principles of harm reduction have been downplayed, in exchange for short-term gains. The logic of reducing harm makes sense to everybody, including the police and other authorities who view eradication of, or abstinence from, drugs as the only standard of success. Remaining neutral about long-term goals has therefore been advantageous, as a tactical concession to proponents of that view.

However, the adoption of an all-inclusive standpoint has certain disadvantages as well. Being co-opted by traditional drug treatment and enforcement confounds the sense of clear priorities established by the early founders of the harm reduction movement. The primary response from harm reductionists has been to reassert their emphasis on public health priorities and further cultivate their "value-neutral" standing.

Establishing a credible evidentiary basis for pursuing harm reduction policies and programs requires empirical assessment of their costs and benefits to determine if they actually are reducing harm. The perspective fostered is, accordingly, neither for nor against recognizing rights of users, nor is it necessarily in favour of drug policy reform. Solutions to drug problems are conceptualized as being determined based on strictly empirical assessment of how these influence the nature and extent of harm (Single, 1999; Strang, 1993). This value-neutral stance has been politically expedient, as a way to gain concessions on pragmatic grounds alone.

Epidemics such as AIDS spread through unsafe sex and drug use forced official recognition and adoption of needed public health initiatives informed by harm reduction. Recognizing that most people do not take illicit drugs, and do not like the idea that other people do, these initiatives take on a value-neutral standpoint and make allowances for some toleration of drug use, in dire circumstances, as a matter of practical necessity. This standpoint is adaptive to a prohibition framework that rejects more liberal conceptions of respect for personal autonomy and individual rights.

Lacking a foundation in humanistic principles for sustaining meaningful drug policy reform, stopgap measures to reduce harm must continue to struggle to survive after the crisis is contained. Despite its evident advantages, harm reduction's neutral language may also be strategically shortsighted. Among its chief shortcomings, from the standpoint of observers frustrated with the absence of significant reform, the movement's (obvious) emphasis on harm and, by extension, harm reduction, may be problematic.

The objective of reducing harm, for status quo defenders, is difficult to justify, despite its pragmatism (or perhaps, more accurately, because it is pragmatic). For its opponents, harm reduction represents a dangerous compromise that threatens the ideal of a drug-free society. Arguably, encouraging safer drug use only encourages more drug use, thereby reinforcing undesirable behaviour.

Continuing resistance to harm reduction education is an illustration of the ideological conflict inherent in drug education (and drug treatment programs), namely whether they are *about* as opposed to *against* using drugs. Shifting the objective of intervention from the problem of use (as viewed by non-drug users) to problems with use (as experienced by users) requires some recognition of the benefits of drug use, from the point of view of substance users. In failing to articulate the nature of demand, harm reduction arguments that focus on harm only are severely limited in scope.

Harm reduction's primary concern has been reducing drug-related adverse events in populations of drug users suffering severe symptoms of abuse. Yet the majority of harm is represented by illicit drug consumers, whose problems are less visible and relatively minor because their population is exponentially larger (Mugford, 1993). Promoting public health priorities and harm reduction measures for the vast majority of users has therefore been neglected, although statistically, on aggregate, they constitute the lion's share of harm.

Pursuit of hedonistic ends, like pleasure and excitement, is not easy to defend within a harm reduction framework. Cost-benefit analysis, from a value-neutral standpoint, inevitably drifts toward an antidrug position or a one-sided emphasis on reducing harm. This is a tactical concession that has evident shortcomings, if the aim is to initiate significant reform.

Neutralizing or conceding the immorality of drug use, as a tactic for prioritizing drug-related harm, tacitly engages with endangerment discourses that trump other types of claims about drug users having rights. Remaining value-neutral in public policy debates, with due respect for scientific evidence, has rarely been successful in achieving law reform (Richards, 1982). Where legislative changes have occurred in North America—as in the case of new protection for the rights of same-sex couples—these have tended to result from a shift in moral judgments as opposed to scientific arguments.

Where existing moral judgments remain unchallenged and unchanged, legislative changes have been negligible at best. The unrealized potential of the harm reduction movement as a catalyst for meaningful drug policy reform is an indication of the limits of employing value-neutral, scientific arguments alone.

Drug Policy Activity in the New Millennium

Harm reduction's emphasis on science is advantageous in the context of increasing calls for rational debate. But its progression through a quarter-century, as an official guiding principle, illustrates some weaknesses with this approach as well. The most significant Canadian drug policy developments of the new millennium shed more light on the political conflict that continues to thwart advocates for change.

Whereas a technical approach to harm reduction is strategic, as a tactic for avoiding ideological disputes, the place of rights is clearly becoming a contentious and divisive theme within the movement. Two philosophies of harm reduction are emerging (Hunt, 2004) in response to challenges from advocates for further articulation of the movement's fundamental values. A **weak rights view** prioritizes public health dimensions and has already been successful in achieving short-term gains.

From this perspective, public health comes first—a stance implying no obligation to protecting the rights of substance users, nor commitment to drug policy reform. A **strong rights view**, by contrast, seeks to reduce harm while recognizing respect for personal autonomy and rights of substance users. The distinction between strong and weak rights is akin to the difference between positive and negative liberty, as it is commonly referred to by liberal philosophers.

Positive liberty is variously defined as an obligation by the state to guarantee its citizens full participation in the democratic process (i.e., right to vote), and mastery or freedom to choose their own pursuits. Among the rights this may include are access to resources that ensure a minimal standard of living, as well as social services, like health care and education, which facilitate fulfillment of one's full potential.

A guarantee of **negative liberty**, by contrast, does not oblige the State to act. Rather it obliges State noninterference in the lives of individuals. From a strong rights point of view, this is the kind of liberty from government intrusion that would be a marker of significant reform.

Harm reduction is a rather contradictory premise within a prohibition framework, in which the greatest harm is arguably a product of enforcing harmful laws. Where changes have occurred, these ordinarily represent expansion of positive liberty protections by the State. This observation offers further critical perspective on drug policy developments of the past few years.

In 2001, for example, the Liberal government launched a controversial and continually evolving exemption scheme for medical marijuana users. Permitting access to marijuana based on medical necessity, 80 years after the first ban was enacted, demonstrates the potency of legal-political arguments claiming a right to health care.

The aforementioned medicalizing trend in Western culture has enabled similar concessions for drug addicts. The trend has been to redefine the addict as a person with a recognized disease deserving treatment versus punishment. The resulting hybrid system of control, empowering medical authorities in a prohibition framework, however, reinforces the legitimacy of punishment for the vast majority of users. Put otherwise, a weak rights view of drug use has been fostered, which presents an obstacle to meaningful reform.

The House and Senate Reports

Another illustration of the stalemate in drug policy reform-related discourse in the twenty-first century is provided by the findings of two government committees, which are remarkably consistent with Le Dain's (1972) three decades earlier. In 2001, the House of Commons formed (yet another) Special Committee on the Non-Medical Use of Drugs (Grayson, 2008).

Comprising elected Members of Parliament from all parties, the special committee conducted hearings across the country and met with experts, even travelling to Europe and the United States. While its objective was to study drugs policy in general, and the committee had no mandate to initiate reform, it took the step to recommend that growing and possessing 30 grams or less of marijuana be decriminalized.

Consistent with the findings of Le Dain, the consequences of conviction for possession were deemed unfair and inconsistent, or disproportionate to harms due to marijuana use. Substance use was increasingly considered a growing and pervasive problem in Canadian society, which had to be addressed in a public health framework. With a partial nod to harm reduction, the Committee favoured taking measures to improve the health of users, keeping them healthy until they were ready to seek treatment.

At the same time, abstinence was recognized as being the best way to avoid drug dependency. Harm reduction was contentious. The attempt to balance interests between conservatives and liberals appears to have resulted in a policy report as much concerned with law enforcement as concern for public health. There had been little actual consultation with health experts, and much concern for input by police. Whereas harm reduction measures, such as drug courts, were permissible, supporting safe injection sites (a suggested way to mitigate risk to injection drug users) was highly controversial. Notwithstanding its adoption of a public health perspective, the discursive emphasis of the House of Commons committee was placed squarely on maintaining drug controls. This becomes evident when the report is viewed alongside coinciding work, by another special government committee, with sharply differing conclusions. That group posed different questions, and came up with different answers, seeking guidance based on principles that need to be established as a foundation for more meaningful drug policy reform.

In September 2002, three months before the release of the House report, the Canadian Parliament's other sitting body (the appointed Senate) released its own drug policy report. Unlike the House, its focus was on cannabis specifically, but many of its recommendations dealt with drug policy in general. The Senate Committee (like Bertrand of the Le Dain group, three decades earlier) called for legalizing cannabis, as well as amnesty for persons convicted of possession under past or present laws.

The decriminalization option was rejected. Instead they favoured a regulatory system of the sale of cannabis through licensing. Criminal penalties were to be reserved for such offences as illegal trafficking, export, and other activities outside of the scope of regulation. Consistent with a public health perspective, it was argued that legalizing cannabis would enable better monitoring and consistency of products. A regulated system would facilitate replacement of punishment and scare tactics with more realistic education and prevention programs.

Unlike previous committees, this one explicitly asserted the need for the development of clearer guiding principles, founded on respect for freedom, diversity, and tolerance. In particular, the Senate argued that the ban on cannabis undermined the fundamental values of the Charter. Despite some common themes, and overlapping health discourses, the conclusions of the House and Senate sharply differed.

Why so different? One might argue that the Senate's narrower focus, and overwhelming evidence for marijuana law reform, facilitated its adoption of a liberal perspective. Apart from the particular opinions of participants, there are other partial explanations worth considering. It might noted, for example, that because House committees are made up of elected Members of Parliament, the participants have "more to lose" politically than Senators, who are at the end of their political careers.

House committee members had more reason to be moderate, for fear of threatening career prospects or their party standing (Grayson, 2008). Considering the timing of release of the reports, one might also ask if the more radical perspective adopted by the Senate was itself a strategy, or diversion tactic. The Senate's call for legalization was criticized in the media as being an indulgent and irresponsible recommendation. In its wake, the moderate, balanced policy suggestions of the House committee were seen as more politically palatable, permissible, and thereby realistic.

Modest changes like the ones suggested were again largely based on practice by police and in the courts. In retrospect, however, such minutiae seem quite trivial, considering the turn toward conservatism taken in Canadian drug policy of the past few years. Up to this point, I have avoided certain details about politics. Drug policy has not been depicted as the product of a Liberal, Conservative, or New Democratic governing party.

Instead the focus has been specifically on policy activity and discursive strategies, including State authority reflected in drug policies themselves. Politics, of course, is highly relevant to policy. Avoiding partisan discussions is impossible, perhaps. I have not sought to avoid them for fear of prejudicial treatment, nor accusations of bias. Rather such avoidance underscores the observation of inertia in Canadian drug policy for decades.

There have been announcements to the contrary, and even commitment to alternative perspectives. But, as amply illustrated throughout Canada's Drug Strategy, a public health approach was never realized in practice (cf. Erickson, 1998; DeBeck et al., 2009). The prohibition framework has persisted for a century as a control regime that has continued to function (or malfunction) as an entity quite separate from successive ruling parties, individual leadership, or politics.

Although Liberal Party politicians and governments have often been supportive of adopting more liberal drug policies, there have been few changes in the law under their leadership that would demonstrate commitment to significant reform. Indeed, the most significant development to date has been the introduction of the Charter (in 1982 under the Trudeau Liberal government), which says nothing in particular about people using drugs. Rather it asserts a set of principles transcending discussions about evidence, or drugs, or public health.

The recent controversy over supervised injection sites in the city of Vancouver further illustrates the nature of underlying conflict and challenge to reform, under the Conservative Party leadership of Prime Minister Stephen Harper (Box 4.2). It demonstrates a conflict over drug use in our culture that has been evident for decades, even centuries, in the Western world. The context of cultural ambivalence observed in Canada, and elsewhere, is examined further in the next half of the book, which details sociocultural constructions of drug use.

Box 4.2

The InSite Controversy

In September 2003, in an effort to reduce infectious diseases and overdose among injection drug users (IDUs), a facility was opened in Vancouver, British Columbia, where IDUs could inject pre-obtained illicit drugs under the supervision of medical staff. Canada's first medically supervised safer injection facility (SIF) was granted a legal exemption to operate on the condition that its impacts be rigorously evaluated. Scientific evaluation of this pilot project was overseen by an external steering committee and an evaluation team that was entirely external to the operators running the facility. Study findings were published in prestigious medical journals including the *Canadian Medical Association Journal*, *New England Journal of Medicine*, *British Medical Journal*, and *Lancet*. The conclusions largely corresponded with those

Continued

from international studies, which have found that SIFs significantly reduce both drug-related harms, including those that largely stem from prohibition of these substances. Public health concerns directly linked to law enforcement, like the use of drugs in unsafe environments and conditions, are not sufficiently addressed by more limited street-level initiatives like needle and syringe exchanges. In addition, SIFs allow for more direct and timely contact with health and treatment services, while lowering the incidence of overdose fatalities, public injection drug use, and infectious diseases.

Despite the documented evidence of positive health outcomes and InSite's contribution to restoring public order, in September 2006 the Harper government refused to renew its license for another three years beyond the pilot phase. Citing insufficient understanding of its impact, the health minister announced that InSite would stay open through 2007, pending further research on the issue. No more safe injection sites would be allowed in Canada, despite demand in other cities like Victoria, British Columbia (which applied in June 2007 for permission to open three sites of its own), and majority support in the city of Vancouver (76 per cent of adults) for extending InSite's operating license. At the time of this refusal, the health minister remarked, "Do safe injection sites contribute to lowering drug use and fighting addiction? Right now the only thing the research to date has proven conclusively is drug addicts need more help to get off drugs." Beyond the minister's denial of the evidence, the federal government officially served notice that harm reduction was no longer an accepted goal of Canadian drug policy.

"Because if you remain a drug addict," said the prime minister, "I don't care how much harm you reduce, you're going to have a short and miserable life." Harper's skepticism about the aims of harm reduction suggests that focusing on evidence is not on the agenda. In so doing, he asserted the federal government's ideological commitment to the war on drugs, and ending what is viewed as an overly permissive culture of acceptance for drug use. "Enforcement is harm reduction," suggested the health minister. And, referring to mixed messages, for users of illicit drugs, the new message from the government is that "the party's over."

Source: Adapted from Hathaway and Tousaw (2008). With permission from Elsevier.

Chapter Summary

This chapter built directly on the previous discussion of historical perspectives on substance use in Canada. It focused on viewing the contemporary context of Canadian drug policy discussions and debates. With emphasis on looking at drug policy perspectives over the past 40 years, Chapter 4 observed the rise of public health discourses, and the emergence of the harm reduction movement. Additionally, it chronicled the introduction of the Charter, and its implications for drug policy reform.

The central theme developed indicates that there are both advantages and drawbacks of adopting either rights-based or value-neutral arguments alone. It seems that harm reduction arguments can only go so far. As a tactical concession, neglecting deeper principles is perhaps politically expedient. However, it appears that a more meaningful departure from punitive drug policies will require a fundamental change in value judgments. The broader cultural context of drug policy discussion is developed further in the next four chapters.

Questions for Critical Thought

1. What is your position on the proper role of government in legislating and enforcing moral conduct? Do you take a liberal, conservative, or differing perspective on the function of the State?
2. How does your response to the first question inform your policy perspective on controlling substance use?
3. What are your views on harm reduction? What are some positive and negative implications of adopting a public health approach to drugs?

Suggested Readings

Alexander, B.K. 1990. *Peaceful Measures: Canada's Way Out of the "War on Drugs."* Toronto: University of Toronto Press. This book argues that Canada's war on drugs has been a costly failure, and should be replaced by peaceful measures for addressing the harmful effects of drug use.

Giffen, P.J., S.J. Endicott, and S. Lambert. 1991. *Panic and Indifference: The Politics of Canada's Drug Laws.* Ottawa: Canadian Centre on Substance Abuse. This book documents the history of interests influencing the development of Canadian drug policy.

Husak, D.N. 1992. *Drugs and Rights.* Cambridge: Cambridge University Press. This book argues that the war on drugs is a violation of the rights of adults to use drugs for pleasure. Criminal laws against the use of recreational drugs are justified neither by the harm users cause themselves nor by the harm that users cause to others.

Suggested Websites

Canadian Drug Policy Coalition
www.drugpolicy.ca

The coalition is a national network advocating for changes in drug policy by engaging citizens to seek out new solutions.

Canadian Foundation for Drug Policy
www.cfdp.ca

The website of the Canadian Foundation for Drug Policy functions as a forum for exchange of information among drug policy reformers, and to share those views with government, the public, and the media.

Canadian Harm Reduction Network

www.canadianharmreduction.com

This organization's mission is to serve as a virtual meeting place for people across Canada committed to reducing the health, social, and economic harms associated with drugs and drug policies.

Parliament of Canada

www.parl.gc.ca/HousePublications/Publication.aspx?DocId=1032297&Language=E&Mode=1&Parl=37&Ses=2&File=5

The 2002 Report of the House of Commons Special Committee on Non-Medical Use of Drugs: *Policy for the New Millenium: Working Together to Redefine Canada's Drug Strategy.*

www.parl.gc.ca/Content/SEN/Committee/371/ille/rep/summary-e.pdf

The 2002 Summary Report of the Senate Special Committee on Illegal Drugs: *Cannabis: Our Position for a Canadian Public Policy.*

5 Sociocultural Dimensions

Learning Objectives

- To recognize the features of sociocultural ambivalence that characterize existing social attitudes toward drugs.
- To discern indicators of increasing social tolerance of recreational drug use.
- To better understand social factors that influence negative perceptions of recreational and compulsive drug users.

Introduction

This chapter is concerned with sociocultural dimensions of the construction of drug issues in Canada. As we have previously noted, increasing tolerance of differences is a defining characteristic of modern Western culture. This idealistic notion has been seriously tested in the post-9/11 era of conservatism marked by cultural anxiety and distrust of outsiders. But the idea that diversity must be legally protected and encouraged is embedded in our national identity (see Hathaway and Atkinson, 2001).

Social boundaries are becoming more fragmented, and more permeable. In today's diverse, multicultural societies, widespread social tolerance is needed to maintain order and respect for institutions. Whether due to political correctness, respect for pluralism, or expanding Western markets, cultural absolutes about deviance are waning. From a constructionist perspective, this suggests that definitions of deviant (and criminal) behaviour have transformed.

Some illicit drug use in Canada has been normalized so much that the behaviour is regarded as nonthreatening. Although actually illegal according to the law, as a form of **tolerable deviance** (or mere difference), such use is seldom officially challenged (Stebbins, 1996). Despite existing moral norms and criminal controls, neither those who tolerate nor enact this deviance view it as wrongful behaviour. When deviance is banned by law yet widely tolerated, the nature and interpretation of controls become ambiguous.

Among other observations consistent with a sense of cultural ambivalence concerning substance use, changing outlooks on morality ought not be mistaken for relinquishment or absence of control. There is still a stigma around drug use, but it simply coexists with other indications of a normalizing trend. This chapter is a study of related contradictions concerning sociocultural responses to drug use.

Is Drug Use Being Normalized?

Normalizing substance use suggests accommodation of the practice by society, or adjusting moral boundaries to include it in the realm of acceptable behaviour (Scheerer, 1978). Adoption of a **normalization** framework for drug policy favours outright legalization for possession; criminal control is replaced with other forms of regulation.

The term has been used for decades as a policy perspective recognizing the rights of people with disabilities to equal treatment, and accommodation of their special needs, to better integrate them into the community. More recently, it has been employed by the Dutch government as the official goal of drug policy in Holland (see Van Vliet, 1990).

Normalization in the Netherlands was understood to mean commitment to pursuing public health objectives as opposed to police priorities and to making substance use seem boring to young people. The separation of hard and soft drug markets by allowing certain "coffee shops" to sell small amounts of cannabis is a prominent example of the pragmatic Dutch approach. Concerns about drug tourism, and sending the wrong message, eventually resulted in sufficient controversy to stem the earlier mandate for normalizing drugs.

Over the past decade, the term has often been used in reference to high rates of illicit drug involvement by otherwise conventional youth and young adults. A variety of factors have been cited by researchers as evidence of normalization. These include drug prevalence, availability, and accommodation by non-using peers.

A more nuanced and contextually informed consideration of drug issues is suggested by the research in this area. Firstly, it is not substance use that has been normalized per se, but rather the controlled, recreational use of drugs. The substance user, from this standpoint, is a rational consumer capable of making reasoned choices (Williams and Parker, 2001). Risks to health, getting caught, and diminished work performance factor into calculations of costs versus benefits of use.

Distinctive boundaries exist around peer tolerance of drug taking. Accommodation by non-users does not extend to uncontrolled use and the use of hard drugs, such as crack cocaine and heroin. Indeed, users and non-users make surprisingly similar distinctions between risky and dependent use (of hard drugs) and involvement in controlled, recreational drug use. A more detailed introduction of the normalization thesis requires an understanding of the limits of its scope. Far from an endorsement of making drug use normal, it is an indicator or barometer of change (Parker, 2005).

Parker situated his research on normalization within the contemporary context of changes in the process of transition from adolescence to adulthood (cf. Chisholm and Bergeret, 1991; Jones, 1991). The process of becoming an adult, it has been argued, is becoming longer and more complex for youth. A period of extended **post-adolescence** is emerging, due to changes in the nature of the workforce.

Among other implications for society, this trend means added training and credentials for well-paying jobs, and consequent delay of the school-to-work transition. Youth and young adults today have more time for using drugs for recreational enjoyment. Our view of drugs appears to have been changing in response to fluctuations in the amount of time devoted to work and leisure over the past century. In particular, the introduction of the weekend has left ample time for many to use drugs in a way that need not necessarily impact their weekday work performance.

In Western industrial society, productivity is a longstanding dominant cultural value. The use of drugs that weaken productivity is ordinarily considered deviant within this social context. It follows that existing definitions of drug use and abuse are closely connected to the structural organization of industrial society (Dobkin de Rios and Smith, 1977). The connection between youth and the drug culture, in this context, places certain limits on the extent of normalization.

Our social outlook on drug use may be changing in response to a lengthening transition from adolescence to adulthood, and adjustments in the balance between leisure time and work. But what is the significance of the theorized shift in attitudes?

It has long been documented that rates of substance use are higher among young people, who have fewer responsibilities. Surveys indicate that drug use is commonly abandoned when young adults get married, join the workforce, and have children. Put otherwise, cessation of the habit occurs simply as a natural outcome of the maturation process. To make a case for drug use normalization beyond adolescence requires a focus on more long-term or sustained use among people with adult roles and obligations to fulfill (Hathaway, 2004a).

Research on the transition into young adulthood suggests that drug use patterns and motives tend to shift. Substance use for pleasure and excitement in social settings is less commonly reported by adults than are other motives like relaxation and reducing the stresses of the workweek. Rather than abandoning illicit drugs completely, there are signs of more strategic and more moderate consumption in response to changing roles and responsibilities.

Drug repertoires reportedly diminish as the use of party drugs, such as ecstasy and cocaine, becomes sporadic. Hallucinogens and stimulants are used rarely, if at all, and only on occasions coinciding with the weekend. Illicit drug involvement is predominantly limited to the use of cannabis in the evening during the workweek, as well as on weekends, sometimes in combination with alcohol and tobacco.

From a public health perspective, the observed trends are noteworthy for informing harm reduction education programs aimed at users in the general population of adults. More generally, research in this area suggests a need for more attention to the harm reduction function of cultural controls observed by drug users in their own communities of fellow substance users.

The nature of controls observed by substance users was theorized succinctly in work by Howard Becker (1953, 1955). In order to progress from the experimental phase to becoming an occasional drug user, he argued, all users must undergo a process of social learning in the company of more experienced users. One must first learn to get high and to perceive such use as both pleasurable and morally permissible.

To become a regular drug user, the occasional user undergoes another social learning process. Interaction with the substance-using group further diminishes the influence of formal and informal societal controls that stigmatize the practice and discourage use. The institutional authority of law and law enforcement is the most recognizable form of drug control. Restrictions on supply due to a drug's illicit status must be circumvented in order for one to become a regular user.

In addition to obtaining a regular supply, users must be able to keep their use a secret from respected non-users and various authorities who would likely disapprove (e.g., parents, teachers, coaches, bosses and co-workers, in-laws, insurers, landlords, physicians, and police). Societal control based on conventional morality and concerns about rejection by non-users are overcome by users through continued interaction with more experienced others.

The behaviour of these others is regarded as quite normal and demonstrably under control. Accordingly, for Becker, the transition from experimentation to regular drug use is characterized by diminishing societal control and its replacement with that of the drug-using group.

Arguably, the most important formal (or, rather, informal) drug control is the cultural tradition of conventional morality that stigmatizes use of certain drugs. The longstanding Western temperance tradition is characterized by an outlook of suspicion and anxiety about drugs that continues to exist. More specifically, there is a culturally embedded social fear and stigma about loss of control.

To become a regular drug user, one must first adhere to an alternative subcultural perspective. Participation in drug subcultures provides the required setting and ideological support for users to develop positive expectations about psychoactive drugs (Becker, 1967). Recreational drug users, most importantly perhaps, must be able to convince themselves that they control their drug use rather than the other way around.

In Becker's work on marijuana, he made a clear distinction between the use of cannabis and habit-forming drugs, like heroin, which are used compulsively and not for recreation. Notwithstanding this distinction, a variety of studies on the use of heavily addicting drugs have challenged the assumption of an absence of control. Contrasting popular depictions of highly stereotyped behaviours, compulsive patterns of drug seeking are the exception not the norm.

Observations of spontaneous remission from addiction upon removal of the addict from stress-laden environments underscore the primacy of set and setting in determining the course of drug dependence and abuse (Zinberg, 1984). The success of supervised heroin maintenance programs, in returning addicts to productive, stable lives, is an illustration of controlled use of narcotics that contradicts conventional portrayals of addiction. Among other implications, this suggests that prohibition contributes to conditions that elicit instability and compulsive drug behaviour by disrupting other mechanisms of control.

Zinberg's articulation of the **controlled drug use** model has inspired a great deal of contemporary research on normal drug use practices and sources of control (cf. Decorte, 2000; Hathaway, 2004a; Pearson, 2001). Recent studies indicate that attitudes toward drugs are neither positive nor negative, but rather contingent on the circumstances—i.e., why, where, when, and how the drug is used.

Attending to the context in which substance use occurs, research has shed light on how the boundaries of normal and deviant behaviour are socially defined. The vast majority of users of cannabis and cocaine, among other drugs commonly used in social circumstances, observe informal rules around their substance use behaviour. The influence of formal drug controls is less apparent than other rules followed by drug users, namely exercising moderation and discretion in the circumstances of their use.

Illicit drug use may be prevalent and widely tolerated, but there is still a stigma experienced by users and certain risks they readily acknowledge. Marijuana use is particularly prevalent in the general population of youth and young adults. Its ambivalent social status invites a closer look at evidence of normalization, and at the nature of the stigma, which culturally endures.

Marijuana Normalization

Cannabis is by far the most widely used illicit drug in the world. In Canada and other Western nations, marijuana has been a prominent symbol and feature of the drug scene for more than 40 years. Recent studies indicate that its use is not confined to a deviant subculture or the margins of society.

National drug surveys suggest that nearly half of Canadians older than age 14 years have used marijuana at least once, and about one in seven (14 per cent) have used it in the past year (Adlaf et al., 2005a). Younger people are more likely to have used it in their lifetime (more than two-thirds of respondents 18–24 years) and to be recent users of the drug (Figure 5.1). Nearly half of the respondents ages 18 and 19 (and a third of 15- to 17-year-olds) report past-year cannabis use.

Survey data through the 1990s and 2000s show dramatic growth trends in most age categories, and a lowered perceived risk of associated harms (cf. Adlaf et al., 1996; Poulin and Elliot, 1997). Use by young adults (aged 18–29) in the province of Ontario reportedly more than doubled (from 18 to 38 per cent) between 1996 and 2005 (Adlaf et al., 2008). Social attitudes toward marijuana use have shifted from near total condemnation to widespread tolerance of users, as use rates have risen in the general population of otherwise-conforming adolescents and adults.

Marijuana use today occurs in social settings that are less clandestine or anxiety provoking than when it was perceived as a more marginal activity. As social attitudes and settings become less problematic, there are also changes in the nature and extent of participation with the so-called drug subculture. The concept of normalization provides a framework for examining how attitudes and behaviour might be changing. It is cited often in analyses reporting apparent shifts in culture, consumption trends, and social stigma, especially among youth in transition to adulthood.

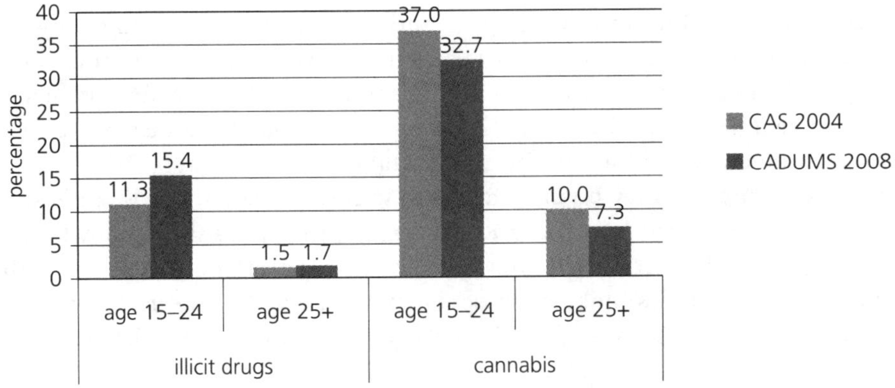

Figure 5.1 Past-Year Use of Cannabis and Other Illicit Drugs, by Age, 2004 and 2008 (CAS and CADUMS)

CAS—Canadian Addiction Survey, CADUMS—Canadian Alcohol and Drug Use Monitoring Survey

Source: Addictions and Mental Health Research Laboratory (2010). Reprinted with permission.

Certain drugs, particularly cannabis, are becoming sufficiently widespread that their use seems unremarkable. The emerging literature on normalization identifies a number of important dimensions for better understanding marijuana use in Canada. In addition to the growing prevalence of use, other indicators of a normalizing process include availability and social and cultural accommodation.

Availability and Access

Easy access to a drug by young people is needed for normalization to occur. Throughout the 1990s, the perceived availability of marijuana increased steadily among youth in Ontario. By the end of the decade, more than half of students surveyed said that marijuana was "easy" or "very easy" to obtain (Adlaf and Paglia, 2003).

Access to marijuana for most users is maintained through casual transactions among friends, and in distribution networks usually limited to cannabis. Most users buy from friends connected to a dealer or from a friend who only deals small quantities. Impersonal transactions with street dealers are avoided.

Long-term users indicate supply-related problems have decreased in recent years. So has their criminal involvement, due to separation of the soft (e.g., cannabis, ecstasy, mushrooms) and hard (e.g., cocaine, heroin) drug markets (Hathaway, 2004a). Therefore, in practice, not unlike the coffee shops in Holland, it appears that cannabis supply networks have been normalized.

Unlike the Dutch approach, however, separation of drug markets has evolved informally, and unofficially, among users and suppliers in a prohibition framework. Normalizing access to cannabis supply reduces the perceived risk of detection and arrest, and the deterrent effect of the law on the drug user.

Prevalence of Use

Another indicator of normalization is increased experimentation with illicit drugs. National drug surveys done in Canada have shown that the rate of experimentation with marijuana is increasing, especially among young adults. Recent estimates suggest approximately two-thirds of 18- to 24-year-olds have used it at least once (Adlaf et al., 2005a). Surveys also indicate increasing rates of use among older age cohorts into their thirties and beyond.

To provide additional perspective on these trends, the use of alcohol, tobacco, and pharmaceuticals is known to be associated with illicit substance use. Put otherwise, drug users—whatever drugs they use—have a higher likelihood of using other drugs. Interestingly, however, the prevalence of marijuana use does not appear to be associated with increasing rates of other substance use.

For example, surveys of Canadian undergraduates conducted between 1998 and 2004 (see Adlaf et al., 2005b) found that the rate of alcohol consumption remained stable, with tobacco use decreasing while marijuana use increased. Although the use of other drugs was found to be decreasing, marijuana use had risen to the point that more than half of undergraduates had tried it, and one in six (17 per cent) had used it in the past four weeks.

In addition to increasing prevalence of use, normalization is concerned with changes in the way that drug use patterns are established and maintained into adulthood. The influence of parents, peers, and siblings in this process, and the surrounding context or cultural environment, are critical determinants of the level of drug access and substance use continuation patterns.

Studies of committed long-term marijuana users indicate a pattern of evolving moderation, and the discontinuation of most other substance use. Whereas the majority intends to keep on using, the tendency is also for them to expect (and demonstrate) a downward trend in levels of consumption. The development of stable patterns of controlled use is associated with reporting fewer problems than users whose use patterns are more varied or sporadic (Hathaway, 2004b).

Further, notwithstanding upward prevalence statistics, the meaning of drug use at different stages of our lives is more difficult to measure than either its prevalence or reported levels of consumption over time. With particular regard to use context, for example, people tend to use marijuana in a wider array of circumstances than other kinds of substances. The diffusion of the practice from the margins to the mainstream is an indication of increasing social tolerance and accommodation of the drug.

Social Tolerance of Users

The social tolerance dimension of the normalization process includes the attitudes of peers who abstain from using drugs. Examining these attitudes means studying non-users to identify their outlook on drug-using peers, different drugs, and different types of use. A variety of studies have found evidence of growing tolerance of controlled, recreational drug use among law-abiding adolescents and adults (cf. Boys et al., 1999, 2000; Parker et al., 1998; Pearson, 2001). As noted previously, both users and abstainers have been found to make similar distinctions between risky or dependent use (of drugs like crack cocaine and heroin) and sensible, controlled use (most often marijuana). Apart from a small subset of non-users who refuse to tolerate any illicit drug use whatsoever, these studies show non-using peers respect the right of others to use certain drugs for recreational enjoyment.

There are signs of a convergence in the ways that substance users see themselves as regular, ordinary citizens and how they are identified by others (Hammersley et al., 2001). This suggests that new lines are being drawn between acceptable and unacceptable use of drugs. These new lines or boundaries do not necessarily correspond with formal definitions and controls (see Figure 5.2).

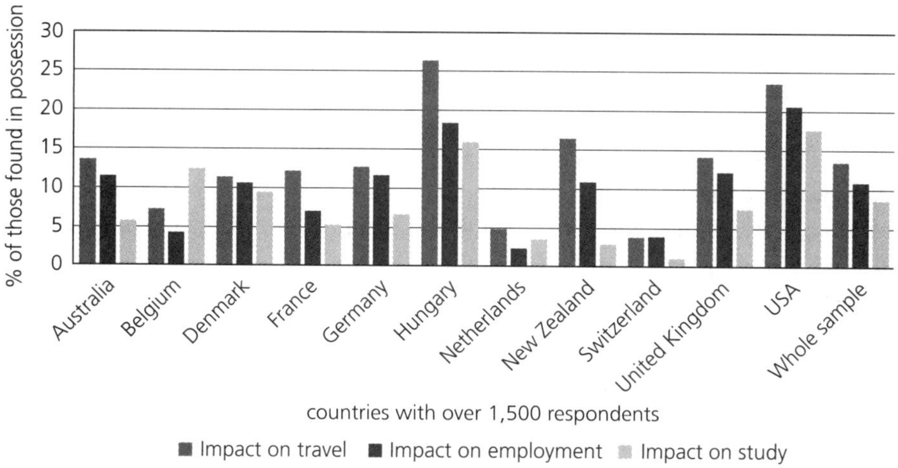

Figure 5.2 Reveals significant national differences in the impact on travel, study, and employment of being charged with possession of cannabis. The United States was one of the worst places to be charged, with more than 20 per cent of respondents reporting a negative effect on their travel and employment, and nearly one in five reporting an adverse effect on their studies.

Source: *Global Drug Survey* (2014). Reprinted with permission.

Cultural Accommodation

In addition to increasing social tolerance of users, there are other signs of growing cultural acceptance and accommodation of recreational drug use. Cultural accommodation of some illicit drug use, particularly the use of marijuana, for example, is evident in media portrayals of drug users. In television, film, and other mainstream media, we are witnessing more neutral, even positive portrayals, of illicit drug use presented to the public.

Television shows like *Weeds* and *That '70s Show* in the 2000s depicted marijuana use as normal, represented by frequent, even daily, use by ordinary people. Most importantly, they did so in a way that corresponded with the actual experiences of marijuana users who used the drug routinely with few adverse consequences (other than those stemming from their status under law).

Admissions of past drug use by respected famous people, including politicians in positions of authority, have become more commonplace. It seems such candour is no longer cause for shame or scorn, or even public controversy. That said, acknowledging current substance use is less common, though not unheard of, by well-known public figures in North American society. Admitting marijuana use has become so unremarkable that it scarcely qualifies as news. To note a memorable exception in Canadian experience, the famous author Pierre Berton, in what would be his final televised appearance, went on CBC primetime (*The Rick Mercer Report*, 18

October 2004) and cheerfully educated viewers on the most efficient way to roll the "perfect joint." He was in his eighties.

Canadian news media are giving more exposure to alternative perspectives of drug issues that directly contradict traditional antidrug discourses. There is evidence of greater balance in reporting and input from participants in drug policy debates. While still facilitated or created by the media, due to coverage that is often heavily biased and distorted, drug scares are less likely to go publicly unchallenged.

The ineffectiveness of law and law enforcement in preventing drug-related problems for society and users is an observation that is gaining more exposure and increasing public support for law reform. Laws that target cannabis possession, in particular, are increasingly debated and presented in the media as an unjustified or questionable use of state resources. And gradually, the harm reduction movement has made progress, as suggested by its presence in drug policy discussions in the news and other mainstream media sources (see Hathaway and Erickson, 2004).

Evidence of cultural accommodation in mass media depictions of drug issues is indicative of an evolution in the way that drug use is portrayed and understood. Media representation of the use of marijuana and other drugs sheds more light on both cultural ambivalence and accommodation of illegal substance use.

Public Attitudes and Policy Activity

Public attitudes toward drug policy in Canada can be studied more directly and precisely using survey methods in addition to analyses of media. Opinion polls conducted over the past few years show that most Canadians favour loosening restrictions and relaxing penalties for cannabis possession (see Hathaway et al., 2007). Recent surveys indicate that more than half of those surveyed favour fully legalizing use. Opinions vary significantly by sex, education, income, ethnicity, and country of birth (Table 5.1).

Support for legal access for health purposes is higher, with nearly 90 per cent of respondents favouring exemption from the law for medical consumers of the drug. Public attitudes are broadly harm reduction–oriented. They are aligned more closely with concern for public health than current policy provisions, which emphasize police priorities and enforce criminal controls. In that respect, they correspond with principles asserted in Canada's Drug Strategy a quarter-century ago.

Returning to examine recent policy activities, within the context of the theorized normalization process, there is little evidence of actual adoption of public health objectives or commitment to reform. With respect to marijuana, it is increasingly apparent that existing legislation is out of step with social tolerance and public attitudes, which favour making changes to the law.

Four decades after the Le Dain report, however, there are signs of pragmatism, or a hint of realism, in response to widespread use of cannabis. Despite

Table 5.1 Proportion of Toronto Residents Who Believe Cannabis Should Be Legally Available, by Sociodemographic Characteristic (N = 1081*)

Characteristic	Surveyed, n	In Support of Legalization, %	*P* value
Sex			
Men	463	62	< .0001
Women	618	48	
Age, y			
18–34	405	56	.505
35–45	447	54	
≥ 55	229	51	
Education			
Less than high school	50	28	.001
High school graduate	196	50	
Post-secondary	834	57	
Personal income in 2003			
< $30,000	360	45	< .0001
$30,000–$49,999	268	58	
≥ $50,000	364	65	
Country of birth			
Canada	688	62	< .0001
Other	392	41	
Ethnicity			
White	836	60	< .0001
Black	66	36	
Other	179	35	

*Not all participants answered all questions.

Source: Hathaway et al. (2007).

the controversy and reaction to the Senate's 2002 recommendation for legalizing cannabis possession, the exercise is noteworthy. Although legalization was rejected as too radical for most Members of Parliament and the general public to accept, opinion polls increasingly find otherwise. The supporting evidence and rationale is out there for claims-makers to employ in present policy debates.

While their discursive effect on political action is presently uncertain, pro-legalization arguments have gained an aura of legitimacy, having gained more formal recognition and exposure. Although it was rejected also, the more moderate proposal for decriminalizing cannabis by the concurrent House committee was far less controversial, indicating an apparent readiness for implementing actual reform.

Therefore, despite the current stalemate in Canadian drug policy developments for more than 40 years, there is still hope for future legislation that is more consistent with persistent calls for policy reform. Perhaps the most significant drug policy development has been the introduction of a set of regulations that allow for use of marijuana as a medicine.

More than 12 years later, at least 30,000 Canadians with chronic medical conditions are authorized for legal access to the drug. However, would-be legal users still face obstacles to access. Early on it was observed that the guidelines are so restrictive the legislation is illusory for most patients who would benefit from using marijuana (Senate Special Committee on Illegal Drugs, 2002).

There are no official guidelines for prescribing cannabis, and many family doctors have been actively discouraged from participating in the application process. Legal sources of supply have also proven unattractive for many authorized consumers, who complain about high costs, poor quality, and lack of variety in cannabis grown by the State supplier (Belle-Isle and Hathaway, 2007).

Most self-defined medical marijuana users do not meet the shortlist of conditions and criteria for supporting diagnoses by a practising physician. Many others who may qualify are unlikely to apply. Therefore, the vast majority of users who self-medicate with marijuana will continue, in all likelihood, to do so outside of the evolving regulatory schema (Jones and Hathaway, 2008).

Despite the normalizing trends observed—as indicated by high use rates, sociocultural acceptance, and support for medical consumption of the drug—marijuana users still encounter social stigma and face the threat of prosecution. The nature and experience of stigma faced by users is essential to examine for a fuller understanding of the scope and limitations of the normalization thesis.

The social boundaries of tolerance and accommodation of illicit drug use will be investigated further. The next section details the experiences and attitudes of marijuana users to augment our understanding of response to the most normalized of all illegal drugs.

Perceptions and Experiences of Stigma

Notwithstanding indications of a normalizing process marked by greater tolerance, marijuana use is officially prohibited throughout the Western world. In Canada, unauthorized possession is a criminal offence with maximum penalties of up to $1000 and six months in prison for first-time offenders.

Despite the exercise of options (probation, fines, diversion, etc.) to reduce the impact of the law in many cases, marijuana users continue to be arrested and treated as if they are criminals (Table 5.2). The threat of formal sanctions, and the consequences of a conviction to one's career and social standing, is no less present than before.

Those who fail to exercise discretion in their drug use often find themselves excluded, maligned, or undervalued (even in drug-using subcultures

Table 5.2 Charges for Drug Offences in Canada, 2010

Offence	N	Rate per 100,000 Population	Proportion	Change from 2009 (%)
Cannabis				
Possession	56,870	167	52.4	14
Trafficking/production/distribution	18,256	54	16.8	10
Cocaine				
Possession	7256	21	6.7	–6
Trafficking/production/distribution	9729	29	9	–4
Other				
Possession	9462	28	8.7	14
Trafficking/production/distribution	6956	20	6.4	5
Total	**108,529**	**318**	**100**	**10**

Source: Canadian Centre for Justice Statistics (2010).

or peer groups). Users are guarded against open use and openness about use to avoid the threat of intervention by authorities, loss of status, or offending non-users who might disapprove (Hammersley et al., 2001; Hathaway, 2004b). Marijuana users still contend with social stigma, and are often identified as deviant by others. Although the social status of some substance use is changing, there is substantial evidence of moral regulation, or what Garland (2001) describes as a "culture of control." Research on experienced drug users shows their attitudes tend to correspond with a conventional understanding about the general nature of drug use and addiction. Social stigma is internalized by users, and reinforces a tendency to observe mainstream cultural requirements emphasizing self-mastery and control (Hathaway et al., 2011).

Evidence of marijuana normalization must be qualified with reference to the user's own particular perspectives and familiarity with stigma. The experiences of otherwise-conforming, law-abiding adults who are careful when and where they use the drug supports the observation that in Canada marijuana possession is not a high-priority offence.

Exercising due discretion, moderation, and control appears to be sufficient for most users to alleviate concerns about detection and arrest. Taking measures to reduce the risk of intervention effectively protects them from the impact of the law. Most marijuana users indicate that law enforcement does not affect their use, and many say they have no fear of legal penalties at all (Hathaway, 2004a).

Experiences of stigma are related more directly to informal mechanisms of control. Marijuana use is hidden from non-users, such as family and co-workers, who may not be as tolerant as normalization might suggest. Users who fail to exercise appropriate discretion in their interactions still report encounters with non-users that result in status loss or social disapproval.

Marijuana users, not surprisingly, reject misconceptions (stemming from the *Reefer Madness* era) still evident in stigmatizing attitudes today (i.e., that the user is lazy, unmotivated, unintelligent, and deviant). A more nuanced understanding of the practice is preferred, which emphasizes self-control, responsible behaviour, and normalcy in all respects, despite the use of cannabis.

In addition to maintaining patterns of controlled use, and suitable discretion interacting with non-users, there are other ways that users seek to distance themselves further from the social stigma of illicit substance use. The stigma of addiction has an influence—drug users readily acknowledge the potential for dependence and adverse effects of use.

Measures taken to avoid developing dependence correspond with statements on the need for moderation. Some users note that periods of abstinence are needed, if use becomes excessive, in order to re-establish or demonstrate control (Hathaway, 2004b). Distancing themselves from other substance users who refuse or fail to do the same alleviates users' concerns about addiction and adverse effects.

Users maintain a clear distinction between themselves (and people like them) and those who do not demonstrate control. Those who violate the standards of controlled use (i.e., abuse) are stigmatized by users, much the same way some non-users tend to label marijuana users as a group. Marijuana users who use less frequently differentiate themselves from those who use it daily. Those who use it every day make their own distinctions based on expectations of the proper time of day. Using marijuana in the evening after work, and perhaps on weekends in more social circumstances, is a common pattern of consumption. This pattern is distinguished from the "wake-and-bake" routine of those who use habitually in the morning hours.

Conventional concerns about the influence of drugs are demonstrated in perceptions of role conflict among users (Hathaway et al., 2011). The experiences and attitudes of many are consistent with societal perspectives that consider illicit drug use incompatible with career and family obligations.

The existence of large numbers of "otherwise conventional" marijuana users (at least those who respond to invitations to participate in research) is a compelling indicator of normalization in itself. While use continues in adulthood alongside more demanding roles, there is evidence of maturation also, in the sense that use becomes less frequent and more moderate.

Few marijuana users take the drug before or during work, though this depends upon the nature of employment and job setting. Concerns about impairing work performance or productivity are often less concerning, from the standpoint of the user, than maintaining one's professional identity and status. This attitude exists even among users who are employed in workplaces in which some bosses and co-workers are open and accepting of marijuana use.

Perceptions of role conflict are especially apparent in the attitudes of parents who use marijuana. Mothers are particularly conflicted. Their concerns correspond with cultural assumptions about gender roles and use of drugs. Abstaining during pregnancy and while parenting young children reflects commitment to performing the role of the "proper mother."

Expectations about parents setting good examples, or serving as role models, are particularly evident for marijuana-using parents with pre-teens and adolescents. As their children become older, they increasingly experience significant dilemmas about the hypocrisy of hiding their drug use. The associated conflict is especially apparent among parents of young people who use cannabis themselves.

Concerns about the harm use may inflict on adolescents are more consistent with mainstream cultural assumptions than parents' actual experiences as marijuana users. The extent to which they tacitly, or actively, endorse stigmatizing attitudes toward their own children is an indication that stigma is internalized by users. Substance users play a role in reinforcing definitions that contribute to their own diminished social status.

Drug laws may not prevent use. These laws, however, do exert a powerful influence on attitudes toward drugs, and on substance users' perceptions of themselves. Separating formal and informal kinds of stigma creates a false distinction between legal and non-legal mechanisms of societal control. Authoritative legal and medical discourses shape users' and non-users' understanding about drug use by influencing attitudes, perceptions, and behaviour.

The use of cannabis as medicine may be an indication of broader transformation in societal perceptions and reactions to the use of certain drugs. But the adoption of a public health or medical perspective may not result in stigma disappearing altogether. Even if cannabis were legalized and sold as a commodity, like cigarettes or alcohol, this would not necessarily remove the social stigma stemming from assumptions of abuse or need for treatment (Room, 2005).

The moral dictum to be healthy can be a powerful source of stigma and a strong motivator for regulating use of drugs. Medicalizing drug use offers no assurance that users of these drugs will not be shunned. The experiences of medical marijuana users serve to further illustrate the cultural ambivalence surrounding the most normalized of all illicit drugs.

Experiences of Medical Marijuana Users

Despite continuation of the ban on marijuana, today its use has come to be increasingly regarded as an accepted recreational alternative to alcohol. It is evident as well that using cannabis as medicine enjoys tremendous popular support (Hathaway et al., 2007). Less well understood is the apparent contradiction demonstrated in the actual experience of users. Using marijuana to cope with chronic health conditions is just as threatening, in different ways, as using it for fun.

Discrimination based on having marginal health status (and illicit drug use) intersects with other stigmas in what might be described as a **domination matrix** (see Collins, 2000). Many who use marijuana for medical conditions experience stigma based on the connection between chronic illness, poverty, and illicit drug use.

The matrix theorized by Collins serves to organize, manage, and legitimize oppression of perceived threats to the system. Its structural dimension includes legal, political, economic and religious factors used to organize existing power relations. From an economic standpoint, in a capitalist society, disabled and sick people threaten productivity. They are labelled "social junk"—unproductive citizens who place a burden on government resources.

People suffering from chronic illness are an uncomfortable reminder that Western medicine has few answers of much value for many of the ailments for which we seek relief. Those who choose to use marijuana for this purpose continue to encounter resistance from authorities and related structural controls. Users still experience overt discrimination, despite official recognition that using marijuana is medically effective for some people.

The Domination Matrix

A web of representatives of structural authority extends from the police and courts to landlords and employers, who are more peripheral but equally important to maintaining structural control. None can be assumed to differentiate between recreational and medical consumption of the drug. Being authorized by medical exemption gives no certainty of being protected from harassment or surveillance (Box 5.1).

Box 5.1 The Domination Matrix: Experiences of Medical Marijuana Users

1. The Structural Domain: Experiences of Users with Police, Courts, and Landlords

I've had my medicine taken away by a cop before.... I didn't have very much cannabis (maybe a gram and a half) on me, luckily. She took that away then approached my boyfriend, who was the driver, and I showed her my card immediately. But she seemed more interested in him. She started harassing him about the pot, and pushed herself up in his face. I told her it was my medicine, and that he wasn't using it.... She just replied by telling us how lucky we were, because if she had seen us light it up, she would have impounded the car, and that we would have suffered. Needless to say, needing cannabis scares me in many ways, because the people around me are vulnerable and are going to suffer because of it.

*****

I was busted with one gram of pot on my birthday, and I had custody of my children at the time. The judge asked me, "What will you do to keep your children?" To which I replied "exactly what I have always done. Supply them with a good home and food and shelter and my love." "What about marijuana?" [asked the judge]. "Oh, I'm not going to quit using marijuana." So the court gave custody back to their mother. Just for that one reason... because I would not say that I would quit using marijuana. I've never lied to my parents about it, so why would I lie to the judge about it? I'm not ashamed of smoking marijuana.

*****

I find being a cannabis user very socially restrictive... even with my exemption. I'm excluded from most places to live... [and] that sort of just shuts me out of this huge part of the world I can't live in, because my mobility is already very curtailed, and this is now legally curtailing it.

2. The Disciplinary Domain: Experiences with Health Services and Medical Professionals

The ambulance men came in and said, "we smell marijuana." "Yes," I said, "I smoke marijuana." They slammed me on the gurney at this point, and I was in extreme pain... I was going into septic shock.... They mistreated me because I smoke marijuana.

*****

In my experience, there's no talk about pot with doctors. They don't want to hear anything about it. And they feel insulted if you talk about it. I mean, you're the only doctor I've seen who can relate to it....

[The Federal Medical Marijuana Program] is not a serious program... they're just mocking and humiliating me, and rubbing my face in the fact that I'm using an otherwise illegal product. And that's a social stigma. Just having a hammer taken to your nuts every time you want to deal with the State... and I don't like dealing with the State much to begin with.

3. The Hegemonic Domain: Language, Images, and Values That Sustain Discrimination

The biggest problem is that people have been brainwashed to think it's hippie juice, that medical use is a joke... that it's an excuse to get high, and people don't see the other side of it.... It's incredibly hard to overcome that. And this attitude exists in doctors too, and police.

*****

I'm not able to talk about it with my parents... not out of a lack of love, just understanding. They know the laws of the land and are just being good

Continued

law-abiding citizens...but anything that goes against the law...well it's against the law...so it must be bad. Their understanding of pot...doesn't go much beyond that.

*****

Now that I'm an adult, it's really honestly very weird to speak about marijuana...some people...when you tell them you're using it as medicine, they're like "Yes. Sure you are, pal. Good for you and your drug habit."

4. The Interpersonal Domain: Daily Interactions and Relationships That Influence Identity and Status

   With friends I notice there's a sort of a silence about pot.... I try to bring it up, I try to get the conversation going, but nobody cares. I feel limited and scared.... I want to get out of my house, and be less angry, and learn to socialize, and they're pushing me back in.

   *****

   The people at the house where I live, they don't talk to me because I smoke marijuana.... They play bingo, they play cards, they go drinking. This is their life... I'm not part of it, and that's why they put me down. I'm a turtle. I don't live outside like that. I live inside. The hard knocks they dish out don't touch me...they just remind me continually that I live in hell.

Source: Personal interviews with the author.

Medical marijuana users on disability, who receive a small fixed income, face discrimination due to economic inequality. With no choice but to rent, and with their mobility restricted, medical marijuana users risk intrusions and eviction if they use (or choose to grow) their medicine at home. Many landlords (and proprietors) prohibit smoking on the premises, and few of them are interested in renting space to tenants authorized to grow illegal drugs. Smoking marijuana in public places similarly still attracts attention from non-users and police.

The structural dimension of the domination matrix intersects with disciplinary sources of oppression. These describe how status quo arrangements become managed through bureaucratic organization and methods of control. Of all the domains of domination, argued Collins (2000), the disciplinary and the structural are the most resilient to change.

Disciplinary domination is less tangible or obvious than structural hegemony. People tend to take for granted that medicine, science, and other bureaucratic institutions uphold accepted standards of rational objectivity in their regulatory operations and activities. The disciplinary domain includes health services and other agencies (e.g., social workers, welfare) employing a bureaucratic process that rationalizes the surveillance of certain populations.

Distrust of bureaucrats and medical professionals is no less prominent among users as the threat posed by police. The role of doctors as gatekeepers is contentious among both groups. This situation leads to conflict between doctors and many patients seeking guidance and support for use of cannabis as medicine.

There is a wide variety of physical and mental health conditions for which people use cannabis. What they tend to have in common is a mutual dissatisfaction with the medicine and treatment they receive from their physicians. In recent decades, there has been a loss of confidence and growing shift away from formal medicine toward alternative therapies (cf. CTV/ Angus Reid Group Poll, 1997; Northcott, 1994).

People are now more likely to experiment with treatments, and seek more self-control over health care decisions (Coomber et al., 2003). Definitions of marijuana as a natural herb remedy, as opposed to a synthetic pharmaceutically produced drug, may also influence perceptions in favour of its use (Macnaghtan et al., 1992).

Alternative therapies in medicine are often difficult to evaluate with standard measures of assessment, due to the philosophies from which they are derived. Some are more properly considered lifestyle, cultural, or spiritual practices that transcend the definitions of disease, health, diagnosis, and evaluation of medical science (Hoffer, 2003; Spencer, 1999). Family doctors have been understandably reluctant, as suggested by their attitudes and the experiences of patients, to accept the role of gatekeeper to marijuana medicine (see Jones and Hathaway, 2008).

Expanding medical jurisdiction over access to marijuana has not resulted in lesser scrutiny and stigma against users. Experiences of patients with their doctors and the government (for those who have been authorized to use) demonstrate the operation of rational bureaucracy and exercise of disciplinary power. The gaze of formal scrutiny, surveillance, and disapproval is reflected in the narratives in Box 5.1.

The experiences of medical marijuana users with authorities, bureaucrats, and medical professionals contradict assumptions of the normalization thesis. The narratives of users indicate that accommodation of the practice is less evident than the argument implies. In addition to the structural and disciplinary elements of the domination matrix, which serve to organize and manage certain target populations, there are also critical ideological dimensions.

Ideological Dimensions

The hegemonic domain is concerned with the use of language, images, and ideas that legitimize oppression. Authority functions because people believe in, confirm, and reproduce it in their daily lives. Attitudes and actions that sustain discrimination against nonconformists help to achieve this.

The interpersonal, along with the hegemonic, domain refers to daily interactions and relationships with people who contribute to the formation of a marginal identity. The narratives of medical marijuana users indicate that they are often stigmatized and devalued, and experience diminished social status. This is especially apparent in their treatment by non-users who cast them in the role of the other or outsider.

These findings contrast the perception, suggested in opinion polls, of near-unanimous support for use of cannabis as medicine. Box 5.1 provides further illustrations of how ideological dimensions of the domination matrix contribute to its structural and disciplinary elements.

As multiple dimensions intersect in practice, or work in tandem, it is difficult to separate the influence of formal and informal mechanisms of control. As "unproductive" citizens, who use a drug that history associates with deviance rather than medicine or health, people with chronic health conditions face stigma that is strongly multidimensional.

Medicine that is smoked, which also gets you high, is not a treatment consistent with conventional perspectives about health. The use of marijuana for a wide array of ailments is a discomfiting reminder that, for chronic health conditions, allopathic medicine has not had all the answers—or, by definition, any cures.

Western medicine and culture is characterized by fear of death, and denial of the fact that sick (and old) people do not necessarily get better (i.e., cured). For many, feeling better is the optimal outcome. By alleviating symptoms, coping offers some relief.

Increasing recognition that marijuana is much safer to use than most prescription drugs, and often more effective, is a threat to structural and disciplinary authority. Arguably the threat to legal–medical authority, as well as the institutional arrangements that support this jurisdiction, is greater than that posed by using marijuana recreationally.

The social status of the drug and its many users might be viewed on a continuum that has shown signs of shifting in the direction of increasing accommodation (or indifference), while retaining vestiges of social disapproval. A more nuanced understanding of the normalization thesis, as applied to cannabis and other types of drugs, requires examination of the signs of transformation and nature of the stigmas that have culturally endured.

The following sections are devoted to further exploration of sociocultural dimensions that shape our views on drugs. We have already considered the historical example of Canada's first drug ban, which targeted smoked opium (and therefore Chinese immigrants). We have seen how early legislation can be traced to racist, bureaucratic, and economic interests, among others that explain the timing and the target.

Drug laws serve the interests of the powerful, reinforcing the authority of moral norms at the expense of disenfranchised, criminalized, addicted, or otherwise threatening (and threatened) minority groups. From opium to cannabis, from LSD to khat, and other drugs deemed criminal for much of the past century, repressive antidrug laws stem from racism, intolerance, and cultural oppression often targeted at youth.

Use of synthetic drugs like ecstasy, and other psychedelic drugs, which are often popular with youth, has met with similar reaction since LSD was outlawed in the 1960s. This response from government was linked to growing fears about a burgeoning drug culture.

Societal reaction to the emergence of psychedelic drug use, particularly among youth, differs from responses to (more harmful and addictive) drugs that are more readily accepted by Canadians. Alcohol and cigarettes have been remarkably resistant to attempts to ban them in the past. The following case studies further demonstrate that reactions are contingent on the status of the user as opposed to health effects or evidence of harm.

From LSD to Ecstasy: The Psychedelic Era

Drugs derive their status in society from that of their users. This is well-documented by Canadian researchers. Montigny (2011) brings together an array of authors writing about a wide variety of drugs. A recurring theme of different studies in this area is that societal reactions tend to indicate commitment to legal moralism and paternalistic values, as opposed to a concern for the rights of substance users.

Societal responses, however, vary widely based on characteristics of the substance-using group. The resistance to restrictions on tobacco, for example, is contrasted with the ease with which non-medical use of opium was outlawed in Canada more than a century ago. The widespread cultural acceptance of alcohol has likewise influenced its status in society, preventing health professionals and government authorities from treating it like other substances with potential for abuse.

The perceived threat of illicit drugs has been disproportionate to evidence of harm to the society and user, typically conflated with anxiety concerning their use by socially marginalized groups. Subversive youth have been among those groups deemed threatening.

For example, LSD was criminalized in Canada after a period during which the drug had developed a reputation as a treatment for a variety of medical conditions, including mental illnesses, migraines, and addiction. Attitudes soon changed though, when LSD use became popular in the youth subculture as a symbol of rebellion and rejection of mainstream societal values. Soon, LSD became associated with disorder, degradation, and corruption of white youth. This effectively transformed it from a promising medical treatment to a drug that no longer had the legitimacy afforded to a deluge of other modern pharmaceuticals. The history of LSD in Canada is partly characterized by conflict between medical researchers and authorities about the designation of the drug.

Originally developed as a migraine medication, LSD (lysergic acid diethylamide) became legally available for purposes of research from the Sandoz Pharmaceutical Company in Switzerland in 1943 (Dyck, 2011). The production of pharmaceuticals dramatically expanded over the next two decades into the 1960s, resulting in the development of hundreds of new drugs.

In this era, scientific researchers conducted thousands of experiments involving LSD. It was shown to be nontoxic, non-addicting, and safe for use, with investigators often taking LSD themselves to further scientific understanding of the drug. Among other applications of interest to practitioners, LSD reportedly gave insight into altered perceptions and distortions of reality. In particular, the drug's effects were thought to mimic symptoms experienced by people diagnosed with schizophrenia.

In the treatment of addiction, LSD had been discovered to produce the kind of spiritual awakening and reflection that was often found to facilitate recovery. Psychedelic interventions emphasize inducing a particular *experience* that is therapeutic, unlike other types of treatment, which focus on the physiology of the brain and body.

The term *psychedelic* was originally used by Canadian-based researcher Humphry Osmond to describe the "mind-manifesting" qualities of the LSD experience (Dyck, 2011). Its distinctive features, compared with other drugs like alcohol, opium, methamphetamine, and cocaine, include increased sensitivity, enhancement of the senses, changes in perceptions of space and time, and feelings of being at one with the universe.

In addition to benign and even life-enhancing qualities, LSD also has the potential for psychotic changes when taken by naive users (and even those with more experience, when taken in large doses). These effects—hallucinations, severe anxiety, paranoid delusions, and perceptual disturbances—made the drug attractive to clinicians for the insight it might offer into treating mental illness.

By the early 1960s, reports of positive experiences with LSD were gaining more publicity and increasing attention from participants in the emerging drug scene. Its conversion from a noncontroversial medical treatment to a threatening new symbol of the youthful counterculture led to calls for tightening restrictions on supply.

In Canada, by 1963, it was observed that black-market distribution of LSD was on the rise. Calls for more restrictions to reduce availability forced psychedelic drug researchers to co-operate more closely with government authorities to maintain credibility, and ensure continued legal access to the drug. Whereas medical authority was initially respected, it was ultimately supplanted and rejected by lawmakers.

At the time, LSD (or acid) was becoming a generic label for a chemically diverse variety of street drugs with hallucinogenic properties. The influence of psychedelic gurus like Tim Leary, who encouraged young people to "drop out and turn on," further deepened the connection between LSD and growing concerns about political dissent (Box 5.2).

Reports of LSD abuse contributed to further negative attention in the media and pressure to institute more stringent regulations. Concerns about the dangers of the drug began to outweigh assertions by proponents of its medical potential.

Humphry Osmond, in particular, prominently sought to counter fears of the drug with evidence of its therapeutic value and safety when administered in clinical conditions. Though sympathetic to the aims of New Age seekers of transcendence, he denounced the likes of Leary for what he saw as crass promotion of a drug with far more value as a psychiatric tool.

Laws that targeted LSD were also criticized by Osmond for constraining research and potential applications. These controls had failed to stem black-market distribution of numerous hallucinogens with unknown chemical properties. While often sold as LSD or acid by street dealers, an array of drugs in circulation represented far greater unknown dangers to consumers.

Parliamentary debates during the early 1960s reveal that politicians were exposed to a variety of informed arguments opposing more restrictive legislation. Lawmakers were aware of therapeutic applications of LSD, maintaining a distinction between legal and illegal use, supply, and distribution. They discussed the drawbacks of imposing legal penalties on young Canadians who used the drug with "innocent intentions," for the sake of curiosity and youthful experimentation. There was also some discussion of alternatives to punishment, such as use of public education campaigns.

By 1967, however, the non-medical use of LSD had reached proportions deemed alarming enough to tip the balance in favour of a ban. John Diefenbaker, the prime minister at the time, suggested that the drug be placed under the Narcotic Control Act as a prohibited substance. The proposal was considered by a cabinet committee and deliberated further by discussion in the Senate. The most troubling development observed by politicians was the dark influence of the drug subculture on young people.

By outgrowing its previous underground identity, and through its association with branded radicals like Leary, LSD entered the mainstream. The Canadian Broadcasting Corporation (CBC), *Life Magazine*, and other media outlets were criticized in Parliament for tacitly promoting and glamorizing the use of LSD. This rebuke resulted from the media's broad coverage of the growing counterculture in Canadian society, which did not explicitly condemn the use of drugs.

Box 5.2 Excerpts from Timothy Leary's Banned Canadian Speech

In 1967 Timothy Leary was invited to speak at "Perception '67," a symposium on psychedelic drugs held at the University of Toronto. Leary was refused permission to enter Canada by immigration authorities because of a prior arrest in the US. Several days later, Dr. Leary attempted to deliver a tape-recorded message across the Detroit-Windsor border. The tape was confiscated; Dr. Leary was brought into Canada, detained, and, on his return, arrested by US authorities. The editor of the *Canadian Free Press*, an Ottawa underground newspaper, got Leary to update and re-tape his message. The result was a message to the Canadian people, recorded at his psychedelic ashram in Millbrook, New York. The following passages are excerpts from that tape-recording.

> Hello! This is Timothy Leary speaking from Millbrook, New York. I bring love and blessings to the people of Canada....
>
> HEY!
>
> PEOPLE OF CANADA!
>
> WAKE UP!
>
> WAKE UP!
>
> Who's brainwashed you to think that alcohol, the dangerous, narcotic, addictive intoxicant, is something that should be consumed, and a holy sacrament such as marijuana and drugs like LSD which have been used for thousands of years by spiritual seekers should not be used?
>
> Our children, indeed everyone in our community, regularly use the sacraments of marijuana and LSD just the way people in other religions use their sacraments to find meaning, to weave the pattern of the spiritual life....
>
> The aims of our religion are those of every religion of the past: we seek to find the god within, the divinity which lies within each person's body. We call this process "turning on." And secondly, we seek to express the revelation, the glory, and the confusion and the paradox which comes to us from turning on in acts of glorification, of communication, of expressing the wonder and the meaning. It's this process of acting it out that is called "tuning in." But in order to turn on and tune in, you must of course "drop out." You cannot live a secular, socially conventional life in the country of Canada and pretend that the aim of your life on this planet is spiritual....
>
> Drop out? What do you mean by that? Does Dr. Leary think that students should drop out of school?

Yes, young people of Canada, I'm telling you that you must drop out of school. Your education system is a narcotic, addictive process paid for by old men and women to teach you to become Romans like themselves. You must drop out of school. The aim of Canadian education, like American education, is to narrow your mind, contract your consciousness, get you to accept this reality, the ridiculous game of the television prop scenario of Canadian industrial urban life today. You must drop out.

But people say, "Dr. Leary, you are not saying to middle-aged people with mortgages and car payments that they should drop out of their jobs?" And I say, yes. I say exactly that, as every holy teacher in history has said before, you must drop out....

The Psychedelic Revolution is nothing more and nothing less than a religious renaissance....

Look around you. Above all look down here at these anguished United States of ours. And what do you see? If you see with any clarity, you will record a madhouse. Our government in Washington is sending metal and steel, and atomic energy, and destructive power all over the globe to protect our national security. To other people the fact is that our government in Washington is a supremely materialistic and atheistic society seeking, as every empire has in the past, control, power, control. Aging, almost senile, and probably impotent men in our capitals both east and west are sending young men out to kill for old men's chess games: power and control.

It's time for a new religion...destruction of the Empire by the new religion.

Hey! Did you hear me say the destruction of the Empire? Yes; that is what I said is needed in Canada....

Now in the next few months there is going to be a period of anguish and conflict, because one thing you must remember, middle-aged bureaucratic people in Canada, you cannot stop us. There is no reward and no punishment which your Government has which can seduce us or intimidate us because, like it or not, believe it or not, we have found the ancient meaning through the use of our secret plant, marijuana, and LSD....

The more you repress it, the more hostile you are to your students, and to your college professors, and to the people of Canada who want to hear the new religion, the faster you guarantee that our religion will take over....

It's the old rhythm. It's going to keep coming: drop out, turn on, tune in....

Source: Leary (1967). Reprinted with permission from the Futique Trust.

Such irresponsible depictions, which minimized dangers, were generally agreed to be confusing for young people and contributing to the rapidly increasing rate of use. The objective of protecting youth tipped the scales in favour of imposing a ban on LSD. The sense of balance evident in earlier discussions was replaced by a consensus that the dangers of the drug significantly outweighed its potential medical benefits; stricter measures would be required to control it.

In 1968, LSD was placed in a special category of the Food and Drugs Act. It was listed alongside other substances such as MDMA (better known as ecstasy) that fell into a nebulous grey area between recreational and potentially therapeutic drugs. With bad publicity reducing the credibility of research into such drugs in the eyes of government funders and authorities, the move effectively prohibited the use of LSD.

Existing medical jurisdiction was decisively eroded by the drug's association with permissiveness, disorder, and a wasted generation of drug-addled youth. A generation later ecstasy would undergo a similarly dramatic transformation. It transitioned from a contained drug to one that symbolized the threat posed by young people taking drugs in uncontrolled environments.

Panic at the Disco? Ecstasy and Other "Club Drugs"

Societal concern about the use of ecstasy shares several characteristics of previous drug panics. Not unlike with LSD or opium or cannabis, and other drugs prohibited over the last century, drug panics with ecstasy were less a product of its properties than its association with a particular subgroup. Just as smoking opium in drug dens by Chinese immigrants came to represent an emerging social threat, so did the consumption of synthetic drugs in clubs and raves among subversive youth.

Most drugs that came to be identified as club drugs were criminalized in Canada before any actual concern over, or even evidence of, use. Typically these were added by default to an expanding schedule of banned substances, and their derivatives, to bring Canadian federal law in line with international treaties. Their specific properties were less of a determinant of their designation than were the risks associated with their use in nightclubs or the rave environment (Grayson, 2008).

Beginning with the targeting of opium dens in Canada, the social history of drug regulation has been largely concerned with the containment of drugs in particular locations, either preventing use outside them or removing them entirely. Societal concern about the risks of taking club drugs is partially derived from the perceived threat of young people and other subgroups congregating in unregulated spaces. Clubs and raves are understood as places people go to escape conventional societal restrictions. In the absence of morality, wrongdoing is encouraged, compelling more involvement in criminal activities including drug use, date rape, and deviant sexual behaviour.

An obvious connection between deviant behaviour and drug use is assumed within the club environment, in which certain populations are construed to be a threat. Substance use by gay or bisexual men within club settings, for example, is depicted as a threat to public health. Independently of evidence, the behaviour is assumed to contribute to the spread of HIV or AIDS, due to heightened risk of unprotected anal sex.

The connection between club drugs and sexual assault is reminiscent of our cultural experiences with alcohol. It conforms to cultural assumptions about gender and patterns of victimization. A similar connection was observed with the use of opium in Canada a century ago, when innocent white women reportedly fell victim to sexual slavery and addiction after taking opium. The use of drugs for rape by men in nightclubs is a potent rationale for targeting club drugs.

Controlling populations deemed a risk to health or morals extends the reach of government authority beyond the scope of regulation by enforcement of the law. Harm reduction interventions in the "rave scene," for example, include a wide variety of measures, from distributing information promoting safer drug use to tightening regulations for nightclubs and rave promoters. Concerns about conditions in the club environment that increase the risk of taking certain drugs have been used to justify regulation, pushing the rave scene further underground.

The decline of the rave scene in Toronto, notes Grayson, followed the institution of a regulatory framework requiring the presence of police and trained medical and security staff (in addition to amenities like washrooms, drinking water, and air-conditioning) on site. Though justified in terms of harm reduction, these requirements often undermined the containment of known risks through informal mechanisms of control. Notwithstanding these developments, it appears that ultimately the illicit reputation of drugs used at clubs and rave events outweighed new concern for meeting public health objectives.

By comparison, traditionally accepted drugs such as alcohol, tobacco, and pharmaceuticals prescribed by health professionals have seen less interference or suppression by authorities. Campaigns against tobacco in the early twentieth century encountered much resistance and considerable hostility (Rudy, 2011). Unlike drug use among distrusted subgroups in society, tobacco use was not considered as a threat to social order. Smoking tobacco was, rather, understood to be a pastime popular among respected citizens. As such, despite the risks to health acknowledged by law-makers, the user's ability to moderate and control the ill effects of smoking has been respected. Resulting regulation has tended to prioritize concerns for users' rights and business interests, as opposed to interventions justified by public health objectives. For example, point-of-sale restrictions to prevent minors from smoking went largely unenforced for many decades. It was not until the 1980s that consensus on the dangers of tobacco could no longer be ignored.

Increasing recognition of the health burden of Canadian's alcohol consumption met with similar resistance. Unlike opium, cocaine, and marijuana, and more recent banned substances like LSD and other psychedelic drugs, the risks of using alcohol are not blamed on the drug. From the 1930s onward, alcoholism was constructed as a problem with the drinker not the drink.

Following years of campaigns to restrict drinking, or ban alcohol entirely, its widespread cultural acceptance supports continued treatment as a non-drug drug (Marquis, 2011). As a measuring stick or benchmark for the normalization process, which is arguably occurring for other types of drugs, its reputation is unrivaled. Alcohol remains the "drug of choice" in our society for the majority of people looking for a bit of fun.

Chapter Summary

Chapter 5 examined sociocultural dimensions of drug use in society, with particular attention to responses to the use of different kinds of drugs. The cultural ambivalence toward drugs was documented, with specific reference to the normalization thesis. As the most pervasive and accepted outlawed drug, social attitudes toward marijuana were examined, among other indicators of its status in society.

Notwithstanding evidence of broad accommodation, and support for using marijuana as a medicine, users still encounter disapproval and experience a stigma irrespective of the motives for their use. Although restrictions against using marijuana appear to be increasingly ambiguous and changing, informal and internal regulations continue to manifest in loss of social status and representation of the user as a threat.

Other illicit drugs that have been connected with a subgroup, and represent an associated threat, include LSD, or acid, and the club drug known as ecstasy. The research presented in this chapter reinforces the primary conclusion that societal reactions are based on factors other than drug properties, health risks, research evidence, or scientific facts. Responses to certain drugs are contingent on the social characteristics of the substance user or those of populations that are considered at risk of using the drug in question.

A far more detailed, and more nuanced, understanding of these issues is provided in a number of excellent case studies. Chapter 6 presents an overview of further contributions by Canadian researchers on how drug use is constructed as a marker of identity, group membership, and status.

Questions for Critical Thought

1. In your experience, is drug use becoming normalized in Canada? What is the evidence supporting and refuting this perspective?
2. What are the implications of the normalization thesis for public policies concerning use of drugs? Does it call for stricter, more permissive laws, or other strategies for regulating psychoactive substance use?
3. What are the connections between earlier drug panics and recent scares concerning use of club drugs among youth?

Suggested Readings

Dyck, E. 2012. *Psychedelic Psychiatry: LSD on the Canadian Prairies.* Winnipeg: University of Manitoba Press. This book is the tale of early research in Saskatchewan on the use of LSD for treating mental illness. It documents how growing societal concerns about the counterculture in the 1960s resulted in the criminalization of psychedelic drugs in Canada.

Grinspoon, L., and J.B. Bakalar. 1997. *Marihuana: The Forbidden Medicine.* New Haven: Yale University Press. This book documents the medical benefits of cannabis, and why its use has been forbidden. The authors argue marijuana should be legally available to all patients who need it.

Parker, H.J., J. Aldridge, and F. Measham. 1998. *Illegal Leisure: The Normalization of Adolescent Recreational Drug Use.* London: Routledge. This book introduces the normalization thesis, and documents the evidence informing its development.

Suggested Websites

Canadian Centre on Substance Abuse

www.ccsa.ca/Eng/topics/Monitoring-Trends/Canadian-Drug-Trends/Pages/default.aspx

This website offers summaries of information gathered through national monitoring of drug trends and their impact. Its aim is to support decision-making by producing statistics on drug prevalence in Canada that provide a basis for comparison with trends in other countries.

Health Canada

www.hc-sc.gc.ca/hc-ps/drugs-drogues/stat/index-eng.php

This website reports highlights from the *Canadian Alcohol and Drug Use Monitoring Survey (CADUMS),* conducted annually since 2008.

DanceSafe
www.dancesafe.org

This website provides current news and information about a wide variety of drugs used by youth. Its primary objective is promoting health and safety within the electronic music community.

The Psychedelic Library
www.psychedelic-library.org

This website provides access to an extensive library of literature on psychedelic drugs.

6 Drugs as Symbols

Learning Objectives

- To understand the role of drugs as symbols of conformity, identity, and resistance to convention.
- To distinguish between subcultural and lifestyle perspectives on the use of psychoactive drugs.
- To understand the role of the war on certain drugs in reinforcing boundaries that preserve the social order.

Introduction

What does drug use mean? From a constructionist perspective, the answer to that question depends on whom you ask. If drug use is indeed a social problem, as most law-abiding citizens would probably agree, finding solutions requires agreement about what kind of problems drug use might cause.

The use of drugs has historically been a moral problem. Intoxication on religious grounds or otherwise is widely viewed as irresponsible and indulgent. But calling substance users "bad" is far from satisfying, from an academic point of view. Because fewer people these days are religious, and the bad drugs are the ones that are against the law, it makes more sense to argue that substance users are a criminal problem.

Not all users are bad people—only those who use the drugs that are against the law. This helpful distinction has been challenged by the discovery that drug use is really a medical problem. Drug users—those who use the bad drugs or not-so-bad drugs to excess—are sick people. People who abuse drugs do not require condemnation or imprisonment, but rather treatment for addiction. The most effective form of treatment so far seems to be for the substance user to stop using (the bad) drugs. Viewed in this light, the answer to the question about the nature of the problem is perhaps not so complicated after all.

It is worth observing that, with very few exceptions, each and every one of us is a substance user. Some of us just happen to use drugs that are more likely to be met with punishment or social disapproval. Drug use is a symbol, a symptom, and a tool. Psychoactive substances are valuable commodities that convey meanings about lifestyle, group identity, and status. Drugs are used as symbols of conformity, rebellion, and the presence or absence of personal control. Drug use is a symptom of exploitation, alienation, and social dislocation in a globalizing world.

Drug use represents enslavement. Drug use represents escape. Drug use is a sign of freedom. Drug use is a coping mechanism.

To illustrate the different ways that drug use is constructed, Chapter 6 is focused on the significance of different types of drugs as indicated in Canadian research. In addition to drugs that have been normalized, this chapter looks at those that seem to be as stigmatized as ever, some even more so than they were in previous eras.

Although they occupy opposite ends of the legal spectrum, neither heroin nor tobacco has shown much indication toward normalization. Increasing regulation and restrictions on tobacco demonstrate increasing social disapproval. Usage rates are declining in most age groups due to stigma and concerns about the health effects of smoking. "Heroin chic," the emaciated drug-addicted look popularized in the fashion industry in the 1990s, has likewise not attracted much of a mainstream following. Whereas social fears predictably spike after high profile deaths, there has been little indication or concern that rates of heroin consumption are increasing among youth.

Despite different and fluctuating patterns of consumption among Canadians, and dramatic differences in how each is defined and labelled, these substances fulfill many similar objectives from the point of view of users, as the following case studies will show (Montigny, 2011). The first—a social history of tobacco use in Canada—sheds important light on transformation of its meaning as a marker of identity, rebellion and conformity, depending on the smoker and time period examined.

Cigarettes and Resistance To (and Through) Smoking

Drugs that are used by "respectable" people have not historically been construed as a threat. When the first anti-smoking campaigns were rolling out, in the later years of the nineteenth century, tobacco was still used by upstanding citizens. The movement against smoking had begun much earlier, in the 1890s, by Christian women as part of the larger **social gospel movement** (Rudy, 2011), which lasted until World War I (1914–18).

Contrary to the generally benign view of tobacco, smoking cigarettes was once linked to the deterioration of white Canadian values and a declining superiority over lesser peoples who lacked the constitution to resist such impure habits. Taking on the role of mothers to the nation, Christian campaigners sought to convince the country that smoking symbolized the physical and mental degeneration of young people and was a threat to nation-building.

Because smoking was a predominantly male habit, men were not receptive to the movement against smoking. Evidently they resented and resisted the intrusion. In the early twentieth century, long before the health risks of tobacco were well known, the medical profession was only just beginning to come to a consensus that smoking was potentially damaging to health. But whereas most physicians unequivocally supported efforts to prevent boys from smoking cigarettes, their concerns did not extend to smoking among men. Rather, as a symbol of maturity and manhood, moderate use of tobacco was considered acceptable. Smoking was a performance of control. The known addictive nature of the habit symbolized a risk to be conquered through displays of masculine achievement, self-discipline, and rationality.

In the social context of the early twentieth century, the anti-smoking movement represented an encroachment on traditional national values. The movement's failure to initiate significant reform can be partially explained by its inconsistency with dominant religious and secular perspectives on the proper function of the State and the role of the law.

To protect the nation, Christian women sought to mobilize support for their contention that the government was justified in assuming the traditional role of the parent. This meant cultivating habits that reflected certain values (even if those included preventing adults from smoking). Usurping the rights of the parent to govern their children's behaviour, however, was considered a breach of the boundaries between the role of private citizens and that of the State.

Moreover, the contentions of the social gospel movement also contradicted understanding of the roles entrusted to the Church. Most Protestants and Catholics held similar positions. Despite supporting age restrictions for tobacco use, the Church believed banning smoking altogether was a misguided, inappropriate means of intervention. It was generally agreed that, much like drinking alcohol, tobacco use was not a sin when enjoyed in moderation.

State interference in the moral formation of its citizens denied the Church its role in cultivating certain virtues and values in a nation of self-governing individuals. The existing constellation of interests and beliefs ultimately resulted in a compromise of sorts, which was more consistent with the dominant morality. In 1908 (the same year opium was criminalized), legislation was enacted that prohibited selling tobacco to children younger than 16 years of age.

For the anti-smoking movement, Rudy (2011) notes, the apparent victory was hollow and primarily symbolic. In practice, the modest intervention it achieved was deemed sufficiently intrusive to effectively derail momentum toward stricter regulations on tobacco. Its identity as a benign substance would not be seriously challenged by medical authorities for another half-century.

Despite the known (by then), though underestimated, health risks, after World War I smoking continued to be seen as a respectable, and even advantageous, lifestyle choice. Women in this era used tobacco to challenge conventions of male dominance and power. For middle-class, well-educated women, smoking cigarettes became associated with rebellion and ambition.

By flouting social norms that linked tobacco use to manhood, upwardly mobile and daring young women embraced smoking as a symbol of modern feminine identity and sense of community with like-minded women. Female smoking rates continued upward after that, approaching nearly half of Canadian women by the mid-1970s (Cook, 2011). Though steadily declining from the 1980s onward, recent surveys indicate that nearly one in four women in their early twenties continue to smoke (see Table 6.1).

As a dependable stimulant and appetite suppressant, smoking was attractive for many women (and young men) partially on account of the social pressure to stay thin. There are a wide variety of other explanations, though, ranging from addiction to rebellion to social influences, including mainstream and social media. The role of smoking as a visual performance, reflecting daring, confidence, and sophistication, is another factor explaining the attraction of tobacco use for middle-class women.

By the 1950s, disincentives had diminished to the point, notes Cook, that smoking had been normalized among women. This situation did not change much until the 1990s, and arguably continues to some degree today.

After World War II (1939–1945), an array of social factors contributed to normalizing smoking among women. Chief among these was involvement of more women in paid labour, and the reputation of tobacco as an effective facilitator of civility in social interaction. Whatever the social characteristics or motivations acting on the female smoker, estimated rates of use climbed sharply,

Table 6.1 Smoking Rates in Canada (N = 1,021), United States (N = 1,007), and Great Britain (N = 1,000), 2003*

Demographic	United States (%)	Canada (%)	Great Britain (%)
Total	**26**	**24**	**32**
Men	26	23	31
Women	26	25	33
Children in household	28	29	37
No children in household	25	22	30
Under 65 years of age	28	26	36
65 years of age and older	16	16	21

*Data reflect smoking status in the past week before the survey was administered.

Source: Retrieved from http://www.gallup.com/poll/10762/current-smoking-trends-us-canadabritain.aspx. Copyright © 2003 Gallup, Inc. All rights reserved. This graph is an interpretation of data compiled by Gallup, Inc. and the content is used with permission. However, Gallup, Inc. had no part in the creation of this graphic interpretation and retains all rights of republication.

from about 5 per cent of women before 1914 to one-third of women between World War I and World War II to nearly half of Canadian women by the 1970s.

The social meaning behind smoking in women is reflected in the non-random distribution of rates among region, ethnicity, language, and other demographic characteristics. Women smokers were particularly common in large cities, but prevalence varied between different social groups. Smoking rates in Montreal, for example, are reportedly much higher among French-speaking women. A poll conducted in the 1950s found that two-thirds of Francophone women smoked versus 28 per cent of English-speaking women.

In Canadian society, smoking was accepted as a symbol of maturity, sophistication, and modern values, which at the time were more important to young women than they were to men. Since the 1920s, by rejecting the authority of their parents, young women who smoked (and drank in mixed company) symbolized impurity and social degradation to an anxious older generation of adults.

As women from all segments of society took up smoking, it was normalized, first privately then publicly. Smoking cigarettes became increasingly regarded as an inexpensive lubricant for social interaction, and a convenient marker of identity for women. As a generally accepted rite of passage in society, smoking cigarettes (for half of the last century, at least) was an acknowledged emblem of modern thinking and behaviour.

Canadian women played an active role in normalizing smoking; social attitudes became accepting of the habit and it was encouraged through shrewd marketing campaigns. As the influence of media expanded, cultural icons such as Betty Davis made smoking fashionable and glamorous, and more of a mainstream female behaviour.

As the range of respectable smoking types broadened, female smokers could identify with one (or more) of several: the intellectual, the seductress, the girl next door, the sophisticate, the socialite, or the serious career women, to name a few. The increasing emphasis on good looks as a marker of sophistication and success made smoking a particularly useful prop for women to exploit in social situations. The association between cigarettes and "slim" was exploited likewise in cigarette manufacturers' marketing to women.

A sense of liberation mixed with danger is apparent in the normalization of smoking among women. It took a combination of both powerfully symbolic and practical dimensions to facilitate the process. Before women entered the workforce in large numbers, standards of feminine purity and respectability had disallowed a widespread adoption of the habit. Popular and educational literature continued to depict smoking as more dangerous for women than for men. At the same time, modern women were increasingly expected to behave differently than women from their mothers' generation.

Beginning with young educated women, then expanding across the social spectrum, the meaning of women smoking in public transformed.

Socially, the symbol of the cigarette shifted from rejection of earlier expectations of feminine behaviour to conformity to modern styles of living.

The role of smoking in the formation of identity has both common and diverging significance in the lives of men and women. Promoting cigarettes for weight control, and as a fashionable accessory, is far more evident in marketing to women than to men. The continuing popularity of smoking by young women, despite decreasing use rates in the general population, requires an understanding of its meaning in both practical and symbolic terms, which continually change over time.

As social stigma and restrictions against smoking have expanded—with the mass marketing of cigarettes increasingly replaced by regulations against smoking and public health campaigns—the meaning of the practice is transforming once again. De-normalizing smoking diminishes the range of respectable identities connected with the habit. Reversing the expansion of twentieth-century feminine identities by replacing the "smoking intellectual" and other valued types with derogatory images of the female smoker as trashy or trampy is increasing.

The normalization of smoking among women in the past resembles processes observed with that of marijuana use today. In young people, smoking marijuana has increasingly been theorized as a marker of identity, which is more fluid or adaptable than previously assumed (Box 6.1).

Box 6.1

Marijuana and Identity: A Case Study

Recent studies indicate that attitudes of youth (from early teens to young adults) toward marijuana use have shifted from being mostly negative and skeptical to positive and accepting. This is not to say that use is normal in the sense that everybody uses, but rather normal in the sense that it is increasingly regarded as legitimate behaviour, by both users and non-users.

To better understand the role that marijuana use plays in the identities of emerging young adults, one study conducted interviews with undergraduate students at the University of Guelph. The normalizing process among students was supported by what might be described as a "fluid" view of self. From this perspective, it appears that the identities of "user" and "non-user" are not fixed, but are more contingent on the circumstances in which drug use occurs. Stigmatizing labels are reserved for those "abusing" it, as opposed to the more typical marijuana user who uses drugs responsibly with no adverse effects.

Students' recollections of how they started using were generally consistent with perceptions of non-users: using marijuana is considered normal by most of the young people that they know. Those who did not use it said they wanted to convey an image that is different from other mainstream youth. This suggests that abstinence is the new form of rebellion, as using marijuana is increasingly the norm.

Indeed, while abstinence apparently required more conscious effort, the choice to use appeared to be the default option for many. Marijuana use is infused with a wide variety of meanings—it is either mundane or commonplace or intimately connected to a sense of independence. The majority of users said attending university, another threshold into adulthood, provided opportunities for using marijuana, regardless of whether they used previously or not.

The greater freedom they reported was commonly attributed to the sense of anonymity that the university setting afforded. Marijuana use allowed some students to blend into the environment. For others, it was more of an expression of identity, defining them in ways they were not able to before.

The prevalence of marijuana use by young adults, and the converging attitudes of users and non-users, means we can no longer speak of users as belonging to an identifiable deviant subculture. Rather, use communicates a style that is more accurately described as conventionally unconventional. Indeed, the very notion of a user, or a non-user, has different connotations in this normalizing context.

In today's postmodern world, youths' attitudes, opinions, and use of leisure time are shaped in different ways than in preceding generations. The process of becoming an adult is fundamentally different for contemporary youth. The stages between childhood, adolescence, and adulthood are more complex and longer than before. These theorized changes in the journey to adulthood are reshaping the nature of leisure and pleasure in a way that is specific to the here and now.

Among other implications of a changing workforce and associated changes in the school-to-work transition, youth today have more time to participate in leisure activities and shape their identities through leisure-time consumption. As leisure is commoditized, the use of certain substances (like fashion) is becoming another symbol of consumption that conveys particular meanings about identity and status.

This perspective on drug use shares much with Erving Goffman's early observations on the nature of the self (1969). As opposed to an essential self, which is singular and fixed, Goffman argued that a person is made up of multiple, loosely connected selves. The social world, for Goffman, was quite literally a stage. Unlike at the theatre, though, there is not one mask to hide behind but rather a repertoire of masks to suit the social setting and the role that one must play in that environment.

Goffman's situated self is neither manipulative nor honest. It is not imaginary or real. Rather, it is fluid. Engaging theoretically with Goffman's situated understanding of the self facilitates a more nuanced understanding of the normalization process with respect to cannabis and other substance use.

Source: Mostaghim and Hathaway (2013).

The normalizing trends observed suggest the transformation of marijuana from a symbol of subcultural resistance to one of lifestyle or identity, with different social meanings. Before examining the nature of this process, the next section takes a closer look at functions of subcultures for drug users who use more heavily addicting and strongly stigmatized "hard drugs."

The Heroin Subculture

The formation of subcultures around drug use ordinarily refers to the rejection or defiance of conventions through the use of substances that have been prohibited. Construction of drug use as a subcultural activity did not proliferate in Canada until after World War II. The existence of subcultures reinforces certain boundaries by which the members of the subgroup are depicted as a threat. But belonging to the subgroup, from the standpoint of drug users, is about developing connections and being part of a community of people devalued by society.

Before the counterculture of the 1960s, during which resistance to conformity became in itself a sign of conformity, illicit drug use was uncommon and represented a more significant transgression of existing social norms. Use of injection drugs such as heroin has long been regarded as a serious breech of our antidrug laws. In the postwar period, before the psychedelic era invited other substances into the drug subculture, injecting heroin became the ultimate symbol of defiance and resistance to Canadian societal norms.

Unlike the young drug users who emerged two decades later, espousing more articulated nonconformist values, heroin users were predominantly working class and poor. Their social background and experience differed vastly from the image of burgeoning prosperity, and middle class conformity in Canadian society after World War II. Carstairs (2006) notes that "hypes," as these users were known (because they identified with the hypodermic needles they were sticking into their veins), defied conventional depictions of the socially dysfunctional and isolated addict.

More than simply an escape from desperation and despair, or else a hedonistic impulse to get "high," heroin use was more about identity and bonding than popular portrayals of the habit have presumed. While acknowledging the suffering and problems faced by addicts, Carstairs' research shows that using drugs is functional for users.

Illicit-substance use is central to forming an identity that represents resistance to oppressive governing structures. It refutes the power of State authorities and others who seek to diminish one's self-esteem and social status. Put otherwise, the drug provides the addict with the means, or sense of agency, by which to facilitate resistance through reappropriation of the act and its connotations.

The use of heroin in Canada in the postwar period was restricted to quite a distinctive subgroup of predominantly white, working class young people with few opportunities for upward mobility. This small and homogenous subculture, which consisted of a few thousand steady users in Vancouver and Toronto, represented but a fraction of an estimated 100,000 injection drug users across Canada today. This "dramatic rise" is less dramatic in the context of rapid urban growth and immigration, and a national population, which has tripled since the end of World War II (see also Table 6.2).

Regardless of its prevalence, intense surveillance and harsh punishment make the use of heroin a risky undertaking. Before the 1960s, when drug users' characteristics began to span the spectrum of Canadian society, there was less diversity within this population. Drug users tended to associate, live with, and marry others who participated in the use of drugs. Substance use was more visibly connected to people from abusive backgrounds leading very troubled lives.

Marginalized young people not only found escape and pleasure using heroin. They also found a sense of fellowship and community—belonging—through association with other users. Beyond the numbing qualities, which gave its users solace, using heroin "successfully" required specific knowledge. Those in possession of it acquired a level of prestige or elevated social status. Because of its scarcity and illicit reputation, not just any "square" could locate and purchase heroin. One had to be a trusted insider to learn where and how to buy the drug, prepare it, and inject it.

Table 6.2 Estimated Number and Prevalence of People Who Inject Drugs among the General Population Aged 15–64, 2011

	Injecting Drug Users					
	Estimated Number			Prevalence (%)		
REGION	**High**	**Low**	**Best**	**High**	**Low**	**Best**
Africa	304,925	997,574	6,608,038	0.05	0.17	1.12
America	2,908,787	3,427,561	4,019,041	0.47	0.55	0.64
North America	1,935,144	2,006,470	2,101,572	0.63	0.65	0.68
Latin America and the Caribbean	973,643	1,421,091	1,917,468	0.31	0.45	0.61
Asia	4,328,212	5,692,005	7,031,647	0.16	0.20	0.25
Central Asia and Transcaucasia	659,582	699,191	758,421	1.25	1.33	1.44
East and Southeast Asia	2,959,863	3,786,472	4,677,484	0.19	0.25	0.30
Near and Middle East/ Southwest Asia	462,269	952,948	1,334,013	0.17	0.36	0.50
South Asia	246,498	253,394	261,729	0.03	0.03	0.03
Europe	3,553,859	3,777,948	4,156,492	0.64	0.68	0.75
East/Southeast Europe	2,821,599	2,907,484	2,987,155	1.23	1.26	1.30
Western/Central Europe	732,260	870,464	1,169,337	0.23	0.27	0.36
Oceania	118,628	128,005	158,919	0.49	0.53	0.66

Source: United Nations Office on Drugs and Crime (2014).

Specifically, the user had to be able to avoid police detection and had to develop a technique for using heroin that works. Regular use of the drug required safe injection. The majority of users "mainlined" heroin, injecting directly into the vein. Preparing the syringe and proper dosage was a complex and ritualistic process, which needed to be learned. Possessing special skills and knowledge was an important source of status, or subcultural prestige, within the heroin-using group.

While simple curiosity and the promise of excitement was a common motivating factor for beginners, users were attracted to and continued to identify strongly with feelings of belonging. Using heroin was a criminalized behaviour that aligned with the fiercely rebellious attitudes of the criminal subclass. Those in this subgroup of society typically had lengthy criminal careers and social disadvantages, offering little hope of gaining respect through legitimate routes.

Feeling misunderstood and persecuted by society is a powerful incentive for seeking solace in a community of like-minded people with the same problems and same values. On the downside, drug addiction is far from a solution to the serious personal and structural problems that makes using narcotics attractive to some people. Because heroin addiction is a burdensome affliction, most users eventually get fed up with the lifestyle. Whereas many succeed in kicking the habit, others find it hard to leave the world of drugs behind.

The difficulty in quitting is as much about withdrawal from the sense of group belonging and the identity provided by the heroin subculture as it is about the physical addiction to a powerful narcotic (Cairstairs, 2006). Participation in the drug subculture is a source of daily interaction, community, and status. The nature and extent of this connection with the subgroup is theoretically contingent on societal reactions, and the corresponding need for subcultural support.

The next section takes a closer look at the transformation of the social meaning of drug use within the theorized context of a normalizing trend. As we have seen, there are important limitations to normalization and the extent of the implied social tolerance of drugs. There is a need for caution and particular attention to qualitative research on experiences of users. Marijuana use (again) is the exemplar in this area. Changing attitudes support exploring concepts that make sense of drug use patterns inconsistent with subcultural explanations.

Drug Subcultures and Contemporary Lifestyles

The use of marijuana has undergone a transition from what was once a largely marginalized activity to one that is more generally established in society. In fact, drug use that previously existed within deviant subcultures has become more prevalent and widely tolerated in general. In this process, we have noted, there are signs of convergence between the way users see themselves as ordinary people and how they are identified by others.

Social attitudes toward drugs and the people who consume them are no longer simply positive or negative, but rather contingent on the context in which the drug is used. Investigating circumstances is more informative than trying to identify users as belonging to a "type." Recall that Becker (1963) first explained the nature of the learning process by which societal controls are overcome through interaction and participation in a deviant subculture.

Through participation with more experienced users, drug use becomes more normal and less problematic. Novice users learn where and how to buy drugs, and how to use them, and find the experience pleasurable. Fear of criticism and rejection by non-users diminishes as users gain assurance that they control their drug use rather than it controlling them. There is a corresponding reduction in the influence of controls based on morality and stigma against drugs.

As the use of marijuana has entered mainstream culture, formal (and informal) sources of control are becoming less efficient. The increasing prevalence of use facilitates greater ease of access, through more casual involvement with illicit sources of supply. Distribution is accomplished through extended friendship networks, rather than street dealers or large-scale drug suppliers. By participating in these networks, many users appear able to maintain a sense of distance from the "criminal element." The inefficiency of drug laws in restricting drug supply is demonstrated by reports of their small relevance to users.

The biggest problem with the law, for many marijuana users, is the implication that marijuana use is wrong. Cultural attitudes have changed to the extent that use occurs in settings less clandestine, or anxiety provoking compared with 50 years ago, when Becker's book *Outsiders* (1963) first examined the subculture of marijuana use. The social differences between users and non-users appear to have diminished to the point that many people are relatively open about using marijuana (Box 6.2).

The social practices and experiences relating to drug use are transforming with increasing tolerance of use of certain drugs. In this context, substance use behaviour reflects different lifestyles and associated meanings of drug use. The experience of deviant behaviour is restructured to reflect diversity and practical concerns. These behaviours and concerns reflect the "here and now" of individual lifestyles, as opposed to those of the subgroup.

Participation in drug subcultures provides the needed setting and ideological support for users to develop a positive outlook toward using drugs (Becker, 1967). However, as the setting becomes less problematic, so does the need for group involvement and ideological support. Illicit drug

Box 6.2 Article Published in the *Guelph Mercury* on 21 April 2010, Highlights Marijuana "Holiday"

Hundreds gather at U of G to celebrate pot smokers' holiday

Armed with bongs, plastic bags of weed, pipes and hookahs, thousands packed the lawn of Johnston Green at the University of Guelph Tuesday to celebrate the annual pot smoker's holiday.

Known as 4/20, the celebration brought together several hundred university students.

They brought tents, blankets, lawn chairs and made themselves comfortable in the sunny afternoon as they smoked. Some students sold cookies and cake to the crowd with proceeds going to the Guelph-Wellington Women in Crisis.

A live band played rock and reggae music. The smell of marijuana wafted through the crowds. Some students wore their hair in dreadlocks, covered by brightly-coloured knitted hats. Groups of people passed around pipes or joints.

"There is a lot of unity here," said 21-year-old Frank Gillespie, carrying a nearly five-foot bong through the crowd.

He said the novelty of the bong allows him to meet other people. He allowed at least 15 people to use it.

There seems to be some debate over just how the 4/20 celebration originated, but urban and internet legend has it starting with a group of teenagers at San Rafael High School in San Rafael, Calif., in 1971. The story goes that they used to meet at 4:20 p.m. to smoke pot because 4:20 was when they finished their school detentions.

For 21-year-old Brad Manning, 4/20 is mostly about togetherness.

"It is about being with people that you like surrounding yourself with," he said folding up a plastic bag of weed. "Every single student is out here for the same reason."

It's not all about getting high, Manning said. He called over to a couple of his friends who hadn't smoked anything at all but decided to attend the event.

He said he had smoked a bowl with his friend, who had just spent a year in Africa.

First year student Mitch Speechley stood in a circle with his friends passing around a joint.

"I have never been here before," he said. "I have always heard about it and it exceeded its expectations."

Ron Howard, 20, sat in the midst of a circle of lawn chairs that surrounded a hookah. The water pipe, originally from India, was being used by the group to smoke flavoured tobacco.

His friend held one end of the pipe to his mouth. He pulled his mouth away and let a puff of smoke escape.

"It's a good community thing," Howard said about the event.

Source: Dharmarajah, T (2010, April 21). Reprinted with permission. © Guelph Mercury, Ont. Canada

use becomes meaningful in ways that are more personal. The idea of lifestyle is important for explaining substance use behaviour and associated meanings, which diverge from those observed within a deviant subculture (Hathaway, 1997).

Marijuana users still gain access to the drug, and develop the outlook needed for use to continue through participation with more experienced users. Over time, however, use becomes more independent. Initial motives and use patterns of the subgroup are replaced by personal considerations more characteristic of a lifestyle. Better understanding of marijuana use requires a better understanding of the way it is explained as an integrated aspect of everyday behaviour.

Users fully recognize that marijuana is illegal, and that using it is not acceptable to everyone. Concealing it from various authorities and non-users (at least known or believed to disapprove), marijuana use is rather routinely integrated into the daily lives of ordinary people. This transition from subculture to contemporary lifestyles indicates a weakening of influence exerted by conventional morality as a method of control.

Contemporary culture comprises an array of distinctive lifestyles and consumption habits. People are able to construct and reconstruct identity to suit themselves and groups to which they feel that they belong. Individual choices are reflected in the daily practices and strategies for living that express a person's sense of self, social identity, and status (Beck, 1992; Foucault, 1988). Identities are constantly remade through a reflexive process. This involves both making choices and performing social roles that contribute to construction of a particular lifestyle and a certain narrative of self.

Similarly does substance use behaviour reflect myriad elements from the mainstream culture and drug subcultures, as well as individual aspects of identity formation (Golub et al., 2005). The choice to use a drug is both constrained and shaped by forces reflecting social boundaries and daily circumstances. This process is inseparable from structural conditions that foster shared identities and practices or lifestyles.

Illicit-substance use is therefore increasingly conceptualized as a situated choice or structured action that conveys meaning about identity, group membership, and status (Measham, 2002; Measham and Shiner, 2009). Marijuana use no longer designates a subgroup with a distinct ideology or pattern of behaviour (Hammersley, 2005; Hathaway, 1997). It is but one aspect of a person's daily life. In a context of increasing social tolerance, such drug use need not necessarily become one's master status. As the deviant identity becomes less all-consuming, using drugs is viewed more as a **practice of the self** (Duff, 2004; Lupton and Tulloch, 2002).

Many recreational drug users' drug use patterns remain social, or dependent on involvement with the substance-using group. Others develop more routinely personal use patterns, calling for more attention to the ways drug use becomes integrated into users' daily lives. Moving away from a group-dependent pattern of consumption to one reflecting features of an individual lifestyle marks a crucial shift in the experience of using, and one's identity or status in relation to the drug.

The social outlook of today's marijuana user does not imply rejection of conventional society. Many users still identify with nonconformist values. However, the societal diffusion of the practice makes it more significant for people as a personal practice of the self. Use of the drug, in other words, appears to have a rather vague affiliation with a deviant subculture.

By the late 1960s, marijuana use already was taking place in social groups that previously had no contact with illicit drugs or other criminal behaviour. The ideological and social characteristics of contemporary users are increasingly diverse. This makes them much less different from non-users than previous theories about substance use have suggested.

Because people from all walks of life use marijuana, users and non-users are increasingly uncertain about what characteristics typify a user of the drug. Its symbolic value is ambiguous, no longer suggesting a clear sense of ideological cohesion. The drug's connection to particular ideals has been replaced by an understanding among users of its function as a strategy, or practical tool, for conventional living.

Identification with a marijuana-using group is often required to overcome earlier ambivalence to try it. But for many users this is only a transitional phase in the development of patterns of consumption. Use in social settings is still common. However, personal satisfaction with marijuana use is stronger in the context of use patterns that do not depend on groups.

Developing a positive relationship with marijuana often means establishing more personal use patterns following less satisfying, group-dependent use (Hathaway, 1997). A more positive experience with the drug for some users followed periods of abstinence and an eventual transition to using marijuana independently of others.

Despite the stigma that remains around marijuana use, research shows that regular use patterns are sustainable. Most users are not seriously morally or otherwise conflicted, and anticipate few changes in their use of marijuana as their adult responsibilities increase. This is an indication of successful navigation of reported role conflict. Continued marijuana use is enabled when users continue to observe the rules and boundaries needed to fulfill expected roles.

Establishing a personal pattern of consumption means adapting it to changing roles and needs. Conflicts seldom arise, as one learns to avoid them. Although marijuana use may become more moderate, and even circumscribed, ceasing (or reducing) use is not a necessary outcome of assuming family roles. In fact, family obligations serve to delineate the boundaries of a well-established pattern of controlled, recreational use. Having a non-using spouse, children at home, or a regular nine-to-five job imposes some restrictions, which shape consumption patterns, but do not necessitate abstaining from all use.

Exploring patterns of consumption, which reflect life transitions and boundaries observed by many marijuana users, demonstrates how the meaning of the practice is much different than what it used to be 50 years ago. Developing a better understanding of use motives and lifestyles of contemporary users is essential for informing theoretical explanations that accurately reflect circumstances of drug use.

Manderson (1995) observes that the construction of drug use as a social problem is a product of contested symbols that conceal its real motives and meanings. The symbolism and imagery of drugs reinforce the boundaries between users and society by fetishizing objects that are linked with substance use. As we shall see, however, obsessing over images or symbols has resulted in the very kinds of problems that drug legislation is intended to resolve.

Clashing Symbols

Like any war, notes Manderson (1995), the war on drugs is really an exercise of power. It is maintained through the ongoing disputes between claims-makers over contested cultural symbols. Symbolism around drug use is fraught with ambiguity, which may explain hostile reactions to the use of certain drugs. This response owes less to rationality or reason than the symbolic meaning of the imagery that drives it; that is, what the use of those drugs has come to represent.

Fixation on illicit drugs as symbols leads to an obsession with addiction—and an equally obsessive, grossly disproportionate societal response. The deviance attributed to the substance user is reinforced through imagery that characterizes drugs, and the people who use them, as social pollutants.

Depictions of the opium den, more than a century ago, evoked a sense of filth, revulsion, corruption, and contagion. The drug's association with the unfamiliar odours and exotic habits of distrusted Chinese immigrants suggested a violation of established moral boundaries. Images of the opium pipe, hypodermic needle, and other paraphernalia or objects used for drug use have long been seen as symbols of societal transgression.

The power of imagery to provoke anxiety is greatest when objects transcend existing social boundaries so that the acts with which they are associated suddenly become ambiguous rather than secure. For example, the appropriation of the hypodermic needle, traditionally used in health care, by addicts in order to use illegal substances and maintain "dangerous" habits is seriously repugnant in the view of most Canadians. Another serious transgression of such boundaries is the misuse of household products like solvents, gasoline, and glue. The misappropriation of prescription medications is also an example (albeit evoking less horror). Even getting high on spray-paint fumes by young people suggests a sense of desperation and unpleasantness that rivals, or goes beyond, anxieties about illicit drugs. This is likely because, unlike heroin, these products are safe, familiar, and easy to access by youth and even children with no previous connection to, or experience with, using drugs.

Corruption of the proper purposes of these objects is threatening, says Manderson, because it undermines the certainty of the functions that they serve. Our sense of boundary violation and revulsion is enhanced by the ease by which the natural function is subverted, along with the assumptions that bring order to the world.

Images of objects employed by substance users represent not only violation but also rejection of the social boundaries that designate outsiders. Objects used in rituals of drug use serve as symbols of deviant identity, community, or strangeness, depending on one's social orientation to these boundaries. As symbols of the strange, unfamiliar rituals of others, these objects alienate us, inciting fear and opposition. And as participants in rituals that are strange and unfamiliar, those in possession of the alienating objects are excluded from the mainstream. Drug rituals also make use of language that, like objects, reinforces the social boundaries established between users and non-users. Highlighting the vocabulary, or argot, of drug users brings attention to differences, creating social distance between the subgroup and the mainstream.

Media reports on drug policing, for example, often draw attention to illicit paraphernalia and the peculiarity of language used by users. The strange vocabulary inherent in the drug scene has evident shock value, and has been used as a wake-up call for parents. This has been a strategy employed in recent governmental antidrug campaigns in Canada.

"Your kids are starting to learn a new language" was the message of prominent print media and television advertisement. As shown in Figure 6.1, school-aged children are depicted using street names for illicit drugs like ecstasy ("love drug"), cocaine ("powder"), and methamphetamine ("jib").

Despite some evidence that media representation of drug issues is becoming more balanced and realistic (Hathaway and Erickson, 2004), the imagery around illicit substance use has not changed significantly since the early twentieth century. The use of alien vocabulary by children reinforces images of drug use as a threat to our communities, and indeed the future of Canadian society.

The language of drug users, much like the objects of drug use, is a potent symbol of the distance and boundaries constructed between society and the drug user. Focusing on differences removes any obligation to understand the

Figure 6.1 Antidrug Campaign

Source: http://www.nationalantidrugstrategy.gc.ca/prevention/parents/print-imprimer.html © All Rights Reserved. National Anti-Drug Strategy. Health Canada 2014. Reproduced with permission from the Minister of Health, 2015.

motives of drug users; any similarities are overlooked. It is enough to simply be addicted to drugs; the reasons for addiction are easy to ignore. Failure to attend to circumstances of addiction contributes to mistreatment of drug users, and the prominence of myth making and hysteria surrounding use of drugs.

The past century of drug control in Canada gives ample illustration of the staying power of imagery depicting the degeneracy of addicts and contagion brought by drugs. The intense hostility to the use of certain drugs is an indication of their potency as symbols, which are both ambiguous and always in contention.

Injecting heroin, notes Manderson, exemplifies the role of rituals and objects in constructing a habit with distinctive connotations, which depend on one's relationship with the drug. The sense of alienation and revulsion felt by others make the practice a potent signifier of users' social distance and differences, and their commitment to the subgroup.

Injection, from the standpoint of the heroin subculture, is a rite of passage into a community that views it as the hardest way to do the hardest drug. The social hierarchy observed within the needle culture recognizes varying levels of achievement. Self-injection directly into veins, as opposed to less efficient "skin popping" (injecting into flesh), is the highest-valued indicator of success.

The nature of the identity constructed through this process is shaped by the subgroup's understanding of what the use of heroin really represents. The conventional meaning of the needle—a marker of infection, disease, despair and death—is reinterpreted in ways that invest the use of heroin with the connotations of a sexual experience. From the act of penetration of the needle in the vein, to the near orgasmic sensation of "the rush," the use of sexual metaphors is central to the heroin user's understanding of the drug experience. Most notably, like intercourse, the act of drug injection is invested with a dual sense of pleasure mixed with danger. The sense of violation is horrifying and compelling, a contradiction that may explain the heroin needle's symbolic power.

Among other implications, seeking better understanding of the symbolic meaning of injecting for heroin users can inform development of services that better address important public health concerns. The safe (or unsafe) sex analogy for sharing needles, as an example, has become engrained in public consciousness, ever since the AIDS epidemic formed connections between deviant sexual activity, substance use, disease, and death.

Needle sharing represents both practical and deeply symbolic cultural practices for those who are involved. Risky drug behaviour is a product of scarcity (of clean needles, skill, and safe places to shoot drugs) and factors connected to the values of the subgroup and society. For example, the provision of clean needles, and supervised injection facilities (like InSite in the city of Vancouver) play a documented role in meeting public health objectives. These kinds of services, however, do not significantly alter communal understanding of particular subcultural practices and meanings enacted among users.

Needle sharing and submitting to the needle of another—that is, being injected by somebody else—are not uncommon aspects of the initiation process. The injecting experience is characterized by expectations that reflect cultural assumptions about gender, among other distinctions such as class, age, and race. Female users have historically taken on a passive or submissive role in yielding to the needle. Women rarely injected narcotics alone, and were much more likely than (heterosexual) men to be "shot up" with heroin by somebody else.

For couples that use heroin together ("running partners"), the sex metaphor is found to be particularly fitting. Running partners develop a shared rhythm: this experience includes the physical experience in getting high together, then suffering through withdrawal, then longing to score and experience the rush again. Often replacing the desire for sexual activity, taking heroin together becomes a substitute for sex and an emotional tie unconnected to drug use.

Where there is exclusion, heroin users find community. For Manderson, the key point is that both sides—users and non-users—appear to be obsessed with images and objects of illicit substance use. Drug use represents a deviation from the values attached to rationality and order in our culture. The integrity and primacy of reason are devalued by drugs' association with surrendering control. Altered or ecstatic states of consciousness evoke images that are both appalling and compelling, repulsive and alluring, rejected and inviting, among other contradictions. The fixation of the law on certain drugs is matched by addicts' fixation or obsession with the drugs of their desire. The intensity of feeling about the use of drugs is a reflection of deeply rooted cultural uncertainties and anxieties concerning the meaning of the act. Drug use blurs the lines between irrationality and reason. Drugs are metaphors for social fears that fix our focus on objects of revulsion and attraction, rather than the motivations of the addict. Substances as symbols become the demons, rather than their influence on users—the possessed.

Drug laws reflect the same obsession displayed by the drug addict. The underlying desires (and social problems) of the user are neglected by treating symbols (and symptoms) as if these were the problem. As a result, the object assumes a level of significance that is disproportionate to the cultural anxieties and desires that it now represents. The outlooks of the law-maker and the drug addict are problematic in the way they fetishize the use of certain drugs. The fetishist fixates upon an object of desire. Similarly, the addict is fixated on the drug as if it were the only path to finding the kind of transformation or transcendence generally sought by people who use drugs.

Drugs also symbolize a loss of self-control within our culture; fear of addiction is analogous to possession by a demon. Drug laws treat the substance as if it were responsible. By fixating on the substance as the object of addiction, drug laws actually create the very kinds of risk behaviours that they are intended to prevent. By ignoring addicts' problems and focusing on the addiction rather than the motivation behind it, drug laws create the deviant identity adopted by drug users and inspire the revulsion that society directs at drug users. By treating drugs as if they are to blame, law-makers neglect the reality of problems such as poverty, alienation, and physical and emotional abuse that are not caused by drug use, but that rather lead to drug use.

Manderson's (1995) important work sheds light on how the imagery employed in waging war on drugs contributes to the very problems that drug laws are intended to resolve. The war on drugs is only failing if we assume its aim is to eradicate the use of certain drugs. Banning drugs has been remarkably successful as a strategy for turning drugs into symbols that reinforce the predominant values of established social order. The final section draws on Manderson's examination of the role of drugs as symbols of "possession." This discussion further illuminates the function of maintaining harmful antidrug laws.

The Crime of Drug Possession

Criminal law is established on two principles. It is designed to punish acts deemed both intentional and wrongful. There is no crime, in principle, without both of these elements. The crime of drug possession is anomalous, notes Manderson (2005), in that no such action is required. Because knowing the drug exists is enough to warrant punishment, the act and the intent are relatively passive compared with those of other types of crimes. Most laws against drug possession put the onus on the accused to establish his or her innocence, rather than the court to prove wrongful action and intent. Proximity to outlawed drugs is presumed to be a crime. The object contaminates the person, not vice versa, which is not ordinarily the case. Therefore, the crime of drug possession is the crime of being possessed.

The relationship between drugs and the person, as defined by the law, contradicts the standard interpretation of possession. Objects, unlike people, do not have purpose. Possessions are passive or, in other words, entirely subject to the ends of individuals. But the crime of drug possession requires proximity, not action; its objective is to punish an intention without an act.

Although they are analogous to gun control, there are important differences that make antidrug laws quite distinctive. Whereas the licensing of guns allows for their possession by properly certified (trustworthy) citizens, there is no such allowance for the use of outlawed drugs. The mandate of drug laws is to prevent use altogether.

The difference between gun and drug laws, argues Manderson, has to do with fears about contamination, which are found in most depictions of drug use. Somehow drugs (unlike guns, for most people) inspire powerlessness, and simply having them is proof enough of wrongful intent.

The very existence of drugs makes us fearful, quite apart from their use or misuse. Manderson has traced this disproportionate fixation on drugs to changing perceptions of the early twentieth century. At that time, in many countries of the world, drug use became quite rapidly redefined as criminal. It was no longer simply shameful, unremarkable, or otherwise accepted by society. With this radical shift in our outlook toward them, the crime of possession has come to define drugs. Substances that can be legally possessed are not often considered "drugs" at all in the colloquial sense. Legal drugs are more often represented as either medicines or regular products for consumption.

In Australia, notes Manderson (2005), like Canada and elsewhere, the first antidrug laws—upon which the current global prohibition has been built—targeted opium smoking. Though it was likely no more harmful than the opium consumed in patented medicine concoctions (which remained widely available), the ban on smoking opium seemed a justified intrusion into the affairs of the distrusted Chinese immigrants.

The connection between foreigners and drug use served a purpose that banning immigrants explicitly would not. Dramatizing the connection between opium and immigrants, by outlawing the former in order to alienate the latter, enabled representation of a national identity that was morally superior to that of foreign "others."

The association between opium and sex, and interracial fraternization, made the drug a useful scapegoat in an era of anxiety over national identity. Sex and drugs became the means by which contamination and loss of national identity were taking place. Young white women epitomized the innocence and purity of the "host" society, and fears of miscegenation were countered by taking the onus off the women (who were always "seduced" by members of the racial other, rather than conscious participants in their own actions) and shifting blame to opium itself. By doing so, society was relieved of taking responsibility for so-called problems with the existing social order. Manderson cites the hysteria around drugs as analogous to other historical examples of anxieties derived from threats to the established order, such as the documented witch-hunt craze in seventeenth-century Salem (Box 6.3).

Box 6.3

Fear of Possession in Seventeenth-Century Salem

Much like unease about drug use in the recent modern era, fear of witchcraft was a product of its time. Although the victims of this hysteria and subsequent punishment were women, the general assumption was that the Devil rather than women or society was to blame. The culture of witchcraft threatened the authority of patriarchy generally and the Church specifically. The notion of "possession," in this world view, served a function not unlike more recent constructions of "addiction." By practising witchcraft, women were succumbing to the devil, who, like the drug pusher today, was so seductive that the possessed were at his mercy without a will of their own.

The treatment of addiction as a medical disorder (not unlike religious notions of possession) provides an explanation for a wide range of behaviour seen as deviating from the norm. Because the drug (or the devil) made him do it, the drug addict is not deemed responsible and neither is society. The blame is squarely on the drug itself, not on the substance user. The object of addiction is the demon to be exorcised.

Possession of drugs, like possession of witches, gives tangible proof of an "evil" that could not otherwise be proven, and punished justifiably. Much like the role of witches, that of drugs is to provide proof of the alarming degradation all around us. To thwart them, moral certitude and vigilance is needed. The crime of drug possession is the crime of being possessed.

Source: Manderson (2005).

Drug possession projects, and justifies, fear and anxieties over maintenance of the social order. Drug laws function to alleviate a crisis of identity, whether it be racialized, or otherwise expressed in terms of human reason, autonomy, or purity. If drugs lead to a loss of agency, drug laws inspire confidence in our ability to exercise and retain our individual freedom. Negative depictions of addicts reassure us of their otherness as well as the superiority of our own behaviour. Contemporary drug laws thereby function to preserve a sense of agency and human will in a world that is increasingly disenchanted with ideals of rationality and freedom.

Because drug laws indisputably make drug problems worse, the function of the law is evidently more symbolic. For Manderson, outlawing drugs is not about destroying drugs, but rather dramatizing anxieties. Enforcing drug laws provides a stage on which the drama can occur.

Making a substance illegal turns it into a symbol. The mythology surrounding drugs amplifies what it may be like to lose one's human freedom, identity, and values. The problem of addiction is substantiated when a drug addict is found in possession of drugs. The hysteria of antidrug discourses is derived from their primary function: to defend human agency from an objectified tangible threat. The dramatization of anxieties that drug use represents provides an explanation for hostilities reflected in societal responses to the use of certain drugs.

These observations shed light on current opposition to harm reduction–oriented policies and programs. Seeking to improve the health and functionality of users is fundamentally misguided from an antidrug perspective, which is more concerned with saving souls than promoting better health. Whereas harm reductionists are relativists, believing that harm from substance use depends on circumstances, the predominant perspective is entirely absolutist in suggesting drugs are bad under any circumstances.

The success of harm reduction, argues Manderson, has only intensified anxiety. It is seen as undermining the function of addiction as a marker of the other. Drugs are to be feared because they represent a loss of agency, which threatens cultural values that cherish personal autonomy. Drug use is a contagion that is to be blamed for undermining a sense of order based on freedom and responsibility.

Harm reduction represents surrender, an admission that the war on drugs cannot be won. Drug policy reform, from this perspective, suggests weakness or a retreat from the good fight against the scourge of substance use. The war on drugs, for Manderson, much like the war on witchcraft, insists on the reality of absolutes (good versus evil). There can be no compromise, no **moral relativism**, in the exercise of righteous law.

The resilience and resurgence of **tough on drugs** discourses demonstrates their power as symbols of disorder and contagion. Prohibition reinforces social rules by the enforcement of respect for the distinctions between good drugs and bad drugs. Rather than eradicating drugs altogether, laws prohibiting their use merely dramatize fears. In this context of societal anxiety about drugs, pragmatic policy initiatives like harm reduction suggest surrender to uncertainty, permissiveness, disorder—a world in which boundaries are no longer observed.

Chapter Summary

This chapter asked the question, what does drug use symbolize? We have noted that the significance of drug use varies widely depending on the user, the context, and the drug. Before its status as a public health pariah, cigarettes represented a threat to youth and a marker of conformity to modern living conventions. For women, smoking served a function similar to that observed in subcultures around illicit drugs: namely, defiance of convention and the creation of a niche. The legal status of the drug does not always determine the most important element of what its use represents.

Heroin users also find community and meaning in their perceived mistreatment and exclusion from society. The more stigmatized the substance, the more powerfully it symbolizes commitment to a particular identity, as a result of one's connection to the marginalized, substance-using group. The normalizing trends observed for other drugs like cannabis (not unlike tobacco use by women decades earlier) requires research more attentive to identities and lifestyles than substance use behaviour of a deviant subgroup.

Understanding the hostility to drug use in society requires an understanding of its meaning as a symbol. The objective of the war on drugs is not to prevent drug use, but rather to create boundaries and reinforce distinctions serving the discursive ends of the established order. The construction of "addiction" in this framework serves a function by creating a convenient societal scapegoat.

Chapter 7 takes a closer look at drug addiction as a discursive construct in Canadian society. The concept of addiction as a sickness, or a symptom of a distinct medical condition or disorder, continues to be a highly influential and contentious force in shaping our collective understanding and response to the use of certain drugs.

Questions for Critical Thought

1. How have attitudes toward smoking changed over the past century? Which views are most consistent with those in your social group?
2. Does drug use among your peers exhibit characteristics more consistent with a subcultural or lifestyle point of view? What are the central features of each concept in your view?
3. What was the reaction in your peer group growing up to the antidrug education you received? Is exposure to these messages effective, in your experience? If not, what kind of changes would you like to see?

Suggested Readings

Boyd, S.C. 2004. *From Witches to Crack Moms: Women, Drug Law, and Policy.* Durham, NC: Carolina Academic Press. This book provides a critical feminist analysis of the impact of drug policy on women.

Cook, S.A. 2012. *Sex, Lies, and Cigarettes: Canadian Women, Smoking, and Visual Culture, 1880–2000.* Montreal: McGill-Queen's University Press. This book explores the history of the paradoxical relationship between women and cigarettes. Focusing on the social context of smoking, it describes the many different meanings that the practice has had for Canadian women.

Fraser, S. and Moore, D, eds. 2011. *The Drug Effect: Health, Crime and Society.* New York: Cambridge University Press. This book brings together work by respected scholars in Australia, the US, the UK, and Canada to explore the multidimensional social meanings of drug use.

Suggested Websites

Cannabis Culture

www.CannabisCulture.com

Cannabis Culture is a Canadian online magazine about marijuana and hemp around the world. Since 1994, the magazine has been a source of news and information about politics, activism, cultivation, and all things marijuana.

Erowid.org

www.erowid.org

This website provides information documenting the complex relationship between humans and psychoactive substances. Its mandate is to educate, reduce harms, increase benefits, and support policy changes.

Wikipedia

www.en.wikipedia.org/wiki/List_of_drug_films

This extensive list of drug films found on Wikipedia is a helpful resource for students interested in examining media depictions of drugs and users.

Government of Canada National Anti-Drug Strategy

www.nationalantidrugstrategy.gc.ca/prevention/parents/

This strategy was launched in October 2007. It offers drug prevention messages designed for youth and parents, and presents an Action Plan for Treatment and Enforcement consistent with its tough-on-drugs approach.

7 Drugs as Symptoms: Constructions of Addiction

Learning Objectives

- To recognize the role of medical and moral discourses in shaping understandings of addiction.
- To critically evaluate the sin and sickness models reflected in the punishment and treatment of drug users.
- To understand alternative perspectives on addiction, which view it as a symptom of larger social problems.

Introduction

What is the meaning of addiction? Examination of the literature reveals that there is little in the way of a consensus, but rather coexisting stances that posit addiction as being both a sin and a sickness. With no accepted definition, confusion is inevitable, especially considering the haphazard use of a variety of terms.

Although technically distinctive, according to most experts, much of the standard associated terminology is used interchangeably in practice by laypersons. To further complicate the matter, addictions experts are increasingly considering the term *addict* to be stigmatizing. The less pejorative, preferred term is *substance use dependent*. However, there is no persuasive scientific explanation as to why the preference exists.

The term *user* is even less pejorative, and saying "people who use drugs" is less stigmatizing still. Because the use of labels has important implications for substance users' social identity and status, distinctions of this nature are more than mere semantics. The use of certain language may well be less offensive, but it must be shown the new term actually reduces preoccupation with the punishment (and treatment) of drug users, among other misinformed societal reactions.

Chapter 7 examines the construction of addiction, with particular attention to merging medical and moral views that dominate our attitudes on substance use behaviour. Canadian contributors are once again highlighted for their important insights and contentions that inform constructionist inquiry in this area of research. Previous analyses by Blackwell (1988) and Alexander (1984, 2000) were particularly helpful in developing this chapter. Its focus is directed at competing definitions and assumptions shaping differing perspectives on addiction.

Constructions of Addiction

Alexander's (1984) definition of addiction adequately captures the phenomenon as it is generally accepted by a wide variety of experts and laypersons. He defines it as "compulsive involvement" with drugs, or other similar behaviour. This definition coincides with understandings of dependence.

This chapter looks at standard definitional criteria often used to diagnose a substance use disorder. But first we will examine the transformative construction of the meaning behind the terms *addiction* and *dependence*. Developing this background is essential for engaging in critical reflection on the discursive strategies and practices in evidence today.

There are two interpretations of the nature of addiction that dominate contemporary history, noted Blackwell (1988). One views addiction as a sin or a moral failing, and the other considers it a sickness or disease. The ongoing tension between these questionable assumptions accounts for the considerable confusion in existing societal responses to the use of drugs. In standard practice the two models are combined in public discourse, resulting in the development of policies reflecting the most dubious claims or presumptions of each.

The addiction-as-a-sin interpretation is predominant. This fact is demonstrated by the disparate allocation of public money and resources toward enforcing prohibition (compared with treatment or harm reduction, for example) as well as existing laws that punish drug use or, more precisely, drug possession. However, moral–legal arguments are grossly inconsistent when one considers how users of different types of drugs are treated differently.

The moral-failure model relies on the assumption that addicts must be held responsible for their choices, as individuals in possession of free will. Although they are technically not punished for their addiction per se, users of illicit drugs such as heroin are treated like criminals and those in possession of the drug are as easily condemned. In contrast, widespread use of alcohol is socially acceptable, and there is a general reluctance to condemn drinkers.

Inebriation appears to be so culturally accepted that it has been used historically as a justification for unacceptable behaviour. Though alcohol has had the most consistent relationship with violence and other criminal behaviour, problem drinkers tend to avoid the condemnation that has been directed at the "junkie."

As so-called criminals, those addicted to illegal drugs are given a special deviant identity not afforded to problem drinkers, with the possible exception of the "skid row alcoholic." However, popular portrayals of vagrant drunkards on the street imbue them with a deviant identity and status derived largely from the public visibility of drunkenness and abject destitution on display.

Inconsistent treatment of drug users by society is the main reason behind conditions that perpetuate disparity. Whereas alcohol is readily available, it is generally assumed that users of illegal drugs such as crack and heroin commit crimes to feed their habits. By contrast, crimes committed by drinkers are primarily understood to be a symptom of their intoxication.

There is also greater stigma against crimes associated with withdrawal (from a drug that has been outlawed) than crimes committed under the influence of a legal drug like alcohol, which is regulated openly and typically costs less. Moral condemnation of addiction is neither determined by dependence on the drug nor by the severity of associated deviant behaviour. Rather, condemnation is selectively applied according to the social status of the user and the drug.

Beyond the blatant inequalities reflected in the law, social class continues to be strongly influential in determining reactions to, and stigmatization of, problem use of alcohol and other kinds of drugs. Regardless of the moral–legal status of the substance, people from lower socioeconomic classes have fewer resources. This means that they have fewer alternatives to punishment and fewer ways of avoiding associated labels.

Historically, in Canada, keeping official records of known addicts has helped distinguish between users of illegal narcotics (or **criminal addicts**) and medical professionals who become addicted to their pharmaceutical supplies. Although arguably as culpable, or more so, than non-professionals—who are held accountable or personally responsible for lapses in judgment culminating in addiction—medical professionals are granted special status. Their official standing under law is the equivalent of that reserved for patients who become addicted to narcotic drugs in the course of medical treatment.

This exception is consistent with the more democratic designation found in the disease interpretation of addiction. Much like a diagnosis of mental illness can alleviate responsibility for criminal behaviour (leading to treatment rather than punishment), justifying addiction as an illness serves a similar function in providing an alternative explanation.

The distinction between sin and sickness relies on the assumption of an uncontrollable craving, which relieves the addict of moral responsibility and accountability for deviant behaviour. Regardless of the status of the drug being misused, addiction is defined as a medical condition that must be treated as opposed to being punished or maligned. The inability of modern medicine to produce a reliable "cure" for addiction is a significant shortcoming of the disease interpretation. Unlike many other diseases, moreover, drug addiction is more often seen as self-inflicted. These factors, among others, may explain why the disease model coexists with the antiquated sin model that inspired criminalization.

The addiction-as-a-sickness perspective has gained considerable societal support. But there is far from a consensus on the definition of dependence and the criteria by which a diagnosis should be made. And contradictions still arise in treating problem drug use as a medical condition.

Blackwell traced the origins of the disease model to eighteenth-century England, specifically chronic drunkenness in upper-class elites. The same behaviour by poor people at the time indicated moral failing, as was the case worldwide. In the nineteenth century, this class distinction disappeared, due to the increasing recognition that the "problem" was not confined to persons of either social status. Alcohol and opium addiction were beginning to be understood as diseases by medical professionals.

This interpretation of addiction gained momentum in North America and Britain in the later nineteenth century, as a result of the emergence of the social gospel movement. Temperance doctrine coincided with the medical perspective. Because the use of alcohol hampered free will, it followed logically that chronic drinkers should be treated with social sympathy instead of scorn.

Unlike in North America, in Britain the disease model of addiction was socially entrenched by the early twentieth century. It achieved legitimacy in drug policy discussions as physicians gained prestige and increasing social influence. Physicians were considered the new guardians of morality, having taken on some of the function of the clergy. A variety of ancient sins, from madness to addiction, were redefined as diseases to be treated and thereby under jurisdiction of the medical profession.

The changing role and status of physicians in society ushered in a new era in which evils such as madness came to be known as mental illness, and chronic drunkenness a sickness that is now called alcoholism. American physicians were comparatively reluctant to accept the disease interpretation of addiction, much like in Canada, where the early decades of the twentieth century saw drug control by punishment established as the primary authority in matters of drug use.

In North America, the boundaries of legitimate medical practice have been predominantly defined within a prohibition framework. Despite increasing influence in policy discussion, the medical profession has played a minor role in implementing actual drug policy reform. Conflicting coexisting definitions of addiction contribute to continued confusion and ambiguous drug policy objectives in North America and elsewhere. State officials pay "lip service" to the medical perspective, with no corresponding decrease in the sin interpretation.

Among other explanations, coexistence of the sickness and moral failure models of addiction might be due to the failure to develop a reliably effective treatment to substantiate the disease analogy. Limited success is documented, whether "treatment" employs chemical, behavioural, or psychosocial therapies. Most of these are not conventionally medical interventions. More often, the primary objective is to focus on facilitating personal growth and better health, to better cope with drug-related problems. And, unlike other kinds of untreatable diseases, the poor prognosis is attributed as much to personal failings as it is to the limits of medical science.

Addiction Treatment Models

A recent overview of major approaches to addiction treatment lists the following contemporary models (Herie and Skinner, 2010). **Cognitive behavioural therapy (CBT)** is the most established treatment model. It is employed in a variety of therapeutic settings, and aims to change thought patterns that drive behaviour. In drug addiction, it is used on the premise that drug dependence is a learned behaviour. Dependence, therefore, can be unlearned through CBT techniques designed to foster better coping strategies and a more positive personal outlook. Other treatment models comprise variations on this central theme, and none of the following contradict the basic principles of any of the others. These treatment models include interpersonal group therapy; motivational interviewing; solution-focused, narrative, and structural family therapies; mindfulness meditation; and self-help or mutual support. None of these treatment models necessitate strict abstinence from drug use. Harm reduction psychotherapy is the only treatment model that explicitly rejects the goal of abstinence informing other models' understanding of "the cure."

Often recommended as an adjunct to treatment with a health care professional, the self-help model is by default the predominant approach. Its interpretation of recovery posits that addicts are able to achieve sobriety on their own; to do so, however, the problem drinker or drug user must be sufficiently committed to engaging with others in recovery for mutual support.

The **12-step model of recovery** (Box 7.1), based on a system of beliefs identified most closely with that of Alcoholics Anonymous (AA), is the most influential and recognized perspective. The basic premise of AA is that alcoholism is a sickness that requires the alcoholic to abstain from drinking, and maintain a lifelong commitment to recovery. The 12-step model has been gradually co-opted and extended to treatment for addiction to illegal drugs, then gambling, to other behavioural addictions such as sex and codependence.

The longevity and prominence of AA are arguably the results of its ability to merge the sin and sickness model, in a way that is consistent with the temperance tradition. Addiction is constructed as an unremitting illness. But the

Box 7.1

The 12 Steps of Alcoholics Anonymous

1. We admitted we were powerless over alcohol—that our lives had become unmanageable.
2. Came to believe that a Power greater than ourselves could restore us to sanity.
3. Made a decision to turn our will and our lives over to the care of God as we understood Him.
4. Made a searching and fearless moral inventory of ourselves.
5. Admitted to God, to ourselves, and to another human being the exact nature of our wrongs.
6. Were entirely ready to have God remove all these defects of character.
7. Humbly asked Him to remove our shortcomings.
8. Made a list of all persons we had harmed, and became willing to make amends to them all.
9. Made direct amends to such people wherever possible, except when to do so would injure them or others.
10. Continued to take personal inventory and when we were wrong promptly admitted it.
11. Sought through prayer and meditation to improve our conscious contact with God, as we understood Him, praying only for knowledge of His will for us and the power to carry that out.
12. Having had a spiritual awakening as the result of these Steps, we tried to carry this message to alcoholics, and to practice these principles in all our affairs.

Source: The Twelve Steps are reprinted with permission of Alcoholics Anonymous World Services, Inc. ("AAWS"). Permission to reprint the Twelve Steps does not mean that AAWS has reviewed or approved the contents of this publication, or that AAWS necessarily agrees with the views expressed herein. A.A. is a program of recovery from alcoholism only—use of the Twelve Steps in connection with programs and activities which are patterned after A.A., but which address other problems, or in any other non-A.A. context, does not imply otherwise.

onus in recovery is put squarely on the person to have the moral fortitude to keep sickness at bay. When treatment fails, it is therefore reasonable to blame the alcoholic or drug addict for his or her failure to commit to recovery.

The influence of both the disease and moral-failure models is evident in treatment and recovery discourses. The two models of addiction support glaring contradictions in the treatment of the problem as an illness (cf. Finagrette, 1991; Valverde, 1998). Addressing problems through group membership and moral regulation is a treatment strategy more generally consistent with a sociological understanding of addiction. Adopting a more critical perspective on drug treatment is by no means an assertion that treatment does not work.

Although success rates vary, most types of treatment have been shown to benefit patients. However, it is increasingly recognized that certain kinds of treatment are better suited to some over others (see Hathaway et al., 2009). Different treatment programs employ different diagnoses of addiction, as well as outcome measures, which confound interpretation. Whatever the reported success rates of recovery, it remains to be established in many treatment studies that those who did succeed were no more motivated to begin with (or otherwise economically or socially advantaged) than those who did not. Those with more resources and fewer psychosocial problems—who have been found to be more likely to seek treatment to begin with—can be reasonably expected to have improved ("succeeded") without receiving treatment of any kind at all.

Regardless of shortcomings and advantages of each perspective, the simultaneous acceptance of contradicting definitions of addiction has hampered the development of more effective treatments. The uncomfortable relationship between conflicting models is exemplified, notes Blackwell (1988), by compulsory addiction treatment carried out in penal settings. The treatment of drug addicts in prison has particular political advantages for the criminal justice system. It appeals to those committed to "rehabilitating" criminals, while retaining ultimate respect for the predominant drug policy perspective informing punishment.

When participation in drug treatment is forced, poor results are not surprising. It is difficult to fathom how expectations could be otherwise. Even if treatment can be justified, or even necessary for the sake of the afflicted, such an intervention is undeniably coercive. In penal settings, the patients are first and foremost prisoners. And many "voluntary" patients are in fact compelled to enter treatment because of family or work pressure, by order of the court, or other circumstances that make the decision unavoidable.

Addiction treatment largely depends on the will to change. Those forced to enter treatment have little choice but to co-operate, regardless of their personal commitment to recovery. Real or feigned commitment is essential whether one's objective is to get along, be left alone, "graduate" from the treatment program, or gain eventual release.

Relapse is understandable (inevitable perhaps), considering the coercion and confusion brought about by the treatment of drug criminals like patients and vice versa. In either case, treatment programs have a tendency to treat substance use as if it were the problem. This is evident regardless of whether it is looked at as an illness, or a symptom of an illness, or whatever kind of problem drug addiction is understood to be.

This response is arguably pragmatic. It is easier to treat the behaviour than to treat an illness for which there is no medical (or psychiatric) cure. Moreover, it is easier to fix the behaviour than attempt to fix the social structure or environment in which the illness is at best mislabelled, and at worst, criminalized.

Despite the fact that alcohol is found to cause more problems than all of the illegal drugs combined, it has tended to escape the societal condemnation heaped on other drug use (Blackwell, 1988). Since the 1930s, the way the problem has been framed in North America has shifted from blaming the substance to emphasizing the characteristics of the drinker and patterns of consumption. The emerging influence of AA in the US has strongly influenced this view of the problem. Emphasis is now placed on immoderate drinking as an individual problem. Unlike the earlier temperance movement, AA does not demonize alcohol, nor demand that it be outlawed to protect us from ourselves. Alcoholism is instead seen as a personal vulnerability and the responsibility of the alcoholic.

As alcoholics, AA members believe they must admit their vulnerability to alcohol by remaining abstinent, and committing to recovery by following the 12 steps. Banning alcohol is not required from this perspective, because only alcoholics have the putative disease. Therefore AA makes no policy pronouncements. It does not seek to influence behaviours or activities of drinkers (or non-drinkers) outside the AA group. Because non-alcoholics do not have the disease, it is assumed that they are able to drink in moderation without developing symptoms of dependence and abuse.

The alcoholism concept, notes Valverde (1998), has been successful because it meets the needs of a variety of interests. Alcohol is a socially accepted, highly profitable (and taxed), commodity consistent with both State and business interests, and as a result the drinking problem is effectively confined to a select number of consumers in the general population.

Pathologizing drinkers, as opposed to drink itself, also serves the interests of the medical profession and the treatment industry, including self-help groups, by guaranteeing a continuous, often lifelong, clientele. Although it is widely recognized as a disease, alcoholism supposedly cannot be treated using medicine, a long-accepted fact. This stance supports a dual interpretation of the illness.

Whereas physicians are responsible for treating physical symptoms (such as overdose and liver damage), patients are referred to mutual support groups like AA for help fostering long-term changes in behaviour. The problem of defining threshold levels, which might enable us to distinguish alcoholics from non-problematic drinkers, is strategically avoided by the AA definition. This requires individual recognition of the problem by the drinker.

Self-admission, or "acknowledging the problem," is understood to happen when people hit rock bottom—the point at which point the alcoholic can no longer countenance continuing denial. Alcoholic Anonymous evidently works for a variety of reasons (see Box 7.2), not least of which is solving irresolvable contradictions that have threatened diffusion of the disease model of addiction.

Whatever its apparent inconsistencies—including evidence that people with drug problems are more likely to recover when they have choices beyond abstinence-based treatment (Hathaway et al., 2009)—AA's definition of

Box 7.2 Alcoholics Anonymous's Techniques of Moral Regulation

Alcoholics Anonymous is successful because it incorporates both medical and spiritual components. It has been able to avoid association with political controversies about prohibition and control of alcohol, which was the downfall of earlier temperance movements. And most importantly, the organization has uniquely connected the experience of total transformation, through abstinence from alcohol, to a series of slogans and techniques for dealing with life's problems.

The old temperance movement had its own technique for sobriety, namely the temperance pledge. Signers were committed to sobriety forever. If they drank even once, this represented a complete failure. Conversely, one of the most popular slogans repeated by AA members is "one day at a time," and AA meetings are filled with people who quit drinking for a time, then went back to drinking and returned. Rather than rejecting these individuals as "backsliders," AA responds with countervailing, complementary techniques. One is the custom of celebrating months or years of sobriety with commemorative tokens, a round of applause, and sometimes even a party.

In addition to recognizing and rewarding long-term abstinence, this technique is complemented by the one that is embodied in the popular slogan "one day at a time." By maintaining focus on the short-term goal of staying sober for the next few hours, everyone is equalized. The tendency of "old-timers" to feel superior to others is muted by reminders that recovery is an ongoing process, in which all alcoholics are equally sober. The one-day-at-a-time technique has the power to forgive lapses in sobriety, which saves the relapsed drinker from becoming an outcast or moral failure.

As guilty feelings figure prominently in relapse, it is important to the success of AA to provide a relatively guilt-free way of reconnecting with the group. The apparently inane, even vacuous slogans ascribed to in AA —"keep it simple," "easy does it," and "one day at a time"—wield significant social power. Their simplicity and lack of content are precisely why they play such an important role in the practical management of people's everyday lives.

The remarkable success of AA can be partly attributed to its techniques for governing the self. The organization's hybridized approach to the practice of recovery by self-control suggests that neither medicine nor religion have a complete monopoly over the meaning of addiction. Its longevity and popularity also challenge conventional assumptions about "experts" dominating the moral regulation of everyday life in the decades of the late twentieth century and beyond.

Source: Adapted from Valverde and White-Mair (1999).

addiction is successful because it points to both illness and personal choice. The same duality is evident in standard definitions of addiction used in the clinical practice environment.

As noted previously, in Chapter 1, the most established framework for assessing substance use disorders has been *the Diagnostic and Statistical Manual of Mental Disorders (DSM)*. The diagnostic focus of the *DSM* criteria reflects a dualistic understanding of addiction, informed by medical and psychosocial factors.

Criteria for Substance Use Disorders

For the past 20 years, the *DSM-IV* (although the fifth edition, *DSM-5*, was just released in 2013) has been a commonly accepted diagnostic tool for assessing problematic drug use. It provides a common language, which has facilitated formal shifting of the discourse of drug problems from a moral perspective to a health one (Herie and Skinner, 2010). Yet the war-on-drugs approach continues unabated, in Canada and other prohibition-centric countries.

Images of addicts make them subject to a different kind of social stigma, which coexists alongside other labels such as criminal, sinner, and degenerate (Room, 2005). The implications of diagnosis with a disorder that is stigmatized, and increasingly defined along the lines of mental illness, are significant in terms of social attitudes, identity, and status.

Rather than referring to addiction, the *DSM-IV* employed the terms *dependence* and *abuse* (see American Psychiatric Association, 1994). The reader may recall that the definition of dependence was determined by the presence of three or more of the following symptoms in the previous 12 months (Box 1.1): increased tolerance, withdrawal, using more or for longer than intended, persistent desire or efforts to control use, considerable time spent using drugs, reducing other activities (i.e., work, school, spending time with family and friends), and continuing to use despite negative consequences (e.g., social, legal, physical).

This array of symptoms evidently captures a variety of substance use behaviours, which support an integrated bio/psycho/social standpoint. The first two listed symptoms, tolerance and withdrawal, are arguably the only truly medical criteria. These symptoms are neither necessary nor sufficient to meet the recommended threshold for diagnosed dependence. At least one additional symptom is required, or a combination of three other symptoms.

Substance abuse, as defined in the *DSM-IV*, was a "maladaptive pattern" of drug use "leading to impairment or distress." One or more of four symptoms, within a 12-month period, in that version were required to meet the threshold for abuse: when recurrent substance use interferes with home, school, or work responsibilities; when use is hazardous (e.g., when driving); and when it causes legal and/or interpersonal problems (e.g., arguing with a spouse or family member). Substance abuse could coexist or precede dependence, or occur on its own without a dependence diagnosis.

The *DSM*, first published in 1952, has incrementally expanded, with each subsequent edition increasing the number of recognized mental disorders. Though widely praised for standardizing psychiatric diagnoses, it has been criticized for creating boundaries between normality and illness (that is, medicalizing deviant behaviours that are entirely socially defined) and for reifying loosely defined symptoms of disorders (that is, putting permanent labels on behaviour based on nebulous criteria, which are commonly subjective or open to a broader level of interpretation) (see Thomas, 1990). Drug problems necessarily exist on a continuum (which ranges from imperceptibly subjective to unequivocally objective or visibly extreme). The often-overlapping *DSM* criteria, however, are treated categorically—clinically present and verifiable, or not. When substance use behaviour is treated in this way, as a kind of problem people do or do not have, it creates a sense of certainty that is not justifiable. A line is drawn on the continuum, obscuring recognition that this threshold puts a label on a person without conveying a sense of meaning of the "disorder" diagnosed (see Room, 2006).

The latest version of the *DSM* introduces broader definitions and lower diagnostic thresholds. Both types of changes have expanded psychiatric jurisdiction over substance use behaviour by encompassing more people. The new revisions to the *DSM* continue the tradition of classifying deviant behaviours as clinical disorders to be treated by medical professionals. In the *DSM-5*, for example, the category of substance use–related disorders has expanded to include gambling disorder. This change reflects agreement among experts that addictive behaviours such as gambling (or sex addiction or binge eating) have certain symptoms that mimic those of substance use disorders.

The criteria for substance use disorders have remained consistent between versions, however, with only two exceptions. The substance abuse symptom of "recurrent legal problems" has been omitted in the *DSM-5*, and the new criterion of "craving" has been added. The lines have been blurred between the previous two-pronged diagnosis of dependence versus abuse; the two are now combined in the new version under "substance-use disorder" (Table 7.1).

In order to be diagnosed with a substance use disorder, the *DSM-5* threshold is set at two or more criteria. The previous version recommended three or more symptoms of substance dependence, and one or more of abuse. The new criteria for substance use disorder are accompanied by additional criteria. Among those added are intoxication, withdrawal, medication-induced disorders, and other unspecified substance-induced disorders, where relevant. Withdrawal from caffeine and cannabis has been added as an indicator of addiction to those substances. And tobacco use disorder is included in the new version, using the identical criteria applied to other kinds of substance use disorders. A new measure of severity of substance use disorders

Table 7.1 Changes to Criteria in the *DSM-5*

Criterion	*DSM-IV* Substance Dependence	*DSM-5* Substance Use Disorder
Tolerance	✓	✓
Withdrawal	✓	✓
Taken more/longer than intended	✓	✓
Desire/unsuccessful efforts to quit use	✓	✓
Great deal of time taken by activites involved in use	✓	✓
Use despite knowledge of problems associated with use	✓	✓
Important activities given up because of use	✓	✓
Recurrent use resulting in a failure to fulfill important role obligations		✓
Recurrent use resulting in physically hazardous behavior (e.g., driving)		✓
Continued use despite recurrent social problems associated with use		✓
Craving for the substance		✓

Source: American Psychiatric Association (2013).

has been derived based on the number of criteria endorsed. The resulting classification scheme enables the assessor to make distinctions in disorders, enabling diagnoses ranging in severity from mild (two to three symptoms), to moderate (four to five symptoms), to severe (six symptoms or more).

These revisions represent an effort to address or compensate for previous weaknesses—the flaws inherent to thinking categorically about substance use behaviour rather than as something that exists on a continuum—by eschewing a dichotomous perspective on addiction. The blurring of the boundaries between earlier definitions, which clearly separated dependence and abuse, avoids the controversy by removing the distinction. *Substance use disorder* is a less contentious term, comes with less proverbial baggage than the others, and includes a wider range of addictive behaviours not necessarily related to substances.

It is still too early to determine the extent of influence these changes to the *DSM* will have on the diagnosis and treatment of addictions. Whereas the previous criteria explicitly acknowledged that people can abuse drugs without being drug-dependent—and be dependent on drugs without symptoms of abuse—these distinctions have been effectively obscured. The implications of new definitional criteria are most significant for those whose substance use behaviour has been redefined by the new thresholds of disorder. The discovery of cannabis withdrawal in the *DSM-5*, for example, has the potential to dramatically transform demand for treatment of cannabis use disorders.

Another common criticism of *DSM* criteria is the inclusion of recurring legal problems as indicative of cannabis (or any other outlawed drug) dependence, when one could easily argue that such legal problems are a result of government attempts to control use. This criticism has been addressed by the removal of recurring legal problems as a symptom category. By substituting it with *craving,* or *desire to use,* however—as part of a more inclusive framework for substance use disorders—the omission is unlikely to result in fewer users meeting *DSM* criteria for having a drug problem. Often legal problems are the impetus for seeking formal diagnosis and drug treatment to begin with. Therefore, as a symptom, it is arguably redundant. Cravings or desire for drugs, however (to be cynical), is also suitably ambiguous and subjective, whether the dependence is mild, moderate, or severe.

Research shows that symptoms of dependence are subjective. Their interpretation has been found to be contingent on a variety of factors and cultural conditions. Compared with those of users in drug treatment, few studies have focused on the larger population of drug users who report minimal symptoms of substance use disorder. The majority of marijuana users found in the community have no immediate intentions of quitting their drug use.

A Case Study: Marijuana Use Disorders

Research on experienced marijuana users suggests that only a small fraction have any legal problems (Hathaway, 2003). Most, however, at one time or another, have experienced a strong desire or craving for the drug. At the same time, most respondents say their use is under control.

Cannabis-related problems appear primarily subjective. Put otherwise, the problem tends to have more to do with self-perceptions of excessive use (i.e., symptoms of dependence) than adverse consequences (or symptoms of abuse). In the study, symptoms of a cannabis disorder were assessed with reference to *DSM-IV* criteria. To increase the sensitivity of each individual marker, we asked participants both whether they had experienced the symptoms and, if so, whether that had happened during the past year.

About one-third of the respondents had experienced three or more of the listed *DSM-IV* symptoms (Table 7.2). Half this group (or 15 per cent of all respondents) reported having these same symptoms during the past year. The most significant decline in rates from general to past-year experiences involved abuse-related symptoms (versus those related to dependence). Put another way, this means that adverse consequences had reduced more noticeably than symptoms of dependence.

If we reanalyze these data—after lowering the threshold for a substance use disorder, from three to two symptoms (to reflect the new *DSM-5* criteria)—we have doubled past-year prevalence of the diagnosis (from 15 to 29 per cent). Reinforcing the importance of subjective self-perceptions informing diagnosis of a substance use disorder, there is no correlation between levels of consumption and the number of *DSM* symptoms reported.

Table 7.2 Percentage of Participants Meeting *DSM-IV* Criteria for Cannabis Disorder (N = 104*)

Number of Symptoms	Experienced (%)	Experienced in the Past 12 Months (%)
0	25	51
1	26	21
2	19	14
3	18	10
4	7	4
5	5	1
6	0	0

*Sample was obtained from a community-based group of experienced users who were not seeking treatment.

Source: Hathaway (2003). Reproduced with permission of Informa Healthcare.

Past-year symptoms of dependence ranged from one-in-three (who reported having used more cannabis than they intended) to one-in-four (who tried to cut back unsuccessfully). Just over ten per cent or less reported adverse consequences: reduced activities (11 per cent), health problems (11 per cent), problems meeting obligations (12 per cent), or troubled personal relationships (8 per cent).

Cannabis use levels in the general population are lower than those found within the present study. The sample comprised committed long-term users, as opposed to the full spectrum of users in society (which ranges from occasional to chronic levels of consumption of the drug). The prevalence of use-related problems is therefore higher in this study than what is typically observed in general population samples.

The composition of the sample of experienced users allows for a more meaningful comparison of symptoms with those who enter treatment for marijuana use–related problems. Whereas users in community-based studies ordinarily extol the benefits of cannabis, denying serious impairment, those in treatment studies have many symptoms of dependence commonly reported by other substance users. Cannabis treatment seekers, however, do not ordinarily report the kind of personal crises and behavioural dysfunction that lead many substance users to seek treatment (see Hathaway et al., 2009). They are more ambivalent about the need for treatment, and tend to be less confident that they can stop using.

Therefore, experiencing symptoms of cannabis dependence is not a condition necessarily connected to experiencing symptoms of cannabis abuse. To further illustrate this point, cannabis-related problems in my community-based study of experienced users can be compared with those reported in a treatment sample (see Hathaway et al., 2008). The treatment group comprised clients recruited from 13 addiction treatment centres in the province of Ontario.

Findings were reported for participants defining their primary drug problem as cannabis-related (N = 99). They were enrolled in residential (n = 46) and outpatient (n = 53) treatment programs that offered a broad spectrum of intervention models. Whereas daily use of cannabis was common in both samples, there were significant differences in use patterns and amounts (see Table 7.3).

Although use levels in the treatment sample were (not surprisingly) reportedly increasing before treatment, the nontreatment group reported that use levels were declining. Average monthly spending on the drug in the nontreatment group was about one-third ($167/month) of the amount spent by the treatment sample ($500/month) over the previous 12 months.

The nontreatment group scored lower on all measures of impairment. Between-group differences, however, were smaller between symptoms of cannabis dependence than they were for symptoms of cannabis abuse. Adverse consequences were a more distinctive element of the treatment seekers' profile than were symptoms of dependence. Whereas symptoms of abuse are rare, symptoms of dependence are not particularly uncommon among users outside treatment.

Symptoms of compulsive use (i.e., using more than intended or failing to reduce) were found to differ least between the study groups. Such problems are not rare, and indicate transition, reflecting users' efforts to

Table 7.3 Percentage of Study Participants Experiencing *DSM-IV* Symptoms of Drug Dependence and Abuse, by Group (treatment versus nontreatment)

	Treatment (N = 99)	Nontreatment (N = 104)	
	Past 3 Years (%)	Lifetime (%)	Past Year (%)
Dependence criteria			
Used larger amounts or for longer periods than intended	88	51	32
Persistent desire or tried unsuccessfully to cut down on use	86	38	24
Gave up or reduced social, recreational, or work activities	72	19	11
Kept using despite recurring physical or psychological problem	65	20	11
Abuse criteria			
Failed to meet obligations at work or school or home	65	25	12
Had recurring legal problems because of use	33	6	1
Kept using despite recurring social or interpersonal problems	71	17	8

Note: $P < .0001$ for all between group differences.

Source: Hathaway et al. (2008). Reproduced with permission of Informa Healthcare.

establish more control. The dysfunctional use patterns of most users in drug treatment were more life disrupting than the symptoms of dependence they reported—rather, these are more indicative of symptoms of abuse.

These findings contradict the view that drug-dependent persons are categorically distinct from other users of the drug. Drug-related problems exist on a continuum. Sustained abstinence post-treatment is reportedly uncommon, regardless of the type of intervention that is used. Reductions in use levels and fewer problems after treatment, however, have been shown to be realistic goals.

There is a growing need for treatment options more consistent with the goals of users seeking to establish more control. Establishing self-control over use to mitigate drug problems is a treatment goal with more potential to alleviate concerns about dependence among users. Conceptions of dependence and abuse are shaped by culture. Because the concept of addiction has no meaning in some cultures (Room, 2006), such measures are more meaningful in theory than in practice.

The evolving *DSM* criteria for substance use disorders are tied to culturally defined notions about drug use. Symptoms of these problems are primarily subjective, and difficult to qualify for different types of drugs. The use of standard measures appears dubious, considering that these apply to legal drugs like alcohol as well as cannabis and cocaine, which are outlawed and hence subject to entirely different societal reactions.

Symptoms of impairment are, in other words, confounded by the social stigma and resulting consequences created by State policies that criminalize some drugs. Drug-related problems, at work or school or home, cannot be separated from the influence exerted by certain cultural assumptions about the use of drugs.

The *DSM* criteria for substance use disorders appear to be evolving in response to criticism of the kind we have examined—as evidenced by changes between the fourth and fifth edition. It is unclear how these changes will affect demand for treatment and practices of drug treatment providers. The analysis presented indicates that there is little reason to expect the latest version will reduce the medical profession's jurisdiction over drugs.

Despite its primary emphasis on psychosocial variables, which are primarily subjective and culturally conditioned, the *DSM* criteria of substance use disorder conform to the assumptions of the disease model. The addict is constructed as having a disorder that is independent of societal conditions, over which the person has no control.

This passive understanding of addiction corresponds with what Alexander termed the **exposure orientation**, which has emerged alongside other notions of contagion and analogies to illness since the nineteenth-century advent of the disease model. The remainder of this chapter draws on work by Alexander (1984, 2000) that challenges the predominant understanding of addiction.

Exposure and Adaptive Understandings of Addiction

The exposure orientation has persisted in our culture, despite the fact that most people exposed to drugs do not keep using them and most who do stop using later on. Alexander (1984) offers a number of examples contradicting the assumption that addiction is created by exposure to a psychoactive drug.

Research shows that less than 1 per cent of medical patients receiving regular doses of narcotics become addicted. Estimates are similar for the pre–drug prohibition era, in North America and elsewhere, when large quantities of opiate drugs were used without restriction. Despite their widespread use in medicine, and as a relaxant, there were few significant problems with addiction.

The later menace posed by heroin is similarly refuted by research in the United Kingdom, where it was widely used in medicine. As we have noted previously, it has been observed that war veterans who used heroin in Vietnam rarely relapsed to addiction upon return to the United States (see Robins, 1993). Many still used occasionally, however. Their occasional, recreational use patterns are consistent with the behaviour of most people who use heroin (and other outlawed drugs considered dangerously addictive).

Estimates for heroin suggest that casual users outnumber regular users by as much as seven to one. Put otherwise, fewer than one in ten become addicted to this notoriously habit-forming drug. Proponents of the disease model may counter this fact by asserting that only certain people are vulnerable to drug exposure. But the fact that certain users become addicts tells us nothing about the characteristics of those with the so-called disease, other than that they are addicted.

If addiction is indeed some kind of disease, notes Alexander, its incidence in general populations must be minuscule. But there is little evidence that it exists at all. Results of laboratory studies using animals provide some evidence supporting the exposure orientation. The fact that rats in cages self-administer narcotics is not informative, however. It tells us very little about how human beings act in self-injection situations

Most results from these studies are arguably not even generalizable to rats outside the lab. Like humans, rats have little appetite for opiates when they are situated in a natural environment. Moreover, many people "dependent" on narcotics show no visible symptoms of functional impairment.

Regular users of narcotics are subject to withdrawal, which is a standard marker of dependence on a drug. One assumption of the exposure orientation is that addiction is explained by the avoidance of withdrawal. This association is untenable, however, considering the evidence refuting the connection.

It is assumed that physical dependence on narcotics results in agonizing symptoms of withdrawal when the addict attempts to stop using the drug.

The addict, seeking to avoid these symptoms, is filled with an irresistible compulsion to resume. This often-dramatized depiction of drug addicts is so prominent that addiction and withdrawal are often treated as synonymous. Research on the actual experience of addicts, however, shows that relapse to narcotics use is rarely related primarily to physiological discomfort. Opiate withdrawal symptoms are far milder than stereotypical portrayals in the media suggest. Every addict forced to, or wishing to, abstain knows of ways to mitigate symptoms of withdrawal.

In addition to reducing drug use gradually, these strategies include consuming alcohol, cannabis, or other sedatives as substitutes for managing symptoms. Substituting old behaviours with new ones such as meditation, hypnosis, and even exercise may also be effective in alleviating symptoms.

Alexander notes that countless addicts have been forced to go "cold turkey" and detoxify. Most revert back to addiction, despite the fact that they have managed to successfully withdraw. Addictions can occur without withdrawal symptoms, but still produce dysfunctional and ruinous behaviour. Withdrawal is not needed to initiate addiction, nor is it sufficient to explain related problems.

It may be tempting to extrapolate results of laboratory studies. But rats in barren cages do not have the multitude of behavioural options available to people. Even the reduced claim that withdrawal may contribute to becoming drug addicted in some instances is dubious. Alexander (1984) points out that stimulants (like cocaine, amphetamines, and nicotine) do not have conspicuous physiological symptoms. Nonetheless, these stimulants appear to be at least as habit-forming or addictive as opiate drugs.

In summary, it is possible to be physically dependent on drugs without being addicted to drugs. And there are circumstances in which one can be addicted without being physiologically dependent. The exposure orientation is evidently contradicted by modern research and historical experience with drugs.

Alexander favours an **adaptive orientation**, which is more consistent with a psychosocial framework (and the constructionist perspective adopted in this book). The adaptive orientation holds that drug addiction is neither created by disease nor by exposure to the substance. It is rather an attempt to adapt to distress through habitual use of a drug.

Much like the bio/psycho/social understanding of addiction, the exposure and adaptive orientations cannot be accepted simultaneously without logical contradiction. The exposure orientation has persisted, influencing social understanding of the nature of addiction and fuelling corresponding cultural myths and stereotypes.

Images of hapless, enslaved junkies have long been prominent in media depictions and popular imagination. These portrayals serve to justify a combination of medical and legal responses to addiction. The depiction suits the mutual and intersecting interests of law enforcement agencies and the **treatment industry**. Alexander's work contributes to the literature that challenges assumptions of the popular disease model. A more plausible perspective, based on the evidence presented (see also Maté, 2012), is that addiction is an adaptive response to an increasing sense of isolation, dislocation, and despair, among other circumstances of a globalizing world.

From this standpoint, treating addicts as either criminal or sick is a band-aid solution, which neglects the deeper structural pathologies that are at the root of many drug-related problems. To suggest that drugs are causes or symptoms of disease is to ignore the verifiable interpersonal and social problems that most people face at one time or another. Drug addiction is adaptive, representing an attempt to compensate for psychosocial problems and deficiencies, which are increasingly apparent on an unprecedented scale.

The Role of Social Dislocation

Rather than a medical disorder or disease, Alexander (2000) argues that addiction is a symptom of the dramatic global expansion of free markets. Addiction is increasingly pervasive in society because free markets dislocate human beings from traditional sources of psychosocial and spiritual support. A sense of mutual support, or **psychosocial integration**, is provided by belonging to and engagement with a group.

The cause of dislocation can be traced to different sources, all of which result in insufficient psychosocial integration. From natural disasters to economic downturns (which have the potential to destroy entire communities) to child abuse, potential causes for fragmentation on smaller and larger scales are diverse.

Since ancient times, the harshest punishments of criminals and outcasts have included banishment or excommunication, solitary confinement, ostracism and the like. Severe prolonged social dislocation leads to suicide for most psychosocially disintegrated people. However, dislocation is universally applicable if psychosocial integration is systematically disrupted. This appears to be the case around the world today.

The primary contributor to dislocation of individuals from traditional family and community ties has been the expansion of free-market societies. Unrestrained pursuit of wealth is doggedly promoted, because everyone presumably benefits from increasing their financial standing. However, this is not the case. Social dislocation caused by the expansion of free-market societies is linked to behaviours more characteristic of despair. People unable to achieve psychosocial integration often adapt to the deficiency by constructing substitute lifestyles. These sometimes centre on compulsive or excessive use of drugs. As a substitute for psychosocial integration, even the most extreme cases of addiction (and other lifestyles that are widely deemed repugnant) might therefore be considered adaptive behaviour. Identifying as a drug addict is more endurable for some than having no identity at all. Addiction's barren pleasures, argues Alexander (2000), are certainly less painful than the unrelenting aimlessness and feelings of depression resulting from **social dislocation.**

The term *addiction* is appropriate, whether the use of drugs is involved or not. Addiction generally refers to the singular pursuit of, or overwhelming involvement with, a certain habit, to the detriment of living a more balanced way of life. Addiction indicates a lack of psychosocial integration. If taken to extremes, such behaviour has historically been recognized as having disastrous consequences.

The traditional conception of addiction is consistent with the move in medicine to broaden definitions of substance use disorders. As an example, the *DSM*'s inclusion of gambling disorder is a significant first step toward official recognition of the illness. This shows that symptoms of addiction are easily extended to other deviant behaviours. There are no important differences in the behaviour or experiences of drug addicts and that of people addicted to other pursuits.

Social dislocation, as the precursor of addiction, is not the pathological condition of a few. It is universal. Addiction is more likely in societies that destroy relationships among families and communities. Implicating globalization, or the expansion of free markets, is not meant to imply that other social models have none of the same or different problems of their own. That said, Alexander (2000) documents consistent links between free markets and expanding dislocation. Free-market societies can only be established and maintained by the displacement of traditional culture. Paradoxically, establishing free markets requires coercion to destroy traditional societal arrangements concerning use of land, labour, currency, and goods. Coercion is required because traditional arrangements ordinarily maintain greater societal cohesion, and most people are reluctant to part with their traditions.

Ironically, maintaining a "free" market requires powerful control of workers and consumers. Mass media and managers indoctrinate the players (i.e., participants of the free market) to regulate our activities and keep us performing assigned market functions. The primary objective is to undermine traditional social structures and relationships, which tend to resist assimilation. Libertarians may argue that free-market institutions are voluntarily adopted, a freely chosen transformation of the political economy and societal arrangements. On the contrary, historical record shows that free markets tend to be established through coercion.

Two hundred years ago or so, the emergence of free-market society in England was achieved by forced displacement of the rural poor, to work and live in urban slums. Forced dislocation spread first through Britain, then its colonies abroad. Subsequently, accelerated social dislocation has occurred everywhere free markets have emerged.

Today, powerful transnational bodies, like the World Bank and the World Trade Organization, are committed to expanding the scope of the free market into areas like medicine and higher education at a faster, more persistent rate than ever seen before. Social dislocation, as a product of the free market, is not confined to poor people or poorer countries. For poor and rich alike, it seems communities are weakened and destabilized by forces of social dislocation.

People increasingly change families, occupations, nationalities, languages, and ideologies throughout the world today. The resulting social dislocation is destructive of the cultural identity of settled populations. As people are transformed into more migratory beings, psychosocial integration is inevitably diminished.

The democratic character of social dislocation is supported by the evidence of growing social problems among the middle class in North American society. In the United States in particular, and increasingly in Canada, the celebration of free market ideology increases pressure to be competitive, efficient, and successful. The resulting culture contributes to neglect of our own children and disconnection from traditional community and family supports.

Intertwined with the successes of free enterprise, namely evident prosperity, are the downsides. Americans score the highest of all developed countries on rates of economic inequality, child poverty, divorce, single parenthood, and television viewing. Not surprisingly, they also lead the world in new diagnoses of childhood disorders, such as attention-deficit hyperactivity disorder (ADHD), prescribing powerful stimulants to treat these "conditions."

As businesses neglect their obligations to the worker—which may have made work endurable before—there is growing discontent, anxiety, and workplace violence. This is occurring among labourers, executives, and managers. In recent years, the Internet has dramatically expanded globalization's reach, replacing more traditional local-group connections. There appears to be a strong, consistent correlation between severe social dislocation and addiction in societies. Social dislocation has long been implicated as a cause of alcoholism in classic literature; for example, this is a common theme in the works of Charles Dickens, who often wrote about the struggles of London's urban poor.

Social historians have, likewise, often noted a connection between the destructive use of alcohol after the Middle Ages and an expanding free-market society. The use of opium, which had previously been common but rarely problematic, soon became a social issue. In recent decades, recognition of similar afflictions (brought on by too much working, shopping, eating, etc.) has led to a profusion of new problems being recognized—and the proliferation of treatment programs and self-help.

Canadian Examples

Cases of extreme social dislocation yield the most visible examples of substance use disorders and other indications of distress. For Alexander (2000), living in the city of Vancouver provided an ideal backdrop for developing his thesis that addiction is a product of social dislocation. Vancouver has long been Canada's most drug-dependent city—a fact confirmed by annual per capita consumption of alcohol and other drugs, alcoholism, drug addiction, overdose, and arrest rates for drug-related crimes.

Addiction that does not involve alcohol and drugs is not as widely publicized but is even more pervasive, and often more destructive, argues Alexander. Severe addictions to money, power, and work are manifested in the activities of occupants of many corporate boardrooms. These addicts feed their habits by polluting the environment while exploiting people and other natural resources. Although these characteristics are apparent in both public and private institutions throughout free-market societies, the city of Vancouver is a classic example. It is a city that was founded on social dislocation.

Since 1862, when the city was first founded, the appropriation of Vancouver's waterfront for commerce has involved eviction of the Native population; many of its ancient cultural practices were outlawed, or stigmatized, resulting in the gradual extinction of its peoples. Alexander (2000) notes that many of the thousands of homeless addicts populating the Downtown Eastside of Vancouver are descendants of the earliest displaced coastal Natives.

Throughout its history the city has also been the primary destination for immigrants from the east. Displaced persons from all parts of Canada, not only Aboriginals, arrived in droves. And from the beginning, Vancouver has been recognized as a favoured landing point in Canada for displaced populations of East and South Asians. It is commonly observed that most residents of the city of Vancouver were born elsewhere. After completion of the Canadian Pacific Railway in 1886, Vancouver acquired the nickname Terminal City.

Since that time, free-market growth appears to have been unstoppable. Vancouver has long served as a beacon of prosperity, little tarnished by problems of poverty, class struggle, and organized crime found frequently in other North American cities. But whereas social dislocation is a common characteristic of many urban centres, in Vancouver it is extreme.

Rather than comprising common values and institutions, the culture of the city is more accurately described as an unstructured mélange of dislocated people. Most visibly, the policy of cultural assimilation in Canada stripped Natives of their culture and land. The main objective was to displace and reintegrate them into the lowest strata of society as labourers and factory workers.

The residential school system is only one example of the destructive ways in which this policy was manifested. Under the mandate of the program, many Native children were taken from their parents and taught to hate their way of life. The resulting alienation from their families, language, customs, and spiritual practices succeeded in destroying cultural bonds. Ultimately failing to assimilate the Native Canadian population into free-market society, the residential school program now serves as an exemplar of extreme and devastating social dislocation.

Sharing the white-man's taste for "firewater" since he introduced it to them, Natives began to experience a serious alcohol problem with the advent of the assimilation strategy. Along with suicide, domestic violence, and abuse, addiction rates in this population are extreme. The familiar claim that alcoholism among Natives is caused by a disease or else a gene that makes them unable to tolerate or control alcohol is not only racist but entirely unconvincing.

Alexander (2000) notes that Europeans who are subject to extreme conditions of social dislocation develop the same problems almost universally. The Orcadians, for example, from the north of Scotland, were recruited in large numbers by the Hudson's Bay Company to man their isolated outposts throughout the Canadian North. In continuous operation since the 1670s (making it the oldest existing capitalist corporation), The Bay preferred to hire young men from the Orkney Islands, who were known for their sobriety and obedience to authority.

Severing their ties with home in hopes of an adventure, and escape from the restrictions of traditional society, the Orcadians in Canada were exiles from their homelands—and within their new adopted home. Alcoholism in this group was rampant (as was suicide), although the term *alcoholic* had yet to be invented. No matter how many liquor bans it instituted, the Hudson's Bay Company was stymied in its efforts to effectively stem the flow of alcohol and alcohol-related problems. It seems the dislocated young men had been irreparably transformed.

Challenges and Implications

Alexander's (2000) emphasis on social dislocation, resulting in deficient psychosocial integration, is challenged by the notion of **instantaneous addiction.** This concept surged with the emergence of the crack scare in America (Reinarman and Levine, 1995). Reportedly enslaving those who used it only once, regardless of their class or economic situation, the use of crack cocaine was deemed a major social problem across North America by the early 1990s. The associated panic and related propaganda (including frightening images of crack-addicted babies) reinforced the war-on-drugs agenda of law-makers—and the exposure orientation of the medical profession. Support for the disease model, as we have seen, does not indicate rejection of enforcement necessarily. It is a complementary strategy, which forces addicts into treatment. Coercion is excusable, assuming it results in addicts getting help for the disorder. Medical and moral–legal views do not conflict. Each standpoint seeks solutions that are based on false assumptions that in turn rely on individualizing psychosocial problems.

Notwithstanding lurid media depictions (cf. Reinarman and Levine, 1997; Starks, 1982), and corresponding measures by law-makers and police, only a small fraction of crack users become addicts. Those who do become addicted are concentrated in the most visibly displaced segments of society. For young men in urban slums, involvement with the drug trade, whether as a dealer or an addict, is adaptive. These roles bring meaning to their lives, which to many is preferable to taking jobs that are degrading and insulting to their pride.

These observations are not new. In literature they go back centuries, and in the social sciences a hundred years at least. Such insights are familiar in Western cultural experience. However, the predominant role of mainstream media is more concerned with celebrating society's achievements, diverting our attention from the problems in society that might otherwise be exposed by focusing on the downside.

It is easier, of course, to individualize problems in society than it is to address their underlying causes. Even the well-meaning aim of balancing policing and harm reduction, for example, is not a viable solution (assuming the objective is to address addiction). The problem is that addiction is neither criminal nor medical: it is political, argues Alexander (2000).

The problem of addiction is embedded in our culture at a level deeper than attempts to understand it are willing to go. No form of intervention directed at the addict can overcome addiction in any lasting way. Productivity and progress achieved at the cost of misery and social dislocation must be meaningfully addressed. In a world of instantaneous communication, which so often glorifies free markets and worships their achievements, we must seek to find a balance in a way that works toward achieving psychosocial integration, with solutions that foster true belonging, connectedness, identity, and community support.

Increasing psychosocial integration is a problem more complex than simply eliminating poverty by providing opportunities for people in free markets. It is not a problem that is easily addressed by policy provisions of the kind that are envisioned by left-, right-, or centre-leaning groups. Social dislocation is a larger global problem that transcends drug problems in society today.

Envisioning solutions to our addiction to free-market ideology will require a re-examination of cultural priorities, argues Alexander. Optimists may argue this transition has begun, with signs of growing discontent with corporate exploitation. However, finding new resources for reducing dislocation requires reducing our dependence on past models of addiction. An adaptive understanding of addiction is essential for entertaining actual solutions to drug problems.

Chapter Summary

Chapter 7 overviewed constructions of addiction from both moral–legal and medical perspectives. The coexistence of the sin and sickness models has fostered contradictions manifested in solutions that reflect the most presumptive and dubious claims of each. These contradictions are reflected in contemporary policies and drug treatment models. We saw how clinical criteria for substance use disorders reflect the same commitment to promoting the disease model by individualizing what really is a psychosocial problem.

The disease model has persisted, despite evidence suggesting that problems of addiction are primarily adaptive, rather than determined by genetics or exposure. An adaptive orientation shifts the emphasis away from moral–medical perspectives on the nature of addiction. Rather, the emphasis is placed on envisioning solutions to reduce social dislocation and other causes of drug problems that relate to failed psychosocial integration.

The final chapter seeks to further understand actual experiences of most people who use illicit drugs. Whether used for medicine, or for recreation, or to cope with adverse situations or environments, psychoactive substances are functional commodities. Rather than disorders, or symptoms of diseases, drugs are better understood as instruments or tools.

Questions for Critical Thought

1. What is your understanding of the nature of addiction? Do you view it as a sin, as a sickness, both, or neither?
2. How does your understanding of addiction influence your perspective on appropriate solutions to drug problems?
3. Is an adaptive understanding of the nature of addiction consistent with your own experience of people with drug problems? What kinds of evidence do you find most convincing in support of or against the adaptive orientation?

Suggested Readings

Alexander, B.K. 2008. *The Globalisation of Addiction: A Study in Poverty of the Spirit*. New York: Oxford University Press. This book argues that responses to addiction have been too focused on the individual addict. The solution to the problem is rather social and political, requiring society to restructure so that people can find a sense of meaning and belonging in their lives.

Maté, G. 2008. *In the Realm of Hungry Ghosts: Close Encounters with Addiction*. Toronto: A.A. Knopf Canada. This book challenges the notion that drugs cause drug addiction. Addictions rather fill a void created by emotional trauma, a problem only worsened bythe disastrous "war on drugs."

Peele, S. 1998. *The Meaning of Addiction: An Unconventional View*. San Francisco: Jossey-Bass. This book examines individual and cultural variations in addictive experience. It challenges the medical perspective on addiction, by emphasizing the behaviour of real people in real settings, in all of its experiential and cultural complexity.

Suggested Websites

Alcoholics Anonymous
www.alcoholics-anonymous.org

The Alcoholics Anonymous website provides information for problem drinkers, media, professionals, and family members about the organization, and its understanding of the nature of the problem.

American Psychiatric Association
www.dsm5.org

This website provides resources for researchers and practitioners. It offers detailed information on development of the *Diagnostic and Statistical Manual of Mental Disorders, Fifth Edition*, released in May 2013.

Canadian Centre for Addictions
www.canadiancentreforaddictions.org

The Canadian Centre for Addictions is a residential treatment facility whose mandate is to help addicts learn the skills they need to live a drug-free lifestyle. The website advocates that in order to be successful in recovery, the physical, mental, emotional, and social aspects of the addicted person's life must be integrated. Therefore, the centre is committed to creating recovery programs that suit the needs of individual clients.

DRUGTEXT
www.drugtext.org

This website provides a wide array of information about substance use, dependence, harm reduction, and drug policy.

8 Drugs as Instruments or Tools

Learning Objectives

- To recognize the different ways in which substances are used to achieve particular objectives.
- To better understand connections between motivations and effects.
- To understand the perceptions and experiences of drug users.

Introduction

Most drug users are not addicts. Nor will they ever become addicts. People learn that their mental state can be altered by drug use, and that drugs affect perception, consciousness, mood, and personality. This transformation often facilitates the performance of non–drug related behaviours. Doses at which most people voluntarily consume drugs are below the thresholds of toxicity. Psychoactive drug use is a functional adaptation, in that individuals use drugs for their pleasurable effects. Although commonly considered maladaptive, substance use is more accurately characterized as a functional behaviour. Whereas addiction is most certainly a burden to society, and causes significant harm to individuals, the use of drugs per se is unrelated to addiction. To say that people use drugs because they have a problem, or that using drugs is a problem, is not a useful characterization.

Many drugs (such as alcohol, in moderate amounts) enhance the subjective perception of power, and provide the user with predictable short-term pleasure. The perceived benefits and functions of drug use include enhanced performance, productivity, sociability, relaxation, stress reduction, and improved mood. This chapter takes a closer look at psychoactive drug use as functional behaviour for the majority of users, which supports the framework for drug use as an instrument or tool.

Functions of Psychoactive Drug Use

We previously observed that the adaptive orientation theory posits addiction as a coping mechanism or a response to problems due to failed psychosocial integration. Most non-addicted people who use drugs do so because the effects are considered beneficial (Müller and Schumann, 2011). Viewing drugs as instruments or tools suggests a process of seeking and consuming psychoactive substances to revert our mental state back to a previously known one.

Substance use facilitates performance of established behaviours that, in theory, might enable users to attain certain goals that would either be unachievable or would otherwise require more effort. The immediate, mind-altering effects of drugs are but one aspect of the complex processes involved in drug-taking behaviours.

Understanding drug behaviour also requires an understanding of the expectations and environment (set and setting) connected to the change in mental state. Substance use occurs in particular environments and in particular motivational contexts. The motivations of the user and the environments in which they use help shape the perceptions and experiences inherent in substance use behaviour.

Human beings have consumed psychoactive plants, and preparations or derivatives, for at least ten thousand years. The origins of drug use are akin to the selective acquisition and consumption of food sources. Just as seeking and consuming different kinds of food may vary in accordance with particular nutritional needs, drug consumption choices and avoidance also serve preventative and self-medication needs. Choosing drugs to change our mental state is therefore an adaptive behaviour. The connection between food and drug selection is compelling as well. Evolutionary theories about substance use and misuse are further complicated by observed changes taking place between ancestral environments and more modern maladaptations.

As technological advances have dramatically expanded the menu of psychoactive substances available, there is a growing repertoire of substance use behaviours. In addition to synthetic compounds, the purity of substances derived from plants has been enhanced. The availability of powerful psychoactive drugs is now a common feature of our cultural environment, and in turn our societal behaviour, in an increasingly globalizing world.

For people living in modern societies, substance use and misuse are pervasive. Although psychoactive drug use can be functionally adaptive, relatively recent environmental changes have also manifested dysfunctional behaviours. Drugs are used to change our mental states in useful ways, to enhance the duration and magnitude of a desired mental state. To better understand the different functions that drugs serve, these generic motives are expanded to examine some specific goals of substance users. This section takes a closer look at reasons why drugs are used, such as to be sociable, improve cognitive performance, and enhance sensory perception, among other functions outlined in Müller and Schumann's influential review (2011).

Enhancing Social Interaction

The establishment and maintenance of social groups and networks is essential to the maintenance of successful societies. Social interaction is imperative to survival. Interaction, therefore, provides a powerful incentive for a wide range of behaviours.

In the modern world, people spend a great deal of time in structured work or educational environments. A large variety of formal and informal rules are followed, which govern interaction in these spheres. Informal social interactions are systematically suppressed in many of these more formal environments to facilitate performance. The establishment of private social bonds is often purposely restricted in favour of professional interactions, which conform to formal roles and expectations. Social activities and gatherings outside the school or workplace are, accordingly, essential to the formation and maintenance of peer groups and networks that fill our social needs. The use of psychoactive drugs facilitates transition from formal to informal group behaviour.

Many drugs change mental states in ways that have been used to enable the transition to informal group activity. The pharmacological effect (as we have seen) is less important than the social meaning and behavioural expectations of the setting or environment of drug use. A variety of substances—alcohol, cannabis, and stimulants (e.g., nicotine, caffeine, ecstasy, and cocaine)—are often used at doses that facilitate interaction.

Use of psychoactive drugs reduces inhibition, discomfort, and anxiety in social situations. Sexual behaviour is governed by a number of the same restrictions inherent to social interactions. Drug use frequently improves the possibility of sex. Notwithstanding popular depictions, which make lurid links between drug use and deviant sexual activity, certain drugs are commonly used as **social lubricants** for interactions that facilitate human sexual behaviour.

Improved Performance and Coping with Stress or Fatigue

Society puts a great amount of pressure on people to overperform, and often compete, at work and at school. To ward off the inevitable fatigue, not to mention the corresponding reduction in both cognitive and physical performance, the use of drugs is common and familiar to most people.

The rules of formal work environments typically only allow for legal stimulants, like caffeine, and prescription drugs, for this purpose; however, illicit drugs are also sometimes used to help employees stay alert and to cope with on-the-job monotony or boredom. The demand for peak performance in the workplace is often coupled with diminished time and occasion for recovery. The use of drugs to cope with stress in limited spare time is accordingly adaptive.

Moderate alcohol consumption is widely recognized as being an effective strategy in this regard, especially in light of its prevalence. Society accommodates the use of alcohol. Its reputation as a social lubricant suggests a blurring of the lines between self-medication for stress reduction and use for recreational enjoyment. These overlapping functions served by alcohol present a challenge to professionals asserting medical jurisdiction over the use of particular drugs to cope with stress.

The same blurred lines are increasingly apparent with the use of cannabis for health and recreation. Marijuana is the most widespread illicit substance used to cope with stress in Canada. Whether done explicitly (and lawfully) or otherwise, many other substances are used for the same purpose.

Self-Medication for Psychological Disorders

Psychological problems are characterized by the prolonged persistence of an aberrant mental state. People suffering from psychological disorders tend to use drugs fitting certain pharmacological profiles. Psychoactive drugs (be they prescribed or recreational) seldom represent a "cure," but they do offer effective temporary relief from negative or unpleasant mental states. Whether the psychiatric condition is diagnosed professionally or speculatively, using available thresholds for mental health disorders, the use of nonprescription drugs serves self-medicating functions.

Although drug use may exacerbate some psychiatric symptoms, users commonly experience improvements in performance or functioning in ways that they must find helpful. Despite the tendency to frown on, or **pathologize,** self-medication with drug use, it is arguably adaptive. Drug-use benefits depend on the drug as well as set and setting. People with mental health disorders, from this standpoint, often use psychoactive drugs as tools to regain functionality and a sense of control over their mental states.

Expanded Sensory Perception

The use of certain drugs—in particular hallucinogens (such as LSD, ecstasy, and magic mushrooms)—is motivated by the user's desire to profoundly alter perceptions of internal and external stimuli. The "psychedelic" drug experience is understood to facilitate new insights that augment our understanding of ourselves and of our surroundings. This search for novel stimuli, environments, or experiences is a common motivation for nondrug and drug behaviours. New experiences typically breed new insights, or else restructure existing knowledge, which can be rewarding. The connection between use of a new drug and a different sensory experience reinforces drug behaviour, particularly for those chasing a "thrill." Whether repeated or abandoned after initial experimentation, seeking new experiences through psychoactive drug use is a common motivating factor. For this reason, rates of first-time drug use are higher than those of regular use patterns.

Other, more "comfortable" drugs like cannabis, alcohol, and stimulants are also used to transform self and social outlook. These transformations, however, are experienced in predictable ways for experienced users. A common motivation among users of these substances is to temporarily relinquish, yet still maintain, some control over their behaviour and perceptions.

Improved Physical Appearance

In addition to performance expectations, modern societies impose certain ideals for physical appearance. Some drugs facilitate behaviours that can help meet these high expectations. In women, the pressure to stay reed slim is a common motivation for tobacco use, as previously noted, while among men, building defined muscles is often assisted by the use of steroids.

That said, the transformation of traditional gender roles and norms is arguably reducing the historical connection between sex and particular substance use behaviours. The perception of improved physical appearance, like drug-induced euphoria, has secondary benefits for self-esteem and confidence. These benefits, in turn, enhance performances and outcomes of activities like sexual and social interaction.

Getting High

Often philosophized as being life's primary desire, whether as a short-term or long-lasting mental state, the pursuit of happiness is common to us all. Mood enhancement is unarguably an important psychological benefit achieved by using drugs. There are a multitude of benefits that stem from changes in mental state, particularly changes that inspire happiness, which enable more efficient performance of activities.

Critics of this point of view predictably protest that it is a mock benefit and a pathway to addiction. Although technically correct, this is a rather hollow argument. Drug-induced euphoria is generally considered more intense than naturally occurring euphoria, which can lead to repeated pursuit of the high through use of the drug. This has evident advantages and costs. The potential for developing a dependence on these practices and effects is a primary drawback of sustained use of any given drug. Concerns about dependence do not negate the fact that drugs are used as tools to facilitate a wide array of behaviours and achieve certain feelings, whether real or induced. This framework recognizes the combined influence of culture, drug use settings or environments, and expectations that shape experiences of use.

Drug Expectations and Effects

In general, a **psychosocial view of substance use** suggests that drug experiences are largely determined by features of the cultural environment within which use is occurring. Initial drug encounters are especially important—these are culturally embedded with different meanings and expectations, derived from social learning (via media and peer groups, and other familiar sources of information about drugs). Novice users explore drug effects at different doses, sometimes using them in different situations and environments. Drugs that are perceived to be enjoyable and useful are significantly more likely to be used again.

Initial introduction to, and modelling of, drug use is ordinarily provided by more experienced users. Individuals will customize their substance use behaviour to optimize its benefits, depending on drug and setting. In this way psychoactive substance use is integrated with one's lifestyle and individual circumstances. Drug use is unique to each individual, but reflects larger group norms that represent the range of normally acceptable behaviour.

The perceived benefits of substance use, within its social context, must be weighed against the adverse effects of the behaviour (Figure 8.1). Many drugs cause damage to the brain and other organs, and increase pre-existing psychological disorders. What remains to be established, case by case (and

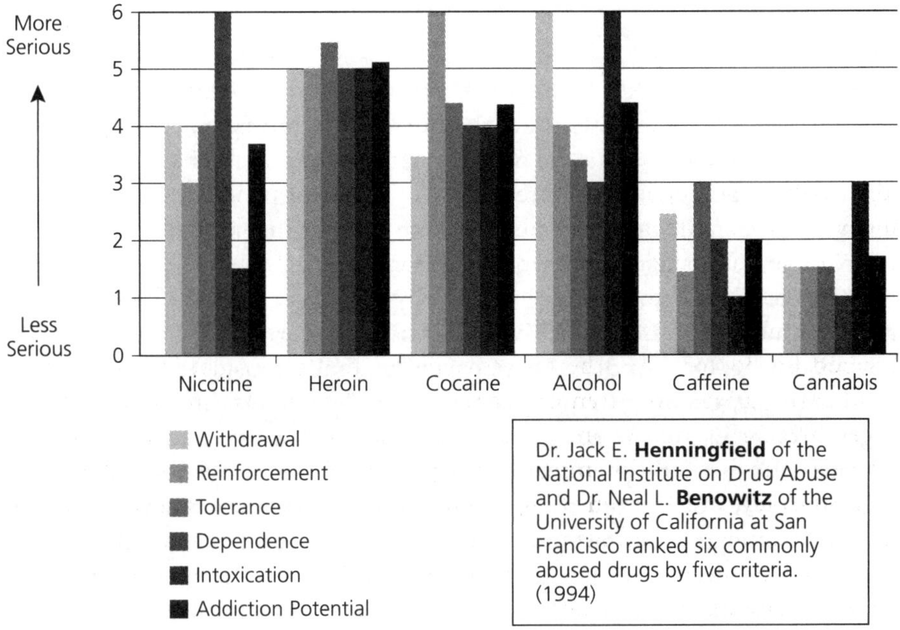

Figure 8.1 Comparing Negative Effects of Different Drugs

Source: CannabisFacts.ca (http://www.cannabisfacts.ca/pdf/HowDoesCannabisCompare.pdf). Reprinted with permission.

by and large), is whether the advantages experienced outweigh the risks to health ascribed to substance use.

As noted previously, one of the costs of instrumentalizing drug use is the potential risk of developing dependence. This understanding has prevented science from developing a better understanding of the use of drugs as tools. People who instrumentalize psychoactive substances are at higher risk of becoming drug dependent. This tells us nothing about who among us are more vulnerable to developing drug use disorders.

What we do know is that addicts tend to seek and consume drugs in a manner that is neither controlled nor goal-oriented. Addiction typically implies an escalating pattern of drug use and toxicity, and corresponding adverse outcomes. The risk of overdose increases, in addition to the long-term deleterious effects of using drugs. Addiction can be functionally adaptive when viewed as a response to social dislocation, as we saw in the previous chapter. By definition, however, **instrumentalizing drug use** means emphasizing controlled drug use that is beneficial as opposed to problematic.

Weighing costs and benefits of drug use is a more philosophical than empirical problem, perhaps. But the instrumentalization framework is well-suited to examining the behaviours and experiences of people who use drugs beneath the thresholds recognized for use disorders.

Research on the benefits of psychoactive drug use (cf. Boys et al., 2001; Morgan et al., 2013; Tupper, 2002) has been overshadowed by the tendencies to conform to dominant assumptions about drugs. Medical and moral–legal viewpoints are predominant, as noted earlier; these determine whether drugs are seen as good or bad. Even so-called value-neutral frameworks (like harm reduction) tend to focus on the risks while disregarding drug use benefits. Emphasizing costs of use defies the logic of cost–benefit analysis. To rectify this oversight and achieve a greater balance, there is a need for more research on benefits of drug use. A truly value-neutral point of view requires as much concern for optimizing benefits as reducing harms.

Despite this, considering the benefits of drug use is viewed as irresponsible, indulgent, or unprofessional. Legal drugs, particularly those prescribed by doctors, are the only drugs deemed beneficial for our health. Medical solutions are often prominent in shaping social understandings of acceptable drug use. At one point or another, alcohol, tea, and coffee have all been encouraged for improving health, vitality, and vigour (Hathaway and Sharpley, 2010), even though the popularity of these drugs as a social lubricant appears to have supplanted most of it health-promoting functions.

Quite unlike tobacco, whose social designation if not its legal status changed significantly in light of its associated harms, marijuana use in Canada is increasingly accepted as a substitute for alcohol and some prescription drugs—which, like tobacco, have been found to have unwanted health effects. In light of these developments, much of this chapter is devoted to examining different reasons for marijuana use. Having overviewed adaptive functions of drug use, we return to cannabis in order to attend more closely to the actual experiences of users.

Expectations and Effects of Marijuana Use

The prevalence of marijuana use in our society makes the practice more comparable to use of legal drugs like alcohol than to that of other outlawed drugs. Despite such widespread use, however, its legal status represents a barrier to research on perceptions and experiences of users (not to mention health benefits and risks) in the general population. Alcohol's unquestioned availability and ubiquity, most notably, have allowed for research across a broad cross-section of drinkers in the general population of adults. Resultant studies have contributed to an understanding of alcohol's mood-altering effects. This is why we know and accept that most people drink for relaxation, in social circumstances, without imbibing to excess or showing symptoms of abuse. Others drink to cope with feelings of anxiety or stress.

Physicians have increasingly pathologized drug use; however, alcohol consumption has maintained a well-established global reputation for its stress-reducing function. While this expectation is fulfilled for many drinkers, self-medication for anxiety may worsen the dysfunction. Using drugs to cope with stress can also lead to other physical and mental health disorders often found among heavy drinkers and recreational drug users (see Hathaway et al., 2013).

Studies of experienced marijuana users indicate that some of their most common expectations of the drug are similar to those attributed to alcohol. The drug is used for coping with anxiety, depression, and a variety of other distressing mental states. Cannabis is also often used for relaxation, as a social lubricant, and as a precursor to various recreational activities. Much like drinkers, few marijuana users report negative effects at moderate use levels. But use for stress or coping may have similar potential to result in adverse, or unwanted, consequences.

Different drugs, as we have seen, have different social meanings, which influence perceptions and experiences of use. Marijuana's "psychedelic" properties have long been celebrated in its subculture. This reputation is supported by anecdotal reports of users who experience expansion of consciousness, enhanced awareness, and other positive insights after taking the drug.

Such experiences, both beneficial and problematic, are intimately connected to the social circumstances (and related expectations) in which cannabis is used. Norms coinciding with specific social roles result in conflicts that arise due to assumptions of appropriate behaviour. Conflicting norms are more predictive of problems than are the quantity and frequency of substance use.

To better understand the relationship between expectations and effects of using marijuana, one study looked at users' motivations and reported positive and negative experiences of use (Hathaway et al., 2013). The primary motivations reported by respondents were relaxation, enjoyment, feeling good, and sociability. Use for coping was a far less important motivation (Table 8.1).

Positive and negative effects of use were measured using survey items beginning with the statement, "As a result of using marijuana, [for example] ... I am happier ... , have more fun in life ... , am less productive ... , [and] less efficient... " (among other commonly reported effects of substance use). Open-ended questions were included in the survey to provide more informa-

Table 8.1 Reasons for Using Marijuana (N = 89; 61% male; mean age 39 y)

Motives*	Respondents (%)
Enjoyment	
To enjoy music, movies or TV	77
To see the world with fresh eyes	40
Relaxation	
To relax	77
To feel less anxious	35
To help you sleep	30
To forget your worries	29
Mood	
To feel good	66
To cope with depression	19
Release	
To blow off steam	43
As a cure for boredom	42
Social	
To be sociable with friends	59
As a symbol of defiance to authority	13
Enhancement	
To get inspiration	40
To feel less inhibited	34
To enhance sex	30
To communicate better	16
Coping	
To get through the day	10
For medical reasons (e.g., pain, nausea)	10
To fight fatigue	4

*Respondents indicated that these motives were important or very important.

Source: Hathaway et al. (2013).

tion about motives and effects. The benefits, and primary objectives, most frequently reported were of the kinds consistent with structured survey items indicating relaxation and enhancement. Results indicated that using marijuana heightened senses, increased creativity, and altered consciousness in a way that gave users a more positive perspective.

Quotes from interviews showed that marijuana was commonly used as a relaxant (e.g., "it chills me out" or "calms me down") and as a complement to other recreational activities. A typical assertion: "it's fun to share with friends, [then] go to the movies, listen to music . . ., go out for a good meal." Positive use outcomes were reported much more often than reported negative effects (Table 8.2). Reported reasons and experiences at various use levels were consistent with each other, indicating wide agreement about the relative importance of different motives and effects.

People who use more cannabis more often tend to experience a higher frequency of every type of motivation and effect (whether these may be defined as positive or negative). Regardless of the use level, however, the rank ordering of motivations and effects appears consistent between groups.

Table 8.2 Marijuana Use Effects (N = 89)

Effects	Respondents (%)
Positive	
As a result of using marijuana	
• I have come to know myself better	61
• I have more fun in life	54
• I have more appreciation for beautiful things	50
• I am more open to other people	45
• I am more balanced	39
• I am happier with myself	36
• I am more open to religious and spiritual matters	33
• My social life has improved	32
• My love life is more intense	24
• I am a better and smarter person	24
• I go out more often	18
Negative	
As a result of using marijuana	
• I take myself less seriously	54
• I am less ambitious	27
• I am less productive	25
• I am slower-thinking	24
• I am less efficient	18
• I have less interest in normal life	15
• I have serious problems	6

Source: Hathaway et al. (2013).

Put otherwise, whatever the level of consumption, using marijuana for relaxation and enhancement was related to more positive experiences of use.

Being employed was related to experiencing more positive effects, while significant predictors of more negative experiences included marriage, use of alcohol, health problems, and being female. Other factors correlated with less positive experiences were use of cannabis as a coping mechanism, lower age of first use, and changes in use patterns due to major life transitions.

Interpretation

There are limitations to fully capturing the experiences of drug users obtained through surveys; more intensive qualitative research is required to do so. The findings of this research, however, do indicate that marijuana use—and use of other substances as instruments or tools—needs to be examined with attention to the motivations behind, and personal and social circumstances surrounding, drug use. Despite the limitations of this research, study findings suggest that life enhancement and relaxation are significant predictors of experiencing more positive effects.

Although using drugs to cope with stress and problems is often a predictor of more problematic use, self-medication need not lead to adverse outcomes. As we have seen previously, new insights can be gained by studying drug users whose experiences are positive. Experiences of stigma based on gender, personal relationships, employment, and health status are all potential sources of role conflict that appear to influence perceptions of use benefits and problems. The association between motivations and effects cannot be determined independently of societal meanings and reactions, which are culturally defined.

People's experiences with banned substances like cannabis differ in important ways from their experience with legal drugs like alcohol. Whether motivations follow or precede the drug behaviour, social norms and attitudes are central to better understanding experiences of use. Drug use motivations are socially constructed phenomena that need to be explained.

Expectations of drug use must be situated socially, historically, and culturally as part of the experience-determining behaviours and associated meanings within the social group. Motivations behind, and effects of, using psychoactive substances are thereby understood as sociocultural descriptions or existing representations of "reality."

Different social groups have different languages, depending on life experiences and social circumstances. Research on the use of drugs as instruments or tools requires an understanding of the background expectations that determine culturally appropriate explanations. To better understand important nuances that shape the connections between drug use expectations and effects, the next section takes a closer look at narratives of people who use marijuana as a medicine for coping with a wide variety of chronic health conditions.

Constructing Cannabis as Medicine

Cannabis has a long medical history, and anecdotal evidence from contemporary users points to an array of therapeutic uses. In Canada, despite its recent history of growing support for use of cannabis to treat disease or alleviate symptoms, there has been little research to determine how it works. Notwithstanding research currently being conducted to scientifically determine marijuana's effectiveness compared with other treatments, experimental medicine sheds no light on how its use is actually experienced by people and what meaning people ascribe to those experiences.

Qualitative research is required to understand perceptions and experiences of people who use cannabis to cope with chronic medical conditions. To better understand the use of cannabis as medicine, in-depth interviews were carried out with 103 users recruited from compassion clubs in three Canadian cities (see also Hathaway and Rossiter, 2007; Jones and Hathaway, 2008; Hathaway and Sharpley, 2010). Drawing from these interviews, this section will explore distinctions made between "recreational" and "medical" consumption of the drug.

Patient narratives in this study include an understanding of chronic pain and illness and the experiences of using cannabis for coping or relief. Cannabis was used to treat a multitude of symptoms of physical and mental chronic health conditions. Of the 25 conditions mentioned, the most prevalent were anxiety, depression, and other mental health disorders (34 per cent); chronic pain (33 per cent); and HIV and hepatitis C (14 per cent).

The common link among respondents was that they suffered from conditions that were chronic or ongoing, and that they were discontent with standard treatments. Descriptions of the benefits of cannabis were often reported alongside side effects of drugs prescribed by doctors. Prescription drugs had either proven ineffective or had unpleasant or debilitating side effects, which outweighed any benefits.

Box 8.1 begins with an excerpt from an interview that gives a colourful description of a drug for epilepsy. The potential side effects listed on the bottle included suicidal ideation. The interviewee had discovered that using marijuana was more effective for controlling his epileptic seizures than this prescribed medication. Though marijuana also has side effects, he found these far more positive. Self-medication using cannabis had much improved his appetite, for example, and countered his insomnia.

Physicians frequently reject anecdotal claims like these as hearsay. Their dismissive attitudes are partly a reflection of financial and professional interests coinciding with those of the drug companies and the medical establishment (see Jones and Hathaway, 2008). Up until the recent past, patient testimony was the primary source of medical knowledge. The trend of formalism over

Box 8.1 Narratives of Medical Marijuana Users

Patients describe their positive and negative experiences with, and reasons for, using the drug in this capacity.

1. Side-Effects

   Here's a few side effects of this lovely new drug they put me on a few years back. This one caused so much confusion and hostility towards my loved ones. It was just bizarre...[reading side effects] "A very small number of people may have thoughts of suicide"—which I did have... I didn't want to live anymore... [continues reading] "the most frequently observed side effects are solemness, weakness, infections such as common colds, dizziness, cold sores. Other side effects include abnormal thinking, amnesia, anxiety, lack of coordination, depression, bruising, emotional liability, mood swings, hostility, nervousness, personality disorder, sore throat, runny nose, stuffy head, tooth disorders and vertigo." Fucking lovely!

2. Alternative Medicine

   I went to San Francisco in 1960 and I was living right in the middle of the Haight-Ashbury for 6 years.... And that's when I started smoking very, very nice marijuana..., [which] in my case has kept me from being a complete vegetable really. I'm very ill, but at the same time, the smoke keeps me doing all the things I want to do at this point in my life. It's keeping me out of the nursing home. It's like a dance, and either you dance or you don't.... I can't dance with Tylenol 3.

3. Self-Discipline and Knowledge

   Smoking to get high and self-medicating [have] a number of different dimensions. One being to numb, to not experience...your problems fall away. And it may give people relief from seemingly intractable problems, but that's not an answer. That's like getting drunk to forget, in a way....

   It's only when people are educated enough and understand the big picture, and how things are all interconnected, with your body, and your state of mind, that you can use it more as a tool.... and I've spent decades looking at specifically these questions.

4. Substitute or Complement to Prescription Drugs

   I consider it my medicine, like the doctor prescribed me amoxycilin or penicillin. Like before I went out and got marijuana, I'd be out at Shoppers Drug Mart and getting my Penicillin. That means I'm sick right? So I consider it like that.

*****

Continued

If you eat it, it relieves more [symptoms] than smoking. And when you eat pot in muffins, it is just as good as Percocet as far as I'm concerned.... Now I don't get high on pot...it's like OxyContin. You don't get high on OxyContin after taking it for a while. It's like any drug, your body gets. You get a sense of well-being, comfortable with yourself maybe. Or maybe you do get a buzz but you don't realize it.

5. Supportive Doctors

My specialist in Vancouver was the one that said, "You should try smoking that marijuana." He says: "I've heard it helps."

*****

My pain doctor—I get spinal epidurals in the hospital once a month—he encourages me to smoke cannabis before I come...and relax, a mild sedative. He gives me a Lorazepam under my tongue to take, and it just relaxes [me]. Because I'm needle phobic... I just don't like needles.

6. Spiritual Healing

After using it medicinally, it's become a spiritual part of my life more and more. Because I believe...our medicines are provided on this earth for us, so why wouldn't cannabis be one of them, when it works the best?

*****

Chronic means it's slowly seeping, it's becoming worse, and then I can hit it with cannabis. But I have to do my visualization. I have to do my breathing which is imagining that there is this hair of light that is non-painful that is on the pain area, that goes around me like a band, and I'm just breathing into that light, and I'm just imagining it getting a tiny bit bigger... and I fall into a deep sleep, and I'll wake up better.

7. "I Don't Get High"

The one I use is Emerald Wonder, an *indica,* because it's for pain and it's for sleep, and those are the two that matter the most to me... and a friend of mine who's a social smoker would give me some and say, "Are you high yet?" And I would say "No, I don't use it for that." And somebody else from the compassion club explained to him that it goes to my pain first, and I thought that makes sense—because I don't get high.

8. Therapeutic Dose and Setting

The environment has to be there for me to be able to smoke it. And when it comes to pain I will sometimes wait until later in the afternoon or early in the evening, because then I don't have to do anything more that day. My phone calls are taken care of, my head isn't as foggy, and I can concentrate... and I really like not having people around when I do it, because I'm looking after myself....

*****

Because I am using it therapeutically… I just can't smoke that much! There's no reason to. Anything over 2–3 tokes… doesn't make any difference really. It costs more money. It's social, I enjoy it, but I'm usually the first person to say no. I'll have one joint and then someone else will roll one and I'll pass. It's just not necessary.

*****

I smoke first thing in the morning, and I smoke every hour and a half these days.

Interviewer: "An entire joint?"

No, I just sprinkle a little bit in a tobacco cigarette…. I've cut down when it hasn't been available. And I find that I have as much therapeutic benefit if I take a pinch, put it in a pipe, and take one toke—it's all I need. Everything after that is recreation.

Sources: Personal interviews with author.

the last century, however, puts more emphasis on evidence-based expertise of the kind procured through formal research methods.

The unregulated use of cannabis as medicine subverts the dominant world view in which experts define what is appropriate medical treatment and what counts as evidence or "proof." Establishing medical efficacy through clinical means alone, however, overlooks myriad psychosocial factors. Alternative approaches are not easy to assess due to the philosophies from which they are derived. These practices transcend formal standards and assumptions of what is meant by health, healing and well-being, and the evaluation methods of conventional medical science.

To illustrate, a different view of "good medicine" was provided by an elderly respondent in the study (Box 8.1.2), who characterizes cannabis as being a transcendental tool that improves well-being and helps her better cope with daily chronic aches and pains. The "high" from using marijuana, in this testimony, is an essential component of its therapeutic benefits.

The vast majority of medical users in this study also used marijuana socially, and although the line between medicinal and recreational use was often blurry, participants did attempt to make distinctions. Using marijuana as medicine was often posited as a deliberate activity, requiring more discipline and self-knowledge (Box 8.1.3). As noted previously, many users made direct comparisons between cannabis and other medications. Most often, using marijuana was described as an effective substitute or complement to pharmaceutical drugs (Box 8.1.4).

Considering the hesitance of doctors to support marijuana use, many patients value the legitimacy afforded by those medical professionals who are supportive (Box 8.1.5). Evidently, Western medicine is not entirely ignorant of the world view of people who self-medicate with cannabis. The need for medical authority to legitimize their choice of medicine was far from universal, though. Others saw the use of medical marijuana as a form of healing and spiritual transcendence (Box 8.1.6).

For those identifying with alternative perspectives on health and health care that depart from standard forms of treatment, the role of the support system provided by belonging to a cannabis compassion club is particularly evident (see Hathaway and Rossiter, 2008). Acquiring marijuana from compassion clubs—as opposed to "street dealers" or other common sources of supply—helped to further justify its use as therapeutic and offered a vocabulary consistent with this image. Most respondents used the term *medicine* to refer to cannabis, as opposed to *marijuana, pot, weed,* or other slang terms employed by recreational users of the drug. Belonging to a community of medical cannabis users also influenced study participants' understanding of the practice as something quite distinctive from using to "get high" (Box 8.1.7).

The use of cannabis as medicine shares many characteristics with the use of other drugs as instruments or tools. The role of social learning in shaping expectations and interpretations of the practice is essential. Ultimately, functionally adaptive use of cannabis—as suggested by the adoption of the term *self-medicate*—requires an element of personal autonomy or choice.

Whereas support from doctors and fellow users was important in constructing use of cannabis as medicine, exerting personal control over drug use circumstances was an essential aspect of the use experience. In defining recreational and medical use patterns, using marijuana therapeutically for many required particular attention to the amount consumed and the setting in which marijuana was used. In particular, distinctions were observed between therapeutic and recreational use settings. Participants often reported using cannabis on a schedule to ensure that its effects remained consistent. Indeed, their use was arguably as chronic as their conditions, with levels of consumption commonly exceeding those of use for recreation.

Medical use patterns are also deliberately distinctive. Using marijuana as a medicine comes with costs that for many present a large financial burden. Fixed incomes can put strict limits on how much these patients can afford. Exercising moderation by necessity is also a demonstration of control, which often was identified as a common attribute of therapeutic use (Box 8.1.8).

Further Implications

The use of cannabis for coping, or as means of adjustment to adverse circumstances, is by no means always a maladaptive habit. Rather, the experience and outcome are contingent on social learning and nuances based on expectations of use and the environment or setting in which the use occurs. With reference to properties of the drug itself, there are important differences between cannabis and stimulants like cocaine (and narcotics, such as morphine, and depressants, such as alcohol and barbiturates).

Physiological dependence on cannabis is rare, and discontinuance of use does not typically result in debilitating symptoms of withdrawal. The drug has been defined as "consciousness expanding" because, quite unlike narcotics or sedating drugs, its use "increases awareness of surroundings and bodily processes," and "serves as a guide to psychic areas which can then be reentered without it" (Solomon, 1966: 443, 446).

Self-reports of cannabis experiences invariably include feelings of euphoria, well-being, and enhanced self-awareness. While many users say it calms them and is useful for relaxing, others paradoxically describe it as a stimulant that invigorates the body, mind, or both. The "high" is therefore experienced in different ways, reflecting a variety of motives, expectations, and effects. Many users credit marijuana for allowing them to disregard distractions that otherwise prevent them from seeing the "big picture" or pick up on nuances that change their perception of any given situation.

Use of the term *recreation* tends to trivialize the role of marijuana in the lives of many users. In that regard, it is worth noting that the essence of the term suggests a deeper meaning in its role to *re-create*. While users generally acknowledge that such benefits are often achievable through other activities, marijuana is deemed to be the most pragmatic method. The next section, accordingly, shifts focus to examine other illustrations of the role of marijuana in the lives of users as an instrument or tool.

Marijuana Use for Work, Leisure, and Transcendence

Using marijuana in our culture is primarily understood to be a recreational activity, enjoyed by young adults on weekends or after work. Although this is a common pattern of consumption, my first study in this area, based on 30 in-depth interviews with recreational users, shows that social use in leisure time is only a single facet of marijuana use behaviour (Hathaway, 1997). Frequently, reasons to use marijuana are more personal, and largely independent of group-oriented use. For some, marijuana is comparable to alcohol. It is commonly depicted as providing an experience that lowers inhibitions in a relaxed informal atmosphere, allowing greater freedom of expression. For other users, the experience of using marijuana is regularly sought outside this social context.

Many regular consumers, for example, use marijuana in order to relax at the end of the workday, as a way to manage stress and get a good night's sleep. Although it is acknowledged there are other ways to do this, marijuana is

Box 8.2

Marijuana and Lifestyle

Regular marijuana consumers describe their relationship with the drug.

1. Superiority Over Alcohol

   It enables me to unwind before bed after a long day of work and helps me sleep without needing a couple of hours to do it.... I enjoy being able to come home and immediately relax in the five to ten minutes it takes to roll a joint. The moment I smoke a joint my brain and all the worries of the day are turned off, and it's just the basic functions left behind. Whatever I'm doing can become the primary focus for me.

2. Enhanced Sensory Experience

   It brightens my mood. I have a great time and see the fun stuff in the world. It helps me remember to appreciate food, colours, beautiful things.... You get so blasé to things in the real world. It's like a re-education—dope says, "Whoa, wait a minute. This is delicious!"

   *****

   To sit in one spot and get stoned is a complete waste. I need to do something—to see and feed my brain, and suck up as much as I can. I feel very confined when I have to stay in one spot. I always try to do something outside where I'm free to move.

3. An Alternative Perspective

   It opens windows that aren't open all the time.... It's just a different way of looking at things, especially as you get older. Being inside your brain for that long gets boring.

   *****

   It allows me to step back a little bit and look at the world in a little more colourful light or warped perspective, instead of taking it so seriously. It lets my sense of humour come out, instead of getting intense and overwrought about things.

considered advantageous for unwinding and alleviating the worries of the day. Compared with using alcohol and other drugs, marijuana is a better tool for many users, allowing them to relax and better refocus their priorities without the cost invoked by a hangover the next day (see Box 8.2.1).

In addition to its use as a restorative relaxant, marijuana is used to induce euphoria, which is experienced as a stimulation of the senses. It heightens consciousness and awareness of surroundings, making leisure-time activities more

4. The Flow Experience

   I like to have my day figured out and be focused first.... Once I have my day figured out, I can have a toke, go out to the studio and focus on exactly what I have to do for hours and hours. Everything has a flow. If it doesn't, I'll stop, have a coffee and a toke, and go back to work, [asking myself] "Now do you have the flow. Now is the perspective better?"

5. Refocusing and Brainstorming

   I often get stoned the day before I write a story. It helps me figure out what's important and interesting in the story. Things that didn't seem important can become crucial to the whole story.

   *****

   My first time going over the data, it allows me to juggle more data and consider more aspects of the data. I take notes and chase them down later when I'm straight.... I may not smoke for two weeks during the technical phase of a project. But the first thing I do when the project ends is smoke a joint. It helps me reset the registers to zero, clear my mind, and get on with the interpretation.

6. A Multipurpose Tool

   There are other activities that will allow me to balance my aggressive reactions to this world with what I need to do to survive and live in it. Most of them require so much time though.... Rather than having to go out and do insane things on a regular basis, marijuana allows me to do it in a very gentle, small way every day.

   *****

   It allows me to be more honest with people I feel I can be honest with. This has helped me to build a really strong relationship with my husband. It has given us some really interesting space to bond in and be together.... Time and work can do the same thing. But dope seems to give you a secret back door to the human condition that gives you access to something fundamentally human, and guides you so that you get to know yourself and other people in different ways.

Source: Adapted from Hathaway (1997).

interesting and enjoyable. The feelings of well-being and euphoria described are enhanced by the full spectrum of sensory experience: sight, sound, touch, taste, and smell (Box 8.2.2).

Enhancing mental and physical awareness facilitates the vigorous pursuit of leisure activities. These descriptions of the marijuana use experience starkly contradict mainstream depictions of the practice, namely the stereotypical portrayal of the lethargic "stoner." Enhanced self-awareness is reported with the use of cannabis, in addition to stimulation of the senses, which for many is considered useful in all aspects of their lives.

For some participants, using marijuana represented little more than an escape from mundane, everyday existence (see Box 8.2.3). For others, the term *escapism* underestimated the value of gaining an alternative perspective on the world. A new outlook, from this standpoint, was considered useful for addressing and resolving real-world problems.

Use of marijuana as a problem-solving tool was especially apparent in the narratives of those who claimed they found it useful in their work. Drug laws that prohibit use, and norms of the work world, commonly prevent people from using on-the-job. Those who worked at home, or in unsupervised environments (or other kinds of workplaces where different rules apply), were not necessarily restricted by these rules.

People who used cannabis while on the job reported using it selectively for an array of tasks. The paradoxical description of its role as both relaxant and stimulant, which complemented leisure-time activities, re-emerged in illustrations of marijuana use at work. For example, one respondent said that her use gave her "a strange ability to focus and not focus at the same time; you can focus but it's on your own terms" (Hathaway, 1997).

As a tool for recreational enjoyment, marijuana was credited with taking the user's mind off work. According to study participants, the drug provided more energy and sensory stimulation thereby enhancing the pleasure found in leisure-time pursuits. Use for work-related tasks was variously described as optimizing the performance of particular activities—often those demanding extra patience, more precision, concentration, and attention to meticulous detail.

A computer programmer in my study, for example, stated: "It allows me to attain perfection in detailed computer work—to take the extra time in the tedious processing of final details to get exactly what I want." Using stimulants at work is relatively common. However, unlike coffee—as has been documented elsewhere, in a study of farm labourers in Jamaica, for example—cannabis is used to alleviate fatigue, as well as to alleviate monotony and boredom (Rubin and Comitas, 1975). Those who find that cannabis enhances work performance are ordinarily discerning, or selective, in its use. For some, its use remains "strictly recreational," even in the workplace. For others, it is integral to doing their jobs.

Optimizing cannabis experiences, more generally, involves a learning process in which users find their own ways of isolating and exploiting the properties they find most useful. With experience, users learn that there are times and places (and work or leisure circumstances) in which cannabis has benefits, and other situations in which it does not. Patterns of selective use for work are determined by demarcating conducive circumstances (Box 8.2.4).

The **flow experience** described above is generally consistent with the descriptions of transcendent, peak, or optimal experience found in **positive psychology**, Eastern mysticism, and other literature exploring altered conscious states (see Hathaway and Sharpley, 2010). Among other benefits ascribed to achieving higher consciousness, the flow experience is characterized as an ability to balance challenges at hand with a capacity to meet them. Often marked by an intense concentration of attention, it includes a clear perception of control over one's actions and what needs to be done from one moment to the next.

The flow experience is optimal in seeking the right balance between adversity and coping skills. The experience reportedly facilitates reduction of understimulation and overstimulation, thereby reducing both boredom and stress. Flow describes a sense of order in oneself and one's surroundings, so that activities are felt to be intrinsically rewarding. Interference from irrelevant distractions is excluded from the field of consciousness. Performance is enhanced by constant feedback from the immediate environment through heightened sensory perception.

Marijuana users feel they benefit from gaining an alternative perspective on their work, and on the world. Looking at things differently reportedly provides a better understanding of how they fit together. Using marijuana is considered advantageous by writers and researchers, for example, in the early stages of a project. It is useful for brainstorming, and often used as a precursor to preparing a project outline (Box 8.2.5). Beyond its applications for enhancing work activity, particularly for those who never use it on the job, marijuana use was credited with shaping users' outlook in a way that changed them for the better.

These illustrations indicate that using marijuana provides serenity of mind and valued insights, which accordingly transcend the boundaries observed between work and recreation. Its influence according to users is unique. Although for others there are other ways of meeting these objectives, using marijuana is reliable, convenient, and better suited for achieving a variety of ends (Box 8.2.6).

Interpretation and Expansion

The previous examples demonstrate that marijuana is routinely used as a tool for work and leisure, and as a means of coping with health problems. Of further note, however, the drug's influence evidently extends beyond those boundaries. Users' narratives invoke a sense of spiritual fulfillment, fascination, or enchantment observed in other literature (see McKenna, 1992). The role of drugs as **plant teachers** is frequently dismissed as a misguided justification for substance use behaviour. The use of psychoactive drugs for spiritual activity and religious purposes, however, is an ancient practice long predating prohibition of these substances.

Taking these claims seriously, accordingly, makes more sense than denying their validity on moral–legal grounds. Using psychedelic drugs is variously argued to foster valuable insights by restructuring prior knowledge. The drug experience is understood to serve a deeper function, beyond the short-term alteration of one's sensory perception.

Taking drugs as tools to foster spiritual experiences is among the earliest documented uses. Psychoactive substance use by shamans indicates that seeking closer contact with the divine through drug experience can reinforce religious ties within the social group. Shamanistic practices of using drugs to help communicate with the otherworldly are an illustration of how altered states of consciousness serve religious purposes in a directed way.

The use of drugs for ritualistic purposes in spiritual and religious practices, however, has largely been forgotten in most parts of the world. Since the arrival and diffusion of Christianity, Judaism, and Islam, drugs have been exchanged for prayer and meditation (see Müller and Schumann, 2011).

The secularization of the Western world may partially explain the popularity of drugs as tools for spiritual enlightenment. The use of psychoactive drugs for ritualistic purposes is evident in clubs, at raves and dance festivals (and pubs), and other places people gather to consume drugs as a group. The individual narratives presented in this chapter illustrate how marijuana users achieve other objectives in their own adaptive and self-directed ways.

Chapter Summary

Building on discussion of addiction as an adaptive response to dislocation in a globalizing world, this chapter's focus shifted to recreational and medical functions of psychoactive substance use. Instrumentalizing drug use recognizes that the practice is conducive to achieving particular objectives, beyond a short-term change in mental state. Drugs are for coping, but also for social interaction, expanding sensory perception, and improving task performance.

The role of social learning was examined in this chapter, with particular attention to how drug expectations and behaviour are influenced by cultural and individual factors. To illustrate the role of set and setting in behaviour, we have explored the use of marijuana, which, though outlawed, is a drug used widely for a variety of purposes. The illicit status of this substance, for most users, has resulted in distinctive patterns of behaviour. We observed that reasons for using marijuana depart from those for using alcohol. Although alcohol is legal and more generally accepted, its functions appear to be more narrowly defined.

The use of cannabis for coping with health problems was examined, with emphasis on how it is constructed as a medicine. Despite increasing tolerance and accommodation of the use of cannabis as medicine in Canada, there is still an associated stigma, which influences perceptions of the practice among users (patients) and non-users. Examining distinctions between medical consumption and marijuana use for recreational enjoyment sheds light on ways that set and setting mediate the drug experience.

Recreational drug use, although often trivialized (and criminalized), is the most common motivation for use, with predominant patterns of behaviour subscribing to this category. Examining the motivations and experiences of users suggests the term *recreation* oversimplifies the matter. In addition to drugs as coping mechanisms and drugs for medicinal purposes, drugs are used as tools for meeting positive objectives.

Drawing on the narratives of marijuana users, who report use of the drug for a variety of reasons, we explored its use for work, leisure, and transcendence. These descriptions often overlap, and it is evident that drawing boundaries between them is difficult to do. The role of marijuana in the lives of many users extends beyond official definitions of drug use as either medical, recreational, religious, or other.

The meaning of the practice is contingent on the social and personal experiences of users of the drug. A common theme emerging in the narratives of users is that they subjectively experience and value the drug's influence for enhancing work and recreational activities. Using marijuana also fosters new perspectives, which are considered useful for achieving certain goals.

Questions for Critical Thought

1. Which of the functions of drug use outlined in Chapter 8 are most consistent with your own motives, or those of people that you know? In your experience, what types of drugs fulfill these different roles?
2. How does the research on connections between motivations and effects compare with your experiences, or those of drug users you know?
3. How do the descriptions of marijuana use for coping and for recreation overlap? How do they differ? Which of these are most consistent with depictions of the practice, or the experiences of marijuana users that you know?

Suggested Readings

Bennett, C., L. Osburn, and J. Osburn. 1995. *Green Gold the Tree of Life: Marijuana in Magic & Religion.* Frazier Park, CA: Access Unlimited. This book documents the ancient history of cannabis in native cultures in North America and around the world.

Tupper, K.W. 2002. "Entheogens and Existential Intelligence: The Use of Plant Teachers as Cognitive Tools," *Canadian Journal of Education* 27 (4): 499–516. This article investigates the use of psychoactive plants as tools to facilitate existential intelligence. It documents the use of plant teachers (or entheogens) for gaining a richer cosmological understanding of the world for individuals and cultures.

Weil, A., and W. Rosen. 2004. *From Chocolate to Morphine: Everything You Need to Know about Mind-Altering Drugs.* New York: Houghton Mifflin. This book is an authoritative resource for unbiased information about how drugs affect the mind and body. It covers a wide range of available substances—from coffee to marijuana, antihistamines to psychedelics, and steroids to smart drugs—including drug effects, precautions, and alternatives.

Suggested Websites

Crack Facts

www.crack-facts.org/drugsetandsetting.html

This website debunks myths about the use of crack cocaine. It further illustrates the influence of set and setting factors in determining experiences and relationships with drugs.

Marijuana—Uses

www.marijuana-uses.com

Dr. Lester Grinspoon's website invites contributions on marijuana's vast array of benefits experienced between its use as medicine and as a social lubricant. It explores the possibilities and effects described by words like therapeutic, enhancement, consciousness exploration and expansion, among others.

MedicalMarijuana.ca

www.medicalmarijuana.ca

This website provides news, information and resources about the use of cannabis as medicine for patients, physicians, and licensed producers.

Conclusion

By adopting a constructionist perspective, my aim has been to offer a distinctly sociological framework for examining drug issues in society. In particular, I sought to problematize the bio/psycho/social standpoint adopted in most textbooks. Beginning with an overview of common themes presented to students taking courses in this area, this book reorients the focus that is typically employed.

Rather than as "facts" we take for granted or assume, the nature of the drug problem is problematized by treating the alleged facts as products of a process of claims-making. Challenging our current knowledge of drugs requires an examination of how drug problems in Canada and elsewhere are constructed, particularly the historical, political, and cultural influences that shape our understanding.

The social history of drug control in Canada reflects racial and class conflict. We have seen how legislation and enforcement of the law is a representation of moral norms and vested interests. The war on drugs was analyzed, with particular attention to ongoing conflicts over values and disagreement over the role of law in regulating moral conduct. The halting progress of the harm-reduction movement serves to illustrate impediments to meaningful drug policy reform. Despite its rational basis in evidence-based knowledge, there are challenges remaining for proponents of implementing public health solutions for drug-related problems.

The sociocultural environment in which substance use occurs was examined closely in this book, with examples highlighting contributions from Canadian research. The analyses provided a variety of insights about the social meaning of drug use from the respective outlooks of users and non-users. Psychoactive substances are valuable commodities. Drugs serve as symbols of conformity, social deviance, and other markers of identity and status in society.

The symbolic function of substance use is often more important than drug properties for developing a better understanding of both the way a drug is used and the consequences of consumption for the user. The last three chapters of the book examined the construction of drug use as a symbol, a symptom, and a tool. Problematic drug use has been variously constructed as a sin and as a sickness, requiring punishment or treatment.

Drug policy today reflects a curious conjoining of the moral-failure and disease models of addiction, and the use of outlawed substances is treated as a problem requiring intervention that addresses both issues. The coexisting moral–legal and medical perspectives offer contradicting explanations of the problem, while instituting the most dubious claims derived from each. To provide a framework for a more balanced perspective, a competing understanding of drug problems was presented.

Instead of as a medical or moral–legal problem, a psychosocial interpretation of addiction was provided. From this standpoint, substance use–related symptoms of addiction are behavioural responses to social dislocation that are arguably adaptive. As a coping mechanism for failed social integration, addiction from this point of view is neither pathological nor limited to problematic substance use.

Psychoactive drugs are used for coping, and as tools for achieving social and personal objectives. Regardless of their status under law, drug users' motivations, perceptions, and experiences provide essential insights into different benefits and costs of substance use. This book provides a framework for examining these issues. It is less concerned with whether drugs are good or bad than with examining how drug-related problems are socioculturally constructed.

Despite the emphasis on claims-making adopted here, it is important to reiterate that a constructionist perspective is by no means inconsistent with that of addiction as a pressing social problem. Substance users seeking treatment have real problems. Many of them benefit by finding ways to cope, employing different medical and psychosocial therapies.

The therapies and services available to addicts have expanded with the diffusion of the public health perspective. However, beyond support for harm reduction and increasing treatment options, which reflect broader expertise and disciplinary knowledge, we must recognize the culture of addiction that sustains drug problems in society today. Inseparable from efforts to treat addiction as a medical or criminal matter, this culture of addiction adopts one or both mechanisms of control.

The expansion of behavioural addictions—such as gambling, sex, codependency, and Internet addiction—is an indication of increasing jurisdiction of the medical profession over a vast range of behaviours. The larger scope of interventions treating different kinds of problems using a variety of psychosocial methods also validates seeking solutions to drug problems in societal conditions and other socializing factors that influence perceptions and standards of behaviour.

Drug-related problems, and the ways in which we understand them, are shaped by class, gender, and ethnicity, among other constructed definitions that divide as they define us. A number of Canadian case studies were presented in this book to document these socializing factors. For example, Manderson's (1995) and Carstairs' (2006) works were cited for the important insights they provided into class-based and gendered definitions of drug problems; these contribute to a better understanding of addiction as a substance use behaviour.

Injection drug use has long symbolized rejection of convention. As the hardest way to do the hardest drug, injecting heroin is invested with dramatically conflicting subcultural and cultural understandings of what the act represents. Interventions in this area require an understanding of the meaning of the behaviour from the point of view of addicts, and the meaning of the intervention for the addict and society. More research is needed to inform harm reduction services for people who inject drugs.

Women who inject drugs (or use any drugs at all) are subject to quite different expectations of behaviour, and their motivations are quite different from those of men. Assumptions about sex and gender roles are influential factors underlying drug behaviour. Cook's (2011) and Rudy's (2011) studies show that smoking cigarettes has, at one time or another, served some of the same functions and subcultural objectives. For women (and for men, to some extent) smoking is a symbol of conformity to certain kinds of values and a symbol of resistance to, or rebellion against, others.

Whether we are recommending harm reduction or prevention—and whether our efforts are aimed at homeless youth or middle-class women—gendered expectations and societal reactions to substance use behaviour must be part of the equation. Gender roles and expectations specifically must be examined and overturned rather than used as status quo to justify a policy or program. High smoking rates, binge drinking, and fetal alcohol syndrome (FAS) are all problems that require a better understanding of problems facing women in society today.

Among other risk groups are young persons who use a variety of substances to fit in, feel good, or cope. Drug use plays a role in the formation of identities; these reflect class, culture, and gendered expectations. Societal reactions concerning substance use reveal race and gender biases, and cultural proscriptions that inevitably distort the meaning of these acts. Harm reduction and prevention interventions must include a deeper understanding of the motives, expectations, and benefits experienced, as well as harms of use. This, in turn, requires an understanding of historical and cultural constructions of what drug use represents. Better educational initiatives that target at-risk youth are necessary, particularly those that differentiate the unique circumstances surrounding socioeconomic class, race, and gender.

The ways we understand drug problems serve a social function by distracting us from different ways of looking at drug issues. For example, sexual assault and FAS are problems "caused" by women drinking, or drinking to excess. This construction of the problem discourages a deeper investigation and discussion of the cultural assumptions and conditions that foster widespread alcohol misuse. Instead of addressing social problems—which would require reflection, hard choices, and societal investment—quasi-medical and moral–legal explanations and evaluations are adopted, which target the symptom not the cause.

Race, like gender, has been shown to influence perceptions and interpretations of substance use behaviour. Higher rates of substance use in certain populations have been used to justify more regulation and restrictions, which reflect conflicting moral norms. Abject poverty and social dislocation, we have noted, have long been understood as major causes of addiction. However, prevention strategies that target "at-risk" populations have a tendency to treat these populations as the problem. The actual causes of the problem are ignored, and shamefully neglected, and drug abuse is either criminalized or pathologized. Alexander's (2000) work has been highlighted in particular. His insights have raised important questions about treating high rates of alcohol abuse among First Nations populations as a "Native problem" as opposed to one that was created by Canadian society.

Such extreme examples of social dislocation, and the destructive tendencies of society itself, support interpretations of addiction as a problem requiring a solution not found in medicine or law. In order to arrive at this conclusion, and contribute to solutions to drug problems *of society*, a better understanding of how substance use–related problems are constructed is a critical necessity. As a starting point for further exploration of these issues, in the social context of Canadian society, I hope this book gives its readers added confidence to do so as students, informed citizens, and claims-makers in their own right.

Glossary

Abuse A term used by clinicians to describe the use of drugs in ways that cause physical or psychological problems, difficulty meeting obligations at home or at work, or legal problems.

Adaptive orientation A perspective on addiction that explains it as a functional behaviour as opposed to a medical disorder.

Addictive personality A psychological perspective suggesting that certain individuals' makeups are more susceptible to drug addiction.

Bio/psycho/social standpoint A multidisciplinary perspective on drug problems, informed by biomedical and psychosocial theories that explain the nature of the problems and the solutions.

Civilizing process A term describing the progression of Western culture to a modern world view informed by science, rationality, and reason.

Claims-making Characterizing social problems with explanations that focus on the process of collective definition.

Cognitive behavioural therapy (CBT) An approach to addiction treatment oriented to the development of strategies enabling the addict to change maladaptive thinking and patterns of behaviour.

Common good A perspective on morality that assumes there is consensus about appropriate behaviour among the majority of citizens that requires protection and enforcement by the State.

Contextual constructionist A sociological perspective that situates claims-making within the context of historical, structural, and cultural influences.

Controlled drug use A way to describe regulated use patterns of many substance users that contradicts assumptions that drug use is problematic.

Criminal addicts The term was historically used to designate users of illegal narcotics who came into contact with the criminal justice system.

Cultural mosaic The idea that Canada is a uniquely multicultural society characterized by diversity and tolerance.

Definition of the situation A sociological perspective that understands behaviour as the product of a process of social definition and subject to interpretation.

Dependence A term used by clinicians to refer to frequent use of psychoactive substances, with symptoms of withdrawal when users stop taking the drug.

Differential association A sociological perspective explaining how definitions favourable to deviant or criminal behaviour are passed along from one generation to the next.

Disease model A biomedical perspective on the nature of addiction, which views it as a sickness or a symptom.

Domination matrix A view of stigma that recognizes its multiple dimensions, which intersect and reinforce oppression in society.

***DSM* criteria** Indicators of substance use disorder listed in the *Diagnostic and Statistical Manual of Mental Disorders.* published by the American Psychiatric Association.

Expectation effects How experiences with drug use are individually influenced and informed by previous understanding of the drug.

Exposure orientation A perspective on addiction that explains it as a biological vulnerability of certain individuals.

Flow experience A term used in psychology to describe a state of consciousness that facilitates task performance and feelings of well-being.

Grounds The rhetorical foundation for interpreting a problem in a particular way.

Harm reduction A drug policy perspective that prioritizes reducing drug use–related harm, instead of substance use itself.

Instantaneous addiction The idea that certain drugs are so habit forming they take hold upon first use.

Instrumentalizing drug use The use of drugs as tools by substance users seeking certain ends beyond a change in mental state.

Labelling theory A sociological perspective that shifts focus of study from rule-breaking behaviour to societal reactions and their effect on rule-breakers' understanding of themselves.

Marxian perspective A branch of conflict theory that views power as existing in the hands of those who own and control the means of production.

Master status The central attribute determining one's identity, outlook, and identification by others.

Moral panic A disproportionate societal reaction to behaviour that is viewed as threatening by the dominant social group.

Moral regulation A sociological perspective emphasizing social processes that shape the definition of acceptable behaviour.

Moral relativism A perspective on the nature of morality asserting that norms or standards of behaviour are socially constructed, as opposed to fixed or absolute.

Nation-building The social process of constructing a national identity that is distinct and different from other national cultures.

Negative liberty Protection from the State that guarantees noninterference in the private lives and personal freedom of its citizens.

Negative reinforcement A psychological perspective suggesting that the continued use of drugs is caused by the avoidance of withdrawal.

Normalization A trend toward more readily accessible, prevalent, and widely tolerated drug use in society.

Overcriminalization The intrusion of the law into consensual activities that are relatively harmless to the actors and to society.

Pathologize To view or characterize something in disease-related terms, with biological causes and medical solutions.

Placebo A chemically inert drug used in studies to account for expectation effects of drug treatment.

Plant teachers The use of certain drugs as tools for personal growth in rituals of self-discovery and spiritual fulfillment.

Pluralist perspective A branch of conflict theory that views power as existing in a multitude of bases of institutional authority.

Positive liberty An obligation by the State to guarantee all citizens full participation in the democratic process, and mastery or freedom to choose their own pursuits.

Positive psychology A psychological perspective oriented to the study of optimal experience and personal well-being, as opposed to diagnosing and treating mental illness.

Positive reinforcement A psychological perspective suggesting that continued use of drugs is caused by seeking and repeating pleasurable experiences.

Post-adolescence A theorized period in the life-course of youth and young adults in which more demanding roles of adulthood are postponed after adolescence in the pursuit of leisure and pleasure; may contribute to the normalization of illicit substance use.

Practice of the self A description of drug use as being personally adapted to suit specific needs of the individual user.

Psychosocial integration The sense of mutual support experienced by belonging to, acceptance by, and engagement with a group.

Psychosocial view of substance use Theoretical perspectives emphasizing psychological and social influences, as opposed to biological or genetic explanations, for substance use behaviour.

Reefer Madness An anti-marijuana film of the 1930s and a resultant term referring to the era of hysteria and propaganda that led to the ban of marijuana in the United States.

Reinforcement theory A psychological perspective that, like economic models, assumes individual behaviour is determined by people's tendency to seek to maximize rewards, while minimizing costs.

Retreatist adaptation A strain interpretation of addiction, which attributes the problem to rejection of conventional means and goals.

Rhetoric of endangerment A claims-making strategy emphasizing risk or danger.

Rhetoric of entitlement A claims-making strategy emphasizing personal freedom.

Rhetoric of rectitude A claims-making strategy emphasizing moral righteousness.

Self-medicate To use drugs as a means to cope with psychological or physical problems.

Set factors The individual motives and expectations that influence experiences of psychoactive drug use.

Setting Features of the social environment influencing individual experiences of drug use.

Social control theory A sociological perspective that attributes crime and deviance to failed socialization to conventional norms.

Social dislocation The breakdown of family, community, and cultural ties that are provided by a sense of mutual belonging, acceptance, and engagement with a group.

Social disorganization A sociological perspective on crime and deviant behaviour as being caused by breakdown of community controls.

Social gospel movement Lobby groups promoting temperance and Christian values, which have been influential in the United States and Canada in campaigns against the use of drugs.

Social lubricant Drugs with effects that assist in social interaction.

Social problems discourse The type of arguments employed by claims-making participants.

Social problems ownership A term describing claims-makers with access to law-makers and recognized legitimacy in claims-making campaigns.

Status politics A term used to describe the use of law by elite interests to criminalize the behaviour of competing social groups.

Strain theory A sociological perspective that views criminal behaviour as the product of unequal opportunity or access to legitimate means of achieving success.

Strict constructionist A sociological perspective that is purely definitional, focusing on claims-making about social problems as opposed to the conditions the claims are about.

Strong rights view A harm reduction standpoint that prioritizes drug users' autonomy and rights.

Temperance mentality An orientation toward substance use behaviour which has shifted from concern for moderation to strict abstinence from drugs.

Tolerable deviance A description that applies to certain deviant behaviours, which are not seen as morally threatening to others and therefore not particularly opposed.

Tough on drugs A policy perspective that insists that substance use is criminal and deserving of strict punishment.

Treatment industry The combined contingent of medical professionals and voluntary organizations providing services to addicts based on the premise that addiction is an illness or disease.

12-step model of recovery A self-help or mutual support approach to treatment for addictions, derived from the traditions of Alcoholics Anonymous.

Vernacular resources A term referring to strategic language used by claims-makers to promote their own social problems definitions.

Warrants The statements made by claims-makers to validate their arguments and justify attention to particular solutions.

Weak rights view A harm reduction standpoint that prioritizes public health, as opposed to rights of drug users or policy reform.

Yellow peril A derogatory term describing fear of Chinese immigrants.

References

Abel, E. 1980. *Marijuana: The First 12,000 Years*. New York: Plenum Press.

Abel, E.L. 2006. *Intoxication in Mythology: A Worldwide Dictionary of Gods, Rites, Intoxicants, and Place*. London: McFarland.

Addiction and Mental Health Research Laboratory. 2010. *Illicit Drug Use*. Edmonton: University of Alberta. Retrieved from: http://www.knowmo.ca/Libraries/Statistics/Statistics_Illicit_Drugs__May_2_10_colour.sflb.ashx.

Adlaf, E., P. Begin, and E. Sawka, eds. 2005a. *Canadian Addiction Survey (CAS): A National Survey of Canadians' Use of Alcohol and Other Drugs: Prevalence of Use and Related Harms: Detailed Report*. Ottawa: Canadian Centre on Substance Abuse.

Adlaf, E.M., A. Demers, and L. Gliksman, eds. 2005b. *Canadian Campus Survey 2004*. Toronto: Centre for Addiction and Mental Health.

Adlaf, E.M., A. Ialomiteanu, and J. Rehm. 2008. "CAMH Monitor eReport: Addiction and Mental Health Indicators Among Ontario Adults, 1977–2005." In *CAMH Research Document Series No. 24*. Toronto: Centre for Addiction and Mental Health. Retrieved from www.dldocs.stir.ac.uk/documents/~CM05Report_final.pdf.

Adlaf, E.M., R.E. Mann, and A. Paglia. 2003. "Drinking, Cannabis Use and Driving Among Ontario Students," *Canadian Medical Association Journal* 168 (5): 565–6.

Adlaf, E., F. Ivis, R. Smart, and G. Walsh. 1996. "Enduring Resurgence or Statistical Blip? Recent Trends from the Ontario Student Drug Use Survey," *Canadian Journal of Public Health* 87: 189–92.

Alcoholics Anonymous General Service Office. 1981. *The Twelve Steps of Alcoholics Anonymous*. New York, NY: Alcoholics Anonymous, Inc. Retrieved from http://www.aa.org/en_pdfs/smf-121_en.pdf.

Alexander, B.K. 1984. "When Experimental Psychology is Not Experimental Enough: The Case of the Exposure Orientation," *Canadian Psychology* 25 (2): 84–95.

———. 1990. *Peaceful Measures: Canada's Way Out of the "War on Drugs."* Toronto: University of Toronto Press.

———. 2000. "The Globalization of Addiction," *Addiction Research* 8 (6): 501–26.

American Psychiatric Association. 1994. *Diagnostic and Statistical Manual of Mental Disorders, Fourth Edition*. Washington, DC: American Psychiatric Association.

American Psychiatric Association. 2000. *Diagnostic and Statistical Manual of Mental Disorders, Fourth Edition, Text Revision*. Washington, DC: American Psychiatric Association.

American Psychiatric Association. 2013. *The Diagnostic and Statistical Manual of Mental Disorders, Fifth Edition*. Washington, DC: American Psychiatric Association.

Arseneult, L., M. Cannon, J. Witton, R.M. Murray. 2004. "Causal Association between Cannabis and Psychosis: Examination of the Evidence," *British Journal of Psychiatry* 184: 110–17.

Beauchesne, L. 1991. "Social Morality and the Civil Rights of Canadian Drug Users," *Journal of Drug Issues* 21 (1): 165–82.

Beck, U. 1992. *Risk Society: Towards a New Modernity*. London: Sage.

Becker, H.S. 1953. "Becoming a Marihuana User," *American Journal of Sociology* 59: 235–42.

———. 1955. "Marihuana Use and Social Control," *Social Problems* 3: 35–44.

———. 1963. *Outsiders: Studies in the Sociology of Deviance*. New York: Free Press.

———. 1967. "History, Culture, and Subjective Experience: An Exploration of the Social Bases of Drug-Induced Experiences," *Journal of Health and Social Behavior* 8: 163–76.

———. 1988. "Herbert Blumer's Conceptual Impact," *Symbolic Interaction* 11(1): 13–21.

Belle-Isle, L., and A.D. Hathaway. 2007. "Barriers to Access to Medical Cannabis for Canadians Living with HIV/AIDS," *AIDS Care* 19 (4): 500–6.
Berger, P.L., and T. Luckmann. 1966. *The Social Construction of Reality: A Treatise in the Sociology of Knowledge*. New York: Doubleday.
Berridge, V. 1978. "Professionalization and Narcotics: The Medical and Pharmaceutical Professions and British Narcotic Use 1868–1926," *Psychological Medicine* 8 (3): 361–72.
Berridge, V. 1980. "The Making of the Rolleston Report, 1908–1926," *Journal of Drug Issues* 10 (1): 7–28.
Berridge, V. 1999. *Opium and the People: Opiate Use and Policy in 19th and Early 20th Century Britain*. London: Free Association Books.
Berrios, G.E. 1985. "Obsessional Disorders: A Conceptual History. Terminological and Classificatory Issues," in W.F. Bynum, R. Porter, and M. Shepherd, eds, *The Anatomy of Madness*, Vol. 1. London: Tavistock, pp. 166–87.
Best, J. 1987. "Rhetoric in Claims-making: Constructing the Missing Children Problem," *Social Problems* 34 (2): 101–21.
———. 1989. "Afterword," in *Images of Issues: Typifying Contemporary Social Problems*. New York: Aldine de Gruyter, pp. 243–53
———. 1995. *Images of Issues: Typifying Contemporary Social Problems*, 2nd edn. New York: Aldine de Gruyter.
Baudelaire, C. [1860] 1971. *Artificial paradise: On hashish and wine as a means of expanding individuality*. New York: Herder and Herder.
Bewley-Taylor, D., and M. Jelsma. 2012. "Regime Change: Re-visiting the 1961 Single Convention on Narcotic Drugs," *International Journal of Drug Policy* 23 (1): 72–81.
Blumer, H. 1971. "Social Problems as Collective Behavior," *Social Problems* 18: 298–306.
Blackwell, J. 1988. "Sin, Sickness, or Social Problem? The Concept of Drug Dependence," in J.C. Blackwell and P.G. Erickson, eds, *Illicit Drugs in Canada: A Risky Business*. Toronto: Nelson, pp. 158–85.
Bonnie, R.J., and C.H. Whitebread. 1974. *The Marihuana Conviction: A History of Marihuana Prohibition in the United States*. Charlottesville: University Press of Virginia.
Boyd, N. 1991. *High Society: Legal and Illegal Drugs in Canada*. Toronto: Key Porter.
Boys, A., J. Marsden, J. Fountain, P. Griffiths, G. Stillwell, and J. Strang. 1999. "What Influences Young People's Use of Drugs? A Qualitative Study of Decision-Making," *Drugs: Education, Prevention and Policy* 6 (3): 373–87.
———. 2000. *Drug Decisions: A Qualitative Study of Young People*. London: Health Education Authority.
Boys, A., J. Marsden, and J. Strang. 2001. "Understanding Reasons for Drug Use Amongst Young People: A Functional Perspective," *Health Education Research* 16 (4): 457–69.
Bozarth, M.A. 1986. "Neural Basis of Psychomotor Stimulant and Opiate Reward: Evidence Suggesting the Involvement of a Common Dopaminergic System," *Behavioural Brain Research* 22: 107–16.
Butters, J.E. 2002. "Family Stressors and Adolescent Cannabis Use: A Pathway to Problem Use," *Journal of Adolescence* 25 (6): 645–54.
Canadian Centre for Justice Statistics. 2010. *Aggregate Uniform Crime Reporting Survey*. Ottawa: Statistics Canada.
Canadian Charter of Rights and Freedoms. 1982. Part I of the *Constitution Act, 1982*, being Schedule B to the *Canada Act, 1982* (UK), c. 11.
CannabisFacts.ca [website]. "How does cannabis compare to other drugs?" Retrieved from http://www.cannabisfacts.ca/pdf/HowDoesCannabisCompare.pdf.
Carstairs, C. 2006. *Jailed for Possession: Illegal Drug Use, Regulation, and Power in Canada, 1920–1961*. Toronto: University of Toronto Press.
Chambliss, W.J. 1969. *Crime and the Legal Process*. New York: McGraw-Hill.
———. 1975. "Toward a Political Economy of Crime," *Theory & Society* 2: 149–70.
———. 1976. "The State and Criminal Law," in W.J. Chambliss and M. Mankoff, eds, *Whose Law? What Order? A Conflict Approach to Criminology*. New York: John Wiley & Sons, pp. 66–106.
Chisolm, L., and J.M. Bergeret. 1991. *Young People in the European Community:*

Towards an Agenda for Research and Policy. Youth Task Force Report. London: Commission of the European Community.
Cohen, S. 1972. *Folk Devils and Moral Panics: The Creation of the Mods and Rockers.* London: Granada Publishing Ltd.
Cole, S.G. 2007. "Finding Dionysus," in D. Ogden, ed., *A Companion to Greek Religion.* Oxford: Blackwell Publishing Ltd, pp. 327–41.
Collins, P.H. 2000. *Black Feminist Thought: Knowledge, Consciousness, and the Politics of Empowerment.* New York: Routledge.
Conrad, P., and J.S. Schneider. 1992. *Deviance and Medicalization: From Badness to Sickness.* Philadelphia, PA: Temple University Press.
Cook, S.A. 2011. "From Flapper to Sophisticate: Canadian Women University Students as Smokers, 1920–60," in E.A. Montigny, ed., *The Real Dope: Social, Legal, and Historical Perspectives on the Regulation of Drugs in Canada.* Toronto: University of Toronto Press, pp. 83–122.
Cook, S.J. 1969. "Canadian Narcotics Legislation, 1908–1923: A Conflict Model Interpretation," *Canadian Review of Sociology and Anthropology* 6: 36–46.
Coomber, R., M. Oliver, and C. Morris. 2003. "Using Cannabis Therapeutically in the UK: A Qualitative Analysis," *Journal of Drug Issues* 33 (2): 325–56.
CTV/Angus Reid Group Poll. 1997. *User Profile, Reasons for Using Alternative Medicines and Practices, Health Care Responsibility.* Toronto: Ontario Press.
Curran, J. 2005. "The Yellow Emporor's Classic of Internal Medicine [book review]," *British Medical Journal* 336 (7647): 777.
Dauvergne, M. 2009. *Trends in Police-Reported Drug Offences in Canada.* Ottawa: Statstics Canada. Retrieved from: http://www.statcan.gc.ca/pub/85-002-x/2009002/article/10847-eng.htm.
DeBeck, K., E. Wood, J. Montaner, and T. Kerr. 2009. "Canada's New Federal 'National Anti-Drug Strategy': An Informal Audit of Reported Funding Allocation," *International Journal of Drug Policy* 20 (2): 188–91.
Decorte, T. 2000. *The Taming of Cocaine: Cocaine Use in European and American Cities.* Brussels: VUB University Press.
Dharmarajah, T. 2010, April 21. "Hundreds gather at U of G to celebrate pot smoker's holiday," *Guelph Mercury.* Retrieved from: http://www.guelphmercury.com/news-story/2742746-hundreds-gather-at-u-of-g-to-celebrate-pot-smoker-s-holiday/.
Dickson, D.T. 1968. "Bureaucracy and Morality: An Organizational Perspective on a Moral Crusade," *Social Problems* 16 (2): 143–56.
Dobkin de Rios, M. and D. Smith. 1977. "Drug Use and Abuse in Cross-Cultural Perspective," *Human Organization* 36 (1): 14–21.
Duff C. 2004. "Drug Use as a 'Practice of the Self': Is There Any Place for an 'Ethics of Moderation' in Contemporary Drug Policy?" *International Journal of Drug Policy* 15: 385–93.
Dyck, E. 2011. "Just Say Know: Criminalizing LSD and the Politics of Psychedelic Expertise, 1961–8," in E.A. Montigny, ed., *The Real Dope: Social, Legal, and Historical Perspectives on the Regulation of Drugs in Canada.* Toronto: University of Toronto Press, pp. 169–96.
Elias, N. 1978. *The Civilizing Process,* Vol. 1: *The History of Manners.* E. Jephcott, trans. New York: Pantheon.
Elias, N. 1982. *The Civilizing Process,* Vol. 2: *State Formation and Civilization.* E. Jephcott, trans. Oxford: Blackwell.
Ericson, R.V., P.M. Baranek, and J.B.L. Chan. 1987. *Visualizing Deviance: A Study of News Organization.* Toronto: University of Toronto Press.
Erickson, P.G. 1992. "Recent Trends in Canadian Drug Policy: The Decline and Resurgence of Prohibitionism," *Daedalus* 121 (Summer): 239–67.
———. 1998. Neglected and Rejected: A Case Study of the Impact of Social Research on Canadian Drug Policy. *Canadian Journal of Sociology* 23 (2/3): 263–80.
———. 2000. "The Harm Minimization Option for Cannabis: History and Prospects in Canadian Drug Policy," in L. Harrison and J. Inciardi, eds, *Harm Reduction.* London: Sage, pp. 155–70.
Finagrette, H. 1991. "Alcoholism: The Mythical Disease," in D.J. Pittman and H.R. White, eds, *Society, Culture, and Drinking Patterns Reexamined.*

Piscataway, NJ: Rutgers Center of Alcohol Studies, pp. 417–38.

Fischer, B. 1994. "Maps and Moves," *International Journal of Drug Policy* 5 (2): 70–81.

Foucault M. 1988. "The Ethic of Care for the Self as a Practice of Freedom," in J. Bernauer and D. Rasmussen, eds, *The Final Foucault*. Cambridge, MA: MIT Press, pp. 1–20.

Gamson, W.A. 1992. *Talking Politics*. Cambridge: Cambridge University Press.

Garland D. 2001. *The Culture of Control: Crime and Social Order in Contemporary Society*. Oxford: Oxford University Press.

Giffen, P.J., S.J. Endicott, and S. Lambert. 1991. *Panic and Indifference: The Politics of Canada's Drug Laws*. Ottawa: Canadian Centre on Substance Abuse.

Global Drug Survey. 2014. "Impact of Being Found in Possession of Cannabis [figure]." Retrieved from http://www.talkingdrugs.org/drug-survey-high-lights-us-cannabis-reform-difficulties.

Glasbeek, A., ed. 2006. *Moral Regulation and Governance in Canada: History, Context and Critical Issues*. Toronto: Canadian Scholars' Press.

Glaser, D. 1956. "Criminality Theories and Behavioral Images," *American Journal of Sociology* 61 (5): 433–44.

Goffman E. 1969. *The Presentation of Self in Everyday Life,* 2nd edn. London: Allen Lane.

Golub A., B.D. Johnson, and E. Dunlop. 2005. "Subcultural Evolution and Illicit Drug Use," *Addiction Research & Theory* 13: 217–29.

Goode, E. 2011. *Drugs in American Society*. New York: McGraw-Hill.

Goode, E., and N. Ben-Yehuda. 1994. *Moral Panics: The Social Construction of Deviance*. Cambridge, MA: Blackwell.

Gouldner, A.W. 1968. "The Sociologist as Partisan: Sociology and the Welfare State," *American Sociologist* 3 (2): 103–16.

Government of Canada. 2010. "Your Kids Are Starting to Learn a New Language [print ad]." Retrieved from: http://addictions.knet.ca/node/11.

Grayson, K. 2008. *Chasing Dragons: Security, Identity, and Illicit Drugs in Canada*. Toronto: University of Toronto Press.

Gusfield, J.R. 1963. *Symbolic Crusade: Status Politics and the American Temperance Movement*. Urbana Ill.: University of Illinois Press.

———. 1975. "The (F)Utility of Knowledge?: The Relation of Social Science to Public Policy Toward Drugs," *Annals of the American Academy of Political and Social Science* 417: 1–15.

———. 1981. *The Culture of Public Problems: Drinking-Driving and the Symbolic Order*. Chicago: University of Chicago Press.

———. 1985. "Theories and Hobgoblins," *SSSP Newsletter* 17 (Fall): 16–18.

Hammersley, R. 2005. "Theorizing Normal Drug Use," *Addiction Research & Theory* 13: 201–3.

Hammersley, R., R. Jenkins, and M. Reid. 2001. "Cannabis Use and Social Identity," *Addiction Research & Theory* 9 (2): 133–50.

Hathaway, A.D. 1997. "Marijuana and Lifestyle: Exploring Tolerable Deviance," *Deviant Behavior* 18 (3): 213–32.

———. 2001a. "Charter Rights of Canadian Drug Users: A Constitutional Assessment of the Clay Trial and Ruling," *Canadian Journal of Law and Society* 16 (1): 29–43.

———. 2001b. "Shortcomings of Harm Reduction: Toward a Morally Invested Drug Reform Strategy," *International Journal of Drug Policy* 12 (2): 125–37.

———. 2002. "From Harm Reduction to Human Rights: Bringing Liberalism Back into Drug Reform Debates," *Drug and Alcohol Review* 21 (4): 397–404.

———. 2003. "Cannabis Effects and Dependency Concerns in Long-Term Frequent Users: A Missing Piece of the Public Health Puzzle," *Addiction Research & Theory* 11 (6): 441–58.

———. 2004a. "Cannabis Users' Informal Rules for Managing Stigma and Risk," *Deviant Behavior* 25 (6): 559–77.

———. 2004b. "Cannabis Careers Reconsidered: Transitions and Trajectories of Committed Long-Term Users," *Contemporary Drug Problems* 31 (3): 401–23.

Hathaway, A.D. and Atkinson, M.F. 2001. "Tolerable Differences Revisited: Crossroads in Theory on the Social Construction of Deviance," *Deviant Behavior* 22 (4): 353–77.

Hathaway, A.D., R.C. Callaghan, S. Macdonald, and P.G. Erickson. 2009. "Cannabis Dependence as a Primary Drug Use-related Problem: The Case for Harm Reduction-Oriented Treatment Options," *Substance Use & Misuse* 44 (7): 990–1008.

Hathaway, A.D., N. Comeau, and P.G. Erickson. 2011. "Cannabis Normalization and Stigma: Contemporary Practices of Moral Regulation," *Criminology and Criminal Justice* 11 (5): 451–69.

Hathaway, A.D., and P.G. Erickson. 2003. "Drug Reform Principles and Policy Debates: Harm Reduction Prospects for Cannabis in Canada," *Journal of Drug Issues* 33 (3): 467–96.

Hathaway, A.D., and P.G. Erickson. 2004. "A Tale of Two Stimulants: An Analysis of Newspaper Coverage of Cocaine and Tobacco in Canada," *Canadian Journal of Communication* 29 (1): 61–80.

Hathaway, A.D., P.G. Erickson, and P. Lucas. 2007. "Canadian Public Opinion on Cannabis: How Far Out of Step with It Is the Existing Law?" *Canadian Review of Social Policy* 59: 44–55.

Hathaway, A.D., M. Kirst, and P.G. Erickson. 2013. "Marijuana Motives and Associated Outcomes: Relaxation and Enhancement Versus Coping Motivations," in M.C. Van Hout, ed., *Drug Use and Abuse: Signs/Symptoms, Physical and Psychological Effects and Treatment Approaches.* New York: Nova Science Publishers, pp. 119–33.

Hathaway, A.D., S. Macdonald, and P.G. Erickson. 2008. "Reprioritizing Dependence and Abuse: A Comparison of Cannabis Clients in Treatment with a Non-Treatment Sample of Users," *Addiction Research & Theory* 16 (5): 495–502.

Hathaway, A.D., and K. Rossiter. 2007. "Medical Marijuana, Community Building, and Canada's Compassionate Societies," *Contemporary Justice Review* 10 (3): 283–96.

Hathaway, A.D., and J. Sharpley. 2010. "The Cannabis Experience: An Analysis of 'Flow,'" in D. Jacquette, ed., *Cannabis: Philosophy for Everyone—What Were We Just Talking About?* New York: Wiley-Blackwell, pp. 50–61.

Hathaway, A.D., and K. Tousaw. 2008. "Harm Reduction Headway and Continuing Resistance: Insights from Safe Injection in the City of Vancouver," *International Journal of Drug Policy* 19: 11–16. With permission from Elsevier.

Haydon, E., J. Rehm, B. Fischer, N. Monga, and E. Adlaf. 2005. "Prescription Drug Abuse in Canada and the Diversion of Illicit Drugs into the Illicit Drug Market," *Canadian Journal of Public Health* 96 (6): 459–61.

Herie, M., and W. Skinner. 2010. *Substance Abuse in Canada.* Don Mills, ON: Oxford University Press.

Himmelstein, J.L. 1978. "Drug Politics Theory: Analysis and Critique," *Journal of Drug Issues* 8: 37–52.

Hirschi, T. 1969. *Causes of Delinquency.* Berkeley: University of California Press.

Hoffer, L.J. 2003. "Complementary or Alternative Medicine: The Need for Plausibility," *Canadian Medical Association Journal* 168 (2): 180–2.

Hunt, A. 1999. *Governing Morals: A Social History of Moral Regulation.* Cambridge: Cambridge University Press.

Hunt N. 2004. "Public Health or Human Rights: What Comes First?" *International Journal of Drug Policy* 15: 231–7.

Hyshka, E. 2013. "Applying a Social Determinants of Health Perspective to Early Adolescent Cannabis Use—An Overview," *Drugs: Education, Prevention and Policy* 20 (2): 110–19.

Ibarra, P.R., and J.I. Kitsuse. 1993. "Vernacular Constituents of Moral Discourse: An Interactionist Proposal for the Study of Social Problems," in G. Miller and J.A. Holstein, eds, *Constructionist Controversies: Issues in Social Problems Theory.* New Jersey: Transacation Publishers, pp. 21–54.

Ignatieff, M. 2001. *Human Rights as Politics and Idolatry.* New Jersey: Princeton University Press.

Jacob, J.C. 2006. "Male and Female Youth Crime in Canadian Communities: Assessing the Applicability of Social Disorganization Theory," *Canadian Journal of Criminology and Criminal Justice* 48 (1): 31–60.

Jones, C., and A.D. Hathaway. 2008. "Marijuana Medicine and Canadian Physicians: Challenges to Meaningful

Drug Policy Reform," *Contemporary Justice Review* 11 (2): 165–75.
Jones, G. 1991. *From Dependency to Citizenship? Transitions to Adulthood in Britain. Longitudinal Strategy in the Study of Youth.* Moscow: Moscow Youth Institute.
Khantzian, E.J. 1985. "The Self-Medication Hypothesis of Addictive Disorders: Focus on Heroin and Cocaine Dependence," *American Journal of Psychiatry* 142: 1259–64.
Kingdon, J.W. 1995. *Agendas, Alternatives, and Public Policies,* 2nd edn. Boston: Little, Brown & Co.
Kirst, M.J., P. Erickson, and C. Strike. 2009. "Polysubstance Use Among Male and Female Street Youth in Toronto, Canada," *International Journal of Social Inquiry* 2 (2): 123–39.
Kitsuse, J.I., and A.V. Cicourel. 1963. "A Note on the Use of Official Statistics," *Social Problems* 11 (2): 131–39.
Ksir C., C.L. Hart, and O. Ray. 2008. *Drugs, Society, and Human Behavior,* 12th edn. New York: McGraw-Hill.
Lang, A.R. 1983. "Addictive Personality: A Viable Construct?" in P.K. Levison, D.R. Gerstein, and D.R. Maloff, eds, *Commonalities in Substance Abuse and Habitual Behavior.* Lexington: Lexington Books, pp. 157–236.
Leary, T.L. 1967. *Leary to Canada: Wake Up! The Banned Speech.* Minneapolis, MN: The Luminist League. Retrieved from www.luminist.org/archives/leary_to_canada.htm.
Le Dain, G. 1972. *Cannabis: A Report of the Commission of Inquiry into the Non-Medical Use of Drugs.* Ottawa: Information Canada.
Lemert, E.M. 1951. *Social Pathology.* New York: McGraw-Hill.
Lipset, S.M. 1991. *Continental Divide: The Values and Institutions of the United States and Canada.* New York: Psychology Press.
Loo, T., and C. Strange. 1997. *Making Good: Law and Moral Regulation in Canada, 1867–1939.* Toronto: University of Toronto Press.
Lupton, D., and J. Tulloch. 2002. "'Life Would Be Pretty Dull Without Risk': Voluntary Risk-Taking and Its Pleasures," *Health, Risk & Society* 4: 113–24.
Mackey, E. 2002. *The House of Difference: Cultural Politics and National Identity in Canada.* Toronto: University of Toronto Press.
Macnaghtan, P., R. Brown, and S. Reicher. 1992. "On the Nature of Nature: Experimental Studies in the Power of Rhetoric," *Journal of Community and Applied Social Psychology* 2 (1): 43–61.
Manderson, D. 1995. "Metamorphoses: Clashing Symbols in the Social Construction of Drugs," *Journal of Drug Issues* 25 (4): 799–816.
———. 2005. "Possessed: Drug Policy, Witchcraft and Belief," *Cultural Studies* 19 (1): 35–62.
Marquis, G. 2011. "From Beverage to Drug: Alcohol and Other Drugs in 1960s and 1970s Canada," in E.A. Montigny, ed., *The Real Dope: Social, Legal, and Historical Perspectives on the Regulation of Drugs in Canada.* Toronto: University of Toronto Press, pp. 219–41.
Maté, G. 2008. *In the Realm of Hungry Ghosts: Close Encounters with Addiction.* Toronto: A.A. Knopf Canada.
McKenna, T. 1992. *Food of the Gods: The Search for the Original Tree of Knowledge. A Radical History of Plants, Drugs, and Human Evolution.* New York: Bantam.
McRobbie, A., and S.L. Thornton. 1995. "Rethinking 'Moral Panic' for Multi-Mediated Social Worlds," *British Journal of Sociology* 46: 559–74.
Measham F. 2002. "'Doing Gender'—'Doing Drugs': Conceptualizing the Gendering of Drugs Cultures," *Contemporary Drug Problems* 29: 335–73.
Measham, F., and M. Shiner. 2009. "The Legacy of 'Normalization': The Role of Classical and Contemporary Criminological Theory in Understanding Young People's Drug Use," *International Journal of Drug Policy* 20: 502–8.
Merton, R. 1938. "Social Structure and Anomie," *American Sociological Review* 3: 672–82.
Mill, J.S. 1901. *On Liberty.* London: Walter Scott Publishing Co.
Mitchell, C.N. 1988. "A Justice-Based Argument for the Uniform Regulation of Psychoactive Drugs," in J.C. Blackwell and P.G. Erickson, eds, *Illicit Drugs in Canada: A Risky Business.* Scarborough: Nelson Canada, pp. 407–43.

———. 1990. *The Drug Solution*. Ottawa: Carleton University Press.

Montigny, E.A. 2011. *The Real Dope: Social, Legal, and Historical Perspectives on the Regulation of Drugs in Canada*. Toronto: University of Toronto Press.

Morgan, C.J., L.A. Noronha, M. Muetzelfeldt, A. Fielding, and H.V. Curran. 2013. "Harms and Benefits Associated with Psychoactive Drugs: Findings of an International Survey of Active Drug Users," *Journal of Psychopharmacology* 27 (6): 497–506.

Mostaghim, A., and A.D. Hathaway. 2013. "Identity Formation, Marijuana and 'the Self': A Study of Cannabis Normalization among University Students," *Frontiers in Psychiatry* 4 (160): 1–7.

Mugford, S. 1993. "Harm Reduction: Does it Lead Where Its Proponents Imagine?" in N. Heather, A. Wodak, E. Nadelmann, and P. O'Hare, eds, *Psychoactive Drugs and Harm Reduction: From Faith to Science*. London: Whurr Publishers, pp. 21–33.

Müller, C.P., and G. Schumann. 2011. "Drugs as Instruments: A New Framework for Non-Addictive Psychoactive Drug Use," *Behavioral and Brain Sciences* 34: 293–347.

Murphy, E. 1922. *The Black Candle*. Toronto: Thomas Allen.

Murray, G.F. 1987. "Cocaine Use in the Era of Social Reform: The Natural History of a Social Problem in Canada, 1880–1911," *Canadian Journal of Law & Society* 2: 29.

Musto, D.F. 1973. *The American Disease: Origins of Narcotic Control*. New Haven: Yale University Press.

Northcott, H.C. 1994. "Alternative Health Care in Canada," in B.S. Bolaria and H.D. Dickinson, eds, *Health, Illness and Health Care in Canada*, 2nd edn. Toronto: Harcourt Brace, pp. 487–503.

Nutt, D.J., L.A. King, and L.D. Phillips. 2010. "Drug Harms in the UK: A Multicriteria Decision Analysis," *The Lancet* 376 (9752): 1558–65.

Parker, H. 2005. "Normalization as Barometer: Recreational Drug Use and the Consumption of Leisure by Young Britons," *Addiction Research & Theory* 13: 205–15.

Parker, H.J., J. Aldridge, and F. Measham. 1998. *Illegal Leisure: The Normalization of Adolescent Recreational Drug Use*. London: Routledge.

Pearson, G. 2001. "Normal Drug Use: Ethnographic Fieldwork among an Adult Network of Recreational Drug Users in London," *Substance Use & Misuse* 36 (1–2): 167–200.

Peele, S. 1985. *The Meaning of Addiction. Compulsive Experience and Its Interpretation*. Lexington: Lexington Books.

Poulin, C., and D. Elliot. 1997. "Alcohol, Tobacco and Cannabis Use Among Nova Scotia Adolescents: Implications for Prevention and Harm Reduction," *Canadian Medical Association Journal* 156: 1387–93.

Pross, J.P. 1975. "Pressure Groups: Adaptive Instruments of Political Communication," in *Pressure Group Behavior in Canadian Politics*. Toronto: McGraw-Hill Ryerson, pp. 1–26.

Quinney, R. 1969. *Crime and Justice in Society*. Boston: Little, Brown and Co.

———. 1974. *Critique of Legal Order*. Boston: Little, Brown and Co.

———. 1975. *Criminology: Analysis and Critique of Crime in America*. Boston: Little, Brown and Co.

———. 1977. *Class, State and Crime*. New York: David McKay.

Reasons, C. 1974. "The Politics of Drugs: An Inquiry in the Sociology of Social Problems," *Sociological Quarterly* 15 (3): 381–404.

Reeves, J.L., and R. Campbell. 1994. *Cracked Coverage: Television News, the Anti-Cocaine Coverage, and the Reagan Legacy*. Durham, NC: Duke University Press.

Rehm, J., B. Taylor, and R. Room. 2006. "Global Burden of Disease from Alcohol, Illicit Drugs and Tobacco," *Drug and Alcohol Review* 25: 503–13.

Reinarman, C. 1988. "The Social Construction of an Alcohol Problem: The Case of Mothers Against Drunk Drivers and Social Control in the 1980s," *Theory & Society* 17: 91–119.

Reinarman, C., and H.G. Levine. 1995. "Crack Attack: America's Latest Drug Scare, 1986–1992," in J. Best, ed., *Images of Issues: Typifying Contemporary Social Problems*. New York: Aldine de Gruyter, pp. 147–86.

Reinarman, C., and H.G. Levine, eds. 1997. *Crack in America: Demon Drugs and Social Justice*. Oakland, CA: University of California Press.

Richards, D.A.J. 1982. *Sex, Drugs, Death and the Law: An Essay on Human Rights and Overcriminalization*. Totowa, NJ: Rowman and Littlefield.

Robins, L.N. 1993. "Vietnam Veterans' Rapid Recovery from Heroin Addiction: A Fluke or Normal Expectation?" *Addiction* 88: 1041–54.

Room, R. 2005. "Stigma, Social Inequality and Alcohol and Drug Use," *Drug and Alcohol Review* 24: 143–55.

Room, R. 2006. "Taking Account of Cultural and Societal Influences on Substance Use Diagnoses and Criteria," *Addiction* 101 (Suppl. 1): 31–9.

Rubin, V., and L. Comitas. 1976. *Ganja in Jamaica: The Effects of Marijuana Use*. Garden City, NY: Anchor.

Rudy, J. 2011. "Unmaking Manly Smokes: Church, State, Governance, and the First Anti-Smoking Campaigns in Montreal, 1892–1914," in E.A. Montigny, ed., *The Real Dope: Social, Legal, and Historical Perspectives on the Regulation of Drugs in Canada*. Toronto: University of Toronto Press, pp. 59–82.

Sarbin, T.R., and J.I. Kitsuse. 1994. "A Prologue to Constructing the Social," in *Constructing the Social*. Thousand Oaks, CA: Sage, pp. 1–18.

Scheerer, S. 1978. "The New Dutch and German Drug Laws: Social and Political Conditions for Successful Criminalization and Decriminalization," *Law & Society Review* 12: 585–606.

Schivelbusch W. 1992. "Tastes of Paradise: A Social History of Spices, Stimulants, and Intoxicants," New York: Knopf Doubleday.

Schlosser, E. 2004. *Reefer Madness: Sex, Drugs, and Cheap Labor in the American Black Market*. Boston: Houghton Mifflin Harcourt.

Schneider, J.W. 1985. "Defining the Definitional Perspective on Social Problems," *Social Problems* 32: 232–4.

Schwartz, M.A. 1981. "Politics and Moral Causes in Canada and the United States," *Comparative Social Research* 4: 65–90.

———. 1986. "Comparing United States and Canadian Public Policy: A Review of Strategies," *Policy Studies Journal* 14 (4): 566–75.

Shaw, C., and H. McKay. 1942. *Juvenile Delinquency and Urban Areas*. Chicago: University of Chicago Press.

Shepherd, R.G. 1981. "Selectivity of Sources: Reporting the Marijuana Controversy," *Journal of Communication* 31 (2): 129–37.

Senate Special Committee on Illegal Drugs. 2002. *Cannabis: Our Position for a Canadian Public Policy*. Ottawa: Information Canada.

Seymour, D., ed. 2012. *Dealing With The Stigma of Drugs. A Guide For Journalists*. East Sussex: United Kingdom Drug Policy Commission. Retrieved from www.ukdpc.org.uk/wp-content/uploads/dealing-with-the-stigma-of-drugs.pdf.

Single, E. 1995. "Defining Harm Reduction," *Drug and Alcohol Review* 14: 287–90.

———. 1999. *A Harm Reduction Framework for Drug Policy in British Columbia*. A Discussion Paper prepared for the British Columbia Federal/Provincial Harm Reduction Working Group.

Single, E., P. Erickson, J. Skirrow, and R. Solomon. 1992. *Drugs and Public Policy in Canada*. Washington: Rand Institute Drug Policy Research Center.

Solomon, D. 1966. *The Marihuana Papers*. New York: New American Library.

Solomon, R. 1988. "The Noble Pursuit of Evil: Arrest, Search, and Seizure in Canadian Drug Law," in J.C. Blackwell and P.G. Erickson, eds, *Illicit Drugs in Canada: A Risky Business*. Scarborough: Nelson Canada, pp. 263–90.

Solomon, R. and Green, M. 1982. "The First Century: The History of Non-Medical Opiate Use and Control Policies in Canada, 1870–1970," *The University of Western Ontario Law Review* 20 (2): 307–36.

Spector, M., and J.I. Kitsuse. 1977. *Constructing Social Problems*. Menlo Park: Cummings.

———. 1987. *Constructing Social Problems*, 2nd edn. Hawthorne, NY: Aldine de Gruyter.

Spencer, J.W. 1999. "Essential Issues in Complementary/Alternative Medicine," in J.W. Spencer and J.J. Jacobs, eds, *Complementary/Alternative Medicine: An Evidence-Based Approach*. St Louis, MO: Mosby, pp. 3–36.

Starks, M. 1982. *Cocaine Fiends and Reefer Madness: An Illustrated History of Drugs in the Movies*. New York: Cornwall Books.

Stebbins, R.A. 1996. *Tolerable Differences: Living with Deviance*. Whitby, ON: McGraw-Hill Ryerson.

Stevenson, G.H., L.P.A. Lingley, G.E. Trasov, and H. Stanfield. 1956. *Drug Addiction in British Columbia*. Vancouver: University of British Columbia.

Strang, J. 1993. "Drug Use and Harm Reduction: Responding to the Challenge," in N. Heather, A. Wodak, and E. Nadelmann, eds, *Psychoactive Drugs and Harm Reduction: From Faith to Science*. London: Whurr Publishers, pp. 3–20

Sullivan, R.J., and E.H. Hagan. 2002. "Psychotropic Substance-Seeking: Evolutionary Pathology or Adaptation?" *Addiction* 97: 389–400.

Sutherland, E. 1939. *Principles of Criminology*. Philadelphia: Lippincott.

Taylor, I.R., P. Walton, and J. Young. 1973. *The New Criminology*. London: Routledge and Kegan Paul.

Thomas, A. 1990. "With Substance Abuse Disorders: A Problematic Diagnosis?" *American Journal of Psychiatry* 147 (2): 173–8.

Tupper, K.W. 2002. "Entheogens and Existential Intelligence: The Use of Plant Teachers as Cognitive Tools," *Canadian Journal of Education* 27 (4): 499–516.

Turk, A.T. 1969. *Criminality and Legal Order*. Chicago: Rand McNally.

United Nations Office on Drugs and Crime. 2014. "Recent Statistics and Trend Analysis of the Illicit Drug Market," in *World Drug Report 2014* (United Nations publication, Sales No. E.14.XI.7). Retrieved from http://www.unodc.org/documents/wdr2014/Drug_use_health_consequences_2014_web.pdf.

Urban Health Research Initiative. 2014. *Drug Policy*. Vancouver, BC: BC Centre for Excellence in HIV/AIDS. Retrieved from http://uhri.cfenet.ubc.ca/content/view/68/82.

Valverde, M. 1998. *Diseases of the Will: Alcohol and the Dilemmas of Freedom*. Cambridge University Press.

———. 2008. *The Age of Light, Soap, and Water: Moral Reform in English Canada, 1885–1925*. Toronto: University of Toronto Press.

Valverde, M., and L. White-Mair. 1999. "'One day at a time' and other slogans for everyday life: The ethical practices of Alcoholics Anonymous," *Sociology* 33 (2): 393–410.

Van Vliet, H. 1990. "Separation of Drug Markets and the Normalisation of Drug Problems in the Netherlands: An Example for Other Nations," *Journal of Drug Issues* 20 (3): 463–71.

Weil, A. 1972. *The Natural Mind: A New Way of Looking at Drugs and the Higher Consciousness*. Boston: Houghton Mifflin.

Williams, L., and H. Parker. 2001. "Alcohol, Cannabis, Ecstasy and Cocaine: Drugs of Reasoned Choice Amongst Young Adult Recreational Drug Users in England," *International Journal of Drug Policy* 12: 397–413.

Wilson, H.T. 2012. *Annual Editions: Drugs, Society, and Behaviour 11/12*, 26th edn. New York: McGraw-Hill.

Wong, D.B. 1984. *Moral Relativity*. Berkeley: University of California Press.

Woolgar, S., and D. Pawluch. 1985. "Ontological Gerrymandering: The Anatomy of Social Problems Explanations," *Social Problems* 32 (2): 214–27.

Zinberg, N. 1984. *Drug, Set and Setting*. New Haven: Yale University Press.

Index